BY WHAT AUTHORITY?

THE VITAL QUESTION
OF RELIGIOUS AUTHORITY IN CHRISTIANITY

MERCER
UNIVERSITY PRESS

Endowed by
TOM WATSON BROWN
and
THE WATSON-BROWN FOUNDATION, INC.

BY WHAT AUTHORITY?

THE VITAL QUESTION
OF RELIGIOUS AUTHORITY IN CHRISTIANITY

edited by
ROBERT L. MILLET

MERCER UNIVERSITY PRESS
Macon, Georgia USA
2010

MUP/P410

By What Authority?
The Vital Question of Religious Authority in Christianity.
Copyright ©2010
Mercer University Press, Macon, Georgia USA
All rights reserved
Printed in the United States of America
First edition

Mercer University Press is a member of Green Press Initiative <greenpress initiative.org>, a nonprofit orgaization working to help publishers and printers increase their use of recycled paper and decrease their use of fiber derived from endangered forests. This book is printed on recycled paper and meets the minimum requirements of American National Standard for Information Sciences—Permanence of Paper for Printed Library Materials, ANSI Z39.48-1984.

Library of Congress Cataloging-in-Publication Data

By what authority? : the vital question of religious authority in Christianity
/ edited by Robert L. Millet. -- 1st ed.
    p.   cm.
Includes bibliographical references and index.
ISBN 978-0-88146-201-2 (pbk. : alk. paper)
1. Authority—Religious aspects—Christianity—Comparative studies.
1. Millet, Robert L.
BT88.B78 2010
262'.8–dc22

2010001574

CONTENTS

    DAVID NEFF

11 On Loving Truth More Than Religion:
    Confessions of a Rebellious Christian Mind 180
    ROGER E. OLSON

    Contributors 192

    Index 193

PREFACE

Professing Christians of various denominations agree that Jesus of Nazareth was born of the Virgin Mary in Bethlehem of Judea; that he "increased in wisdom and stature, and in favor with God and man" (Luke 2:52); that he "went about doing good" (Acts 10:38)—lifting and consoling the weary, enlarging the circle of the accepted and acceptable, demonstrating a willingness to be inconvenienced, and teaching the importance of loving God and loving one's fellow mortals (Matthew 22:35-40).[1] Those who read and accept as fact the New Testament further believe Jesus performed miracles, claimed to forgive sins, demonstrated power over the elements, healed the sick, raised the dead, and taught as one having authority (Matthew 7:29). In short, his actions transcended the natural world, and his deeds challenged naturalistic explanation.

People received him as the Promised Messiah, the Savior and Redeemer of humankind. He declared himself to be the Son of God and acted as though he were God. When he performed healing miracles, for example, there is no account within scripture of Jesus using language such as, "By the authority of Almighty God I hereby . . ." or "Using the power that God has given me, I command you to. . . ." There is no instance in which he turned heavenward and asked his Heavenly Father to perform some sign or wonder. Rather, when Jesus spoke and acted, he did so *with authority*, assuming authority of himself, performing his deeds and transforming his listeners and observers with an authority that was surely beyond anything earthly man possessed. He was God, God the Son, and he never hesitated to bless the faithful by virtue of his own divine authority.

Now it is true that while on earth Jesus was subordinate to the Father, spoke often of carrying out his Father's will, declared regularly that he could do nothing but what God had commanded, and even noted that "my Father is greater than I" (John 14:28). The Apostle Paul wrote of how Jesus the Christ voluntarily "emptied himself" of the fullness of his Godhood in order to minister among men and women and carry out the infinite and eternal atoning sacrifice (Philippians 2:5-8). But he was still Deity, the Incarnate One, Immanuel, God with us.

Note the following verses.

---

[1]Scripture quotations in this preface are from a current edition of the King James Version ("Authorized Version" in the UK; ca. 1611) and are in public domain.

And it came to pass in those days, that [Jesus] went out into a mountain to pray, and continued all night in prayer to God. And when it was day, he called unto him his disciples: and *of them he chose twelve, whom also he named apostles*. (Luke 6:12-13; emphasis added)

And when he had called unto him his twelve disciples, *he gave them power* against unclean spirits, to cast them out, and to heal all manner of sickness and all manner of disease. (Matthew 10:1; emphasis added)

Luke puts it this way:

Then he called his twelve disciples together, and *gave them power and authority* over all devils, and to cure diseases. And *he sent them to preach the kingdom of God*, and to heal the sick. (Luke 9:1-2; emphasis added)

For as the Father raiseth up the dead, and quickeneth them [brings them to life]; even so the Son quickeneth whom he will. For *the Father* judgeth no man, but *hath committed all judgment unto the Son*. . . . For as the Father hath life in himself; so hath he given to the Son to have life in himself; and hath given him authority to execute judgment also, because he is the Son of man. (John 5:21-22, 26-27; emphasis added)

Ye have not chosen me, but *I have chosen you, and ordained you*, that ye should go and bring forth fruit, and that your fruit should remain. (John 15:16; emphasis added)

And when he [the resurrected Lord] had so said, he shewed unto them his hands and his side. Then were the disciples glad, when they saw the Lord. Then said Jesus to them again, Peace be unto you: *as my Father hath sent me, even so send I you*. (John 20:20-21; emphasis added)

As they ministered to the Lord, and fasted, the Holy Ghost said, Separate me Barnabas and Saul for the work whereunto I have called them. And when they had fasted and prayed, and *laid their hands on them*, they sent them away. (Acts 13:2-3; emphasis added)

Toward the end of that first missionary journey, Saul of Tarsus and Barnabas retraced their steps and confirmed the churches they had established:

And *when they had ordained them elders in every church*, and had prayed with fasting, they commended them to the Lord, on whom they believed. (Acts 14:21-23; emphasis added)

Jesus had authority, to be sure. The scriptures seem to attest to the fact that his representatives were given a like authorization, a power to act and officiate in his name, a divine investiture of authority. When at Caesarea Philippi Peter bore witness that Jesus was the Christ, the Son of the living God, he was commended with these words:

> Blessed art thou, Simon Bar-jona: for flesh and blood hath not revealed it unto thee, but my Father which is in heaven. And I say also unto thee, That thou art Peter, and *upon this rock I will build my church*; and the gates of hell shall not prevail against it. And *I will give unto thee the keys of the kingdom of heaven: and whatsoever thou shalt bind on earth shall be bound in heaven: and whatsoever thou shalt loose on earth shall be loosed in heaven.* (Matthew 16:16-19; emphasis added; compare 18:18)

A host of questions have been spawned as a result of Peter's confession and Jesus' commendation, including:

1. What are the "keys of the kingdom of heaven"?
2. Were they given to Peter alone, or were they delivered to all of the Twelve?
3. What is the relationship between these keys and the authority mentioned in the scriptural passages above?
4. Is this passage in Matthew 16 a valid scriptural justification for apostolic succession from Peter?
5. By what authority could Luther and other Reformers make the claim that Roman Catholic apostolic authority was no longer needed?
6. Is a "priesthood of all believers" a scripturally sound concept?
7. How does one derive authority from the Bible?
8. How and in what manner does one derive authority from Truth, and how do authority and truth relate?
9. What of those, like many of the Founding Fathers of America, as well as certain Christian leaders through the years, who felt that apostolic authority had been lost with the death of the apostles and needed to be delivered to earth once again?
10. What is the relationship of authority to scriptural interpretation and the performance of the ordinances (sacraments)?

These are only some of the questions addressed in this book. Represented within the pages that follow are thoughts from representatives of

Roman Catholicism, Eastern Orthodoxy, Evangelicalism, Restorationism, and other Protestant movements.

Authority is a, if not *the*, crucial question among religious traditions that make unique truth claims about Jesus Christ. Some claim apostolic succession and sacred tradition dating to the time of Jesus. Some teach that authority to act in God's name comes to one and all who receive Jesus Christ as Savior and Lord and rely upon individual calls and "giftedness" as well as the Holy Scriptures for their authority. Some believe that the Mother Church had indeed gone off course for a season but that more was required than a reformation; they speak often of returning to the primitive church of the first century and of a restoration of sacred authority and modern revelation. Where is the truth to be found? While this book does not aspire to an uncontested answer, the conversation generated among the various contributors to this volume—persons who demonstrate respect and Christian civility toward one another in comparing and contrasting their respective points of view—makes the exploration itself an informative and rewarding enterprise.

Robert L. Millet, editor

AUTHORITY IN THE CATHOLIC TRADITION

Peter A. Huff

The biblical *locus classicus* for any discussion of authority in Christianity has always been Mark 11:27-33 and its synoptic parallels, where Jesus' opponents confront him in the temple and pose the question: "By what authority are you doing these things?"[1] Since the first century, every Christian tradition has had to face the same question and devise an answer in conformity with its understanding of the essence of Christianity. Some have invoked the authority of books and creeds; others have summoned the power of reason or claimed direct inspiration from God. The model of authority predominant in the Roman Catholic church takes a broadly inclusive approach to the question, balancing a variety of factors that have historically informed Christian life. Richly interwoven sources of authority in the Catholic tradition include subjective phenomena such as reason, conscience, and experience and more objective phenomena such as scripture, liturgy, councils, creeds, and the teaching of bishops and popes. Shaped by centuries of intellectual exploration, spiritual introspection, sacramental worship, and practical application, these integrally related elements constitute the full tapestry of Catholic authority on faith and morals.

In this essay, I will concentrate on two of the characteristic features of the Catholic tradition's multifaceted view of authority. In particular, I will focus on two of the more objective areas in Catholic thought that have proved especially significant in the Protestant-Catholic encounter: (1) the relationship between scripture and tradition and (2) the authority of the church itself. As a convert to Catholicism, with deep personal roots in the evangelical tradition, I am interested in drafting a critical discussion of the issue of authority into the service of an already fruitful ecumenical dialogue between Protestant and Catholic Christians. As a Christian pluralist, active in interfaith affairs on the local and international level, I am also interested in probing the dimensions of the Catholic understanding of authority that bear directly on questions of interreligious relations and a theology of religions. Consistent with its emphasis on the continuity between divine grace and the created order of nature and history, the Catholic tradition has developed a sacramental model of authority that unites a high view of revelation with an inclusive appreciation for cultural institutions as well as non-Catholic and non-Christian forms of religious experience. What makes

---

[1]Unless otherwise noted, all Scripture quotations contained herein are from the New Revised Standard Version (NRSV; see p. iv above).

the Catholic vision of authority distinctive is its synthesis of timeless truth and ecclesial structure with historical dynamism and human imagination.

The Second Vatican Council

For the purposes of this essay, the best place to get a sense of the Catholic tradition's approach to the issue of authority is the collection of official documents promulgated by the Second Vatican Council (1962–1965). In these historic sixteen constitutions, decrees, and declarations, the Catholic church attempted to offer a reason for its hope to a modern world profoundly transformed by the trauma of world war, the anxiety of "cold war," the globalization of the technological revolution, and the erosion of traditional faith. In an unprecedented way, it also expressed its willingness to enter into respectful dialogue with the modern world on issues of contemporary and ultimate significance. Reading the "signs of the times," as they put it, the church authorities who gathered at Vatican II sought to communicate the Christian message in a way comprehensible to "a world that is at once powerful and weak, capable of doing what is noble and what is base, disposed to freedom and slavery, progress and decline, amity and hatred" (*Gaudium et Spes*, 9).[2]

From a Catholic perspective, the Christian community has always been seeking to gain greater self-understanding and enhanced clarity in self-articulation through the process of collective reflection and communal decision making. The Book of Acts describes several pivotal moments in the early church's experience when Christian leaders assembled to formulate common responses to unanticipated problems: the selection of a new apostle after the suicide of Judas (1:15-26), the creation of the institution of the "Seven" for diaconal service (6:1-6), and the incorporation of Gentile believers into a messianic movement previously identified by Jewish standards of belief and practice (15:1-29). The remarks of James at the so-called Council of Jerusalem, traditionally dated around the year CE 50, captured what would become the operative theological understanding of councils in the evolving Catholic tradition: "For it has seemed good to the Holy Spirit and to us . . ." (15:28). The Catholic church historically has seen itself as a

---

[2]All quotations from the documents of the Second Vatican Council are from Austin Flannery, ed., *Vatican Council II: Constitutions, Decrees, Declarations* (Northport NY: Costello, 1996). Citations refer to the Latin title of the document and the relevant section of the text.

living community of faith divinely commissioned to address unique historical challenges in response to the leadership of the Spirit who, according to
Jesus' promise, "will guide you into all the truth" (John 16:12).

Beyond the apostolic councils of the primitive New Testament community, the Catholic church recognizes—along with the Orthodox churches,
the Anglican church, and the confessional Protestant denominations—a
series of ecumenical or worldwide councils of bishops that have contributed
significantly to the consolidation of Christian creed and cult throughout
history, especially during classical Christianity's formative centuries. Since
the Council of Nicea in 325 CE, which officially defined church teaching on
the divinity of Christ, ecumenical councils have tackled a host of disputed
questions dealing with doctrine, worship, organization, and discipline.
According to Catholic reckoning, the Second Vatican Council represents
the twenty-first in the series, the most recent in the wake of two other major
councils in the church's modern period: the Council of Trent (1545–1563),
called to execute programmatic reform in the era of the Protestant Reformation, and Vatican I (1869–1870), best known for its definition of papal
infallibility.[3]

Vatican II, convened by Pope John XXIII at the threshold of a period
of incredible religious and cultural ferment, ranks as the most important
event in contemporary Catholic experience.[4] John Paul II, auxiliary bishop
of Krakow at the time of the council, called it "a great gift to the Church
[and] to the entire human family."[5] Swiss theologian Hans Kung, one of the
leading *periti* or expert consultants at the council, has called it "an epoch-
making and irrevocable turning point" in the history of Catholic Christianity.[6] The premier historian of the council, Giuseppe Alberigo, has summed
up the feelings of many observers in his description of Vatican II as "a

---

[3]See Christopher M. Bellitto, *The General Councils: A History of the Twenty-
One Church Councils from Nicaea to Vatican II* (New York: Paulist Press, 2002).

[4]See Giuseppe Alberigo and Joseph Komonchak, eds., *History of Vatican II*,
5 vols. (Maryknoll NY: Orbis Books, 1995–2006). See also William Madges, ed.,
Vatican II: Forty Years Later (Maryknoll NY: Orbis Books, 2006).

[5]John Paul II, *Crossing the Threshold of Hope*, ed. Vittorio Messori, trans.
Jenny McPhee and Martha McPhee (New York: Alfred A. Knopf, 1994) 157.

[6]Hans Kung, *The Catholic Church: A Short History*, trans. John Bowden (New
York: Modern Library, 2003) 182.

masterpiece . . . of the subtle workings of the Holy Spirit."[7] The council inaugurated an era of collective renewal and self-examination so dramatic and so extensive that even after forty years it continues to be the single most important reference point for the definition of international Catholic character and purpose.

The pastoral reforms of the council, initiated by the almost 2,500 bishops who participated in its sessions, reflected the attempt to enact Pope John's agenda of *aggiornamento* ("updating") in the most important areas of modern Catholic identity and outreach. The conciliar "fathers" envisioned the church at the intersection of "the earthly and the heavenly city," uniquely positioned to probe the record and promise of modernity "in light of the Gospel and of human experience," while "carefully distinguishing the everlasting from the changeable" (*Gaudium et Spes*, 40, 46, 52). The sixteen documents produced by the council focus on subjects such as liturgy, education, ecclesiology, revelation, religious freedom, missions, ecumenism, and interreligious dialogue. The conceptual embodiment of the council's extraordinary legacy, they still exercise enormous influence in virtually every aspect of church life. The most relevant for an examination of the issue of authority in Catholicism are *Dei Verbum*, the Dogmatic Constitution on Divine Revelation, and *Lumen Gentium*, the Dogmatic Constitution on the Church.

Scripture and Tradition

About a hundred years before Vatican II, in opposition to the Protestant *sola scriptura* of his day, John Henry Newman, the archetype of the nineteenth-century Catholic convert, asserted that "ecclesiastical authority" was the "supreme rule and appropriate guide for Catholics in matters of religion."[8] In a sense, of course, he was correct. Contrary to textbook stereotypes, Catholicism cannot be properly categorized as a "religion of the book." The Catholic trajectory in Christian spirituality has always emphasized a divinely appointed teaching church as the matrix that gives rise to both scripture and the sacramental pattern of Christian experience. For modern intellectual converts such as Newman, especially pilgrim souls from

---

[7]Giuseppe Alberigo, *A Brief History of Vatican II*, trans. Matthew Sherry (Maryknoll NY: Orbis Books, 2006) 128.

[8]John Henry Newman, *The Idea of a University*, ed. Martin J. Svaglic (New York: Holt, Rinehart, and Winston, 1964) 8.

evangelicalism, the journey to Catholicity has invariably included a transformative encounter with the concept of tradition as a living phenomenon and the New Testament portrayal of "the church of the living God" as "the pillar and bulwark of the truth" (1 Tim. 3:15).

At the same time, however, Newman's reference to the supremacy of ecclesial authority in Christian life profoundly misstated the historic Catholic view of the priority of church over scripture. Perhaps reflecting more of the convert-cardinal's embattled position as apologist and polemicist in Protestant Victorian England than a strict interpretation of Catholic doctrine, the remark misrepresented the central place of the Bible in Catholic belief and practice. The formulas have fluctuated over time, but the basic principle has remained roughly the same: scripture constitutes the written standard of sacred revelation, but tradition—broadly expressed in liturgy, creed, preaching, polity, and interpretation—serves as scripture's divinely ordained natural context, apart from which the text can be neither efficacious nor comprehensible.

Contemporary Catholic scripture scholars point to an affirmation of the authority of tradition within the Bible itself.[9] Paul, they explain, employed the category of *paradosis* or tradition ("handing on") in a positive, definitive manner. He encouraged Christians at Thessalonica to "hold fast to the traditions that you were taught by us, either by word of mouth or by our letter" (2 Thess. 2:15). He commended Corinthian believers "because you . . . maintain the traditions just as I handed them on to you" (1 Cor. 11:2). He thanked God for the Roman church's obedience to "the form of teaching to which you were entrusted" (Rom. 6:17). The prefaces to his description of the Last Supper—Christianity's first written account of the Eucharist— and his celebrated declaration of Christ's Resurrection, framed according to the conventions of early Christianity's *kerygma* ("proclamation"), both demonstrate the crucial function performed by tradition in Paul's theology: "For I received from the Lord what I also handed on to you . . ." (1 Cor. 11:23, cf. 15:3 NRSV). Arguably his trope of "treasure in earthen vessels" (2 Cor. 4:7 KJV, RSV) sprang from insights into the curious interplay of divine revelation and human creativity in his own experience. From a

---

[9]See Joseph T. Lienhard, *The Bible, the Church, and Authority* (Collegeville MN: Liturgical Press, 1995). See also Raymond E. Brown, Joseph A. Fitzmyer, and Roland E. Murphy, eds., *The New Jerome Biblical Commentary* (Englewood Cliffs NJ: Prentice-Hall, 1990).

Catholic point of view, New Testament references to "the apostles' teaching" (Acts 2:42), "the standard of sound teaching" (2 Tim. 1:13), and "the faith that was once for all entrusted to the saints" (Jude 3 NRSV) suggest a similarly dynamic interpenetration of scripture and tradition at all levels of early Christian life.

Before the twentieth century, official Catholic rhetoric favored language that spoke of two seemingly independent sources of revelation: written scripture and unwritten tradition emanating from Christ and the apostles. The Council of Trent, partly in response to Protestantism's high view of scripture as the sole authority, gave the impression that medieval scholasticism's two-source theory of revelation was an unchanging tenet of Catholic faith—an impression reinforced by numerous church documents including Pius XII's encyclical *Humani Generis* (1950). During the nineteenth and first half of the twentieth century, however, several new currents in Catholic intellectual life challenged this long-standing perception: Catholic modernism's incorporation of historical-critical methods into biblical and historical research, the neopatristic *Nouvelle Theologie*'s shift from propositional to personalist models of revelation, Teilhard de Chardin's synthesis of evolutionary science and Christian mysticism, and a variety of other efforts seeking a *ressourcement* ("return to the sources") and a rediscovery of Catholicism's rich theological pluralism. These pioneering movements promoted an ethos of increased historical consciousness in Catholic scholarship and sparked a tendency to emphasize greater continuity between scripture and tradition. Despite a series of setbacks, and in some cases overt ecclesiastical opposition, they served as catalysts for Vatican II's more nuanced approach to scripture and tradition.[10]

Especially influential in this process was Newman's concept of the development of doctrine. Newman saw the Christian faith not as a static set of propositions fixed in biblical texts but as a dynamic course of insights expanding naturally and gradually under unforeseen historical circumstances. In his unfinished masterpiece *An Essay on the Development of Christian Doctrine* (1845), he articulated the principle of doctrinal development with an arresting metaphor from nature:

> It is indeed sometimes said that the stream is clearest near the spring. Whatever

---

[10]See T. M. Schoof, *A Survey of Catholic Theology 1800–1970*, trans. N. D. Smith (New York: Paulist Press, 1970).

use may fairly be made of this image, it does not apply to the history of a philosophy or belief, which on the contrary is more equable, and purer, and stronger, when its bed has become deep, and broad, and full. . . . In time it enters upon strange territory; points of controversy alter their bearing; parties rise and fall around it; dangers and hopes appear in new relations; and old principles reappear under new forms. It changes with them in order to remain the same. In a higher world it is otherwise, but here below to live is to change, and to be perfect is to have changed often.[11]

Many Newman scholars have seen in these words a prophetic "anticipation" of the Second Vatican Council's progressive openness to new ideas. Some have even dubbed the council "Newman's Council."[12]

Dei Verbum's Theology of Revelation

According to Vatican II, Catholic teaching on the authority of scripture and tradition is best understood in the context of a holistic vision of God's universal self-disclosure to humanity—recognizing, as former-*peritus* Joseph Ratzinger (now Benedict XVI) has urged, that God's revelation "is always greater than what can be contained in human words, greater even than the words of Scripture."[13] The council documents reassert the First Vatican Council's position on the possibility of certain knowledge of God through creation, conscience, and the natural light of reason. They also affirm authentic knowledge of revelation independent of explicit knowledge of Christ or the Christian faith. The council's Decree on the Church's Missionary Activity, for example, refers to "elements of truth and grace," hidden "seeds of the word," and a "secret presence of God" in the world's various religious traditions (*Ad Gentes*, 9, 11). The landmark Declaration on the Relation of the Church to Non-Christian Religions maintains that "spiritual and moral truths" outside the visible boundaries of Christianity "often reflect a ray of that truth which enlightens all men and women" (*Nostra Aetate*, 2).

    The council's Dogmatic Constitution on Divine Revelation, hailed as

---

[11]John Henry Newman, *An Essay on the Development of Christian Doctrine* (Notre Dame IN: University of Notre Dame Press, 1989) 40.

[12]Ian Kerr, *John Henry Newman: A Biography* (Oxford UK: Oxford University Press, 1988) 411.

[13]Joseph Ratzinger, *Milestones: Memoirs 1927–1977*, trans. Erasmo Leiva-Merikakis (San Francisco: Ignatius Press, 1998) 127.

"a genuine watershed in the history of Roman Catholicism,"[14] presents a
theology of revelation that synthesizes classical understandings of scripture
and tradition with modern insights into the study of the Bible and salvation
history. At the time of the council, readers were most impressed by the document's endorsement of historical-critical methodology, its respect for the
divine-human character of biblical literature, and its designation of biblical
study as "the very soul of sacred theology" (*Dei Verbum*, 24). Many praised
its call for a revival of the art of preaching and the practice of *lectio divina*
as well as its hope for "a new impulse of spiritual life" (*Dei Verbum*, 26).

Today *Dei Verbum* provides an eloquent summary of the contemporary
church's position on the authority of revelation. The document is frequently
reprinted in Catholic Bibles and forms the basis for the section on revelation
in the *Catechism of the Catholic Church*.[15] It is often credited with
contributing to the renaissance of biblical studies still very much observable
in Catholic academic culture. Its distinctive approach to revelation—a four-
dimensional model uniting tradition, scripture, episcopal authority, and the
Holy Spirit—has become a standard component of postconciliar Catholic
theology, superseding the premodern two-source theory:

> [I]n the supremely wise arrangement of God, sacred tradition, sacred scripture
> and the magisterium of the church are so connected and associated that one of
> them cannot stand without the others. Working together, each in its own way
> under the action of the one holy Spirit, they all contribute effectively to the
> salvation of souls. (*Dei Verbum*, 10)

Perhaps the most notable features of *Dei Verbum*'s theology of revelation are its consistent emphasis on the dynamic quality of divine revelation
and its accompanying accent on revelation's organic character. Without
mentioning him by name, Vatican II adopted an evolutionary scheme
analogous to Newman's notion of doctrinal development in order to underscore the "living and active" nature of God's word in tradition and scripture
(Heb. 4:12). Just as the Virgin Mary "treasured all these words and
pondered them in her heart" (Luke 2:19), the council maintained, so the
church's ongoing process of nurturing its understanding of revelation yields

---

[14]Donald Senior, "Dogmatic Constitution on Divine Revelation," *Vatican II and Its Documents: An American Reappraisal*, ed. Timothy E. O'Connell (Wilmington DE: Michael Glazier, 1986) 139.
[15]See *Catechism of the Catholic Church* (Ligouri MO: Liguori, 1994) 50-141.

greater penetration into the mystery of the Gospel. New public revelation after Christ is denied, but so is exclusive dependence upon the letter of the Bible. The "living teaching office" of the church's bishops, grounded in the "single sacred deposit of the word of God" formed by tradition and scripture, makes "the voice of the holy Spirit sound again and again" (*Dei Verbum*, 10, 21):

> The tradition that comes from the apostles makes progress in the church, with the help of the holy Spirit. There is growth in insight into the realities and words that are being passed on. . . . Thus, as the centuries go by, the church is always advancing towards the plenitude of divine truth, until eventually the words of God are fulfilled in it. . . . Thus God, who spoke in the past, continues to converse with the spouse of his beloved Son. (*Dei Verbum*, 8)

Likewise, *Dei Verbum* represents a virtual canonization of Paul's "treasure in earthen vessels" motif. At its heart is a vision of a God whose self-communication is mediated through particular conceptual and linguistic systems embedded in the corporate life of specific cultures around the world. The document's generous definition of tradition recognizes the "many and various ways" in which God has revealed the divine personality to humanity (Heb. 1:1) and the culturally conditioned character of the public channels that have transmitted divine wisdom throughout the centuries. Its treatment of scripture is equally remarkable for its emphasis on the Bible's inerrancy with regard to salvation and its acknowledgement of the cognitive and cultural limitations of the Bible's human authors: "God speaks through human beings in human fashion" (*Dei Verbum*, 12).

What ultimately distinguishes the conception of authority articulated in *Dei Verbum* from alternative theories in global Christianity is its conviction that genuine Christian authority rests on a concrete—and nearly sacramental—conjunction of ancient teaching, communal insight, evolving ecclesial structures, and ongoing spiritual renewal. Such an embodied view of revelation, the council suggested, is an example of the "marvelous 'condescension' of eternal wisdom," not unlike the incarnation of the Word in the "weak flesh of human beings" (*Dei Verbum*, 13).

The Authority of the Church

The Second Vatican Council's document on revelation clearly perceives the Bible as the church's book. Scripture functions properly, it maintains, only when effectively connected to the church's tradition of spiritual, intellectual, and liturgical life. Its correct meaning, moreover, is dependent upon the church's leadership: "Catholic exegetes and other workers in the field of sacred theology should work diligently together and under the watchful eye of the sacred magisterium" (*Dei Verbum*, 23). Newman's remark about the supremacy of "ecclesiastical authority" in Catholic life, as I have suggested, may have overlooked the role of scripture in the Catholic worldview, but it did not underestimate the enormously important place of the church in Catholicism's comprehensive vision of authority.

From a Catholic vantage point, Christianity has always been a highly communal faith. The New Testament portrait of early Christianity, sketched against the background of the Hebrew Bible's concept of covenant, depicts a self-consciously social entity conspicuous for its common values and practices, increasingly structured patterns of leadership, and clear identity boundaries distinguishing it from other groups and movements. The ideal vision of the Christian assembly (*ekklesia*) in the Book of Acts emphasizes the collective dimension of the new tradition:

> They devoted themselves to the apostles' teaching and fellowship, to the breaking of bread and the prayers. . . . All who believed were together and had all things in common; they would sell their possessions and goods and distribute the proceeds to all, as any had need. Day by day, as they spent much time together in the temple, they broke bread at home and ate their food with glad and generous hearts, praising God and having the goodwill of all the people. (Acts 2:42-47)

Paul's image of the Christian fellowship (*koinonia*) as the "body of Christ" (1 Cor. 12) and the description of Christian believers as "this new breed of men" in the second-century Epistle to Diognetus illustrate the importance of the social dimension for formative Christianity. Likewise, Ignatius of Antioch's stress on the centrality of the bishop (*episkopos*) in the Christian community and his felicitous association of *katholou* ("universal" or "whole") with *ekklesia* make it abundantly clear that ecclesiology was becoming a major doctrinal enterprise within the developing phenomenon of Christian theology.[16]

Church historians routinely point out that, while other ecumenical councils concentrated on a single dogmatic problem related to Christology or soteriology, Vatican II was uniquely and intentionally a pastoral council,

---

[16]See *Early Christian Writings*, trans. Maxwell Staniforth and Andrew Louth (London: Penguin Books, 1987).

particularly focused on the doctrine of the church. Arguably the main purpose of the council was to clarify ecclesial identity in the unsettling atmosphere of modernity. Official council documents on the ministry of bishops and priests, the renewal of religious life, the apostolate of lay people, and the task of ecumenical dialogue directly address questions of ecclesiology in an age of uncertainty. The council's Pastoral Constitution on the Church in the Modern World, the longest document produced by any ecumenical council,[17] explicitly states its desire "to set down how [the council] understands the presence and function of the church in the world of today" (*Gaudium et Spes*, 2).

The Ecclesiology of *Lumen Gentium*

Lumen Gentium, Vatican II's Dogmatic Constitution on the Church, contains the core of the council's reflections on the communal dimension of Christianity. With the phenomenal range of its eight chapters, it represents a much more extensive endeavor than the council's document on revelation—nearly five times its length. Like *Dei Verbum*, however, it has been recognized by the vast majority of Catholic theologians as a seminal work in Christian thought. Its abiding influence can be seen not only in the universal *Catechism* and subsequent magisterial teaching but also in landmarks of ecclesiological scholarship such as Hans Kung's *The Church* (1967), Avery Dulles's *Models of the Church* (1974), Leonardo Boff's *Church, Charism and Power* (1986), and Joseph Ratzinger's *Called to Communion* (1991). One commentator has described *Lumen Gentium* as "a revolution in the Church's self-understanding."[18]

The document reviews the major images for the church in scripture and patristic literature and anchors its ecclesiology in themes of the church's sacramental "mystery" and its status as the pilgrim "people of God" on earth. The church, it says, is "a sacrament—a sign and instrument, that is, of communion with God and of the unity of the entire human race" (*Lumen Gentium*, 1). As a "visible sacrament" of God's reconciling activity, the church is also by definition a community—but a community unlike any other on earth. Natural yet supernatural, historical yet eschatological,

---

[17]Justo L. Gonzalez, *The Story of Christianity*, 2 vols. (San Francisco: Harper & Row, 1985) 2:354.

[18]John Linnan, "Dogmatic Constitution on the Church and Decree on the Pastoral Office of Bishops in the Church," *Vatican II and Its Documents*, 43.

mystical yet visible and sociological, human yet divine, the Christian church transcends "at once all times and all boundaries between peoples." "For this reason," the document explains, "the church is compared to the mystery of the incarnate Word" (*Lumen Gentium*, 8, 9).

Lumen Gentium traces the roots of the church's authority back to the covenant heritage of ancient Israel and the messianic mission of Jesus. By the time of the council, many New Testament scholars, both Protestant and Catholic, had already begun to posit a fundamental disjunction between the "Jesus of history" and the "Christ of faith." Increasingly academics associated the "kingdom of God" exclusively with the eschatological expectation of the Jewish Jesus of Nazareth, while "church" was becoming a term reserved for the post-Easter Christian community more and more focused on doctrine and cult. In contrast to what is still the trend in early Christianity studies, *Lumen Gentium* retains the traditional link between ecclesiology and the "kingdom of God" in Jesus' message and ministry:

> To carry out the will of the Father, Christ inaugurated the kingdom of heaven on earth and revealed his mystery to us; by his obedience he brought about the redemption. The church—that is, the kingdom of Christ already present in mystery—grows visibly in the world through the power of God. . . . [T]he church, equipped with the gifts of its founder and faithfully observing his precepts of charity, humility and self-denial, receives the mission of proclaiming and establishing among all peoples the kingdom of Christ and of God, and is, on earth, the seed and the beginning of that kingdom. (*Lumen Gentium*, 3, 5)

More importantly, *Lumen Gentium* closely associates the present-day Catholic church with the church founded by Christ and affirmed for centuries as "one, holy, catholic, and apostolic." The Catholic church historically has seen itself as the authoritative body entrusted with the "keys of the kingdom of heaven" and the responsibility of binding and loosing on earth and in heaven (Matt. 16:19, 18:18)—a community continuous with both the *ekklesia* built on the "this rock" (Matt. 16:18) and the post-Resurrection *koinonia* "built upon the foundation of the apostles and prophets, with Christ Jesus himself as the cornerstone" (Eph. 2:20). According to *Lumen Gentium*, the particular marks of the Catholic church's unbroken continuity with the church founded by Christ include its ongoing participation in the three-fold ministry of Christ as prophet, priest, and king and its unceasing engagement, through the "common priesthood" of lay people and the "ministerial or hierarchical priesthood" of presbyters and bishops, in the celebration of the seven sacraments of baptism, confirmation, penance, eucharist, matrimony, ordination, and anointing of the sick (*Lumen Gentium*, 10, 50).

Of considerable importance in this regard are the teaching and administrative offices of bishop and pope, the magisterium of the church. These ministries *Lumen Gentium* locates in the highest context of Trinitarian theology and salvation history:

> Jesus Christ, the eternal pastor, established the holy church by sending the apostles as he himself had been sent by the Father (see Jn. 20:21). He willed that their successors, the bishops, should be the shepherds in his church until the end of the world. In order that the episcopate itself, however, might be one and undivided he placed blessed Peter over the other apostles, and in him he set up a lasting and visible source and foundation of the unity both of faith and of communion. (*Lumen Gentium*, 18)

Through the ritual imposition of hands and the gift of the Holy Spirit, bishops inherit the evangelistic responsibilities of the apostles and govern the church as representatives of Christ. They exercise collective authority in conferences, synods, and worldwide councils, and they oversee their respective dioceses with full pastoral authority, not as papal vicars or autonomous agents. Most of all, bishops are charged with fostering and safeguarding "the unity of the faith and . . . the discipline which is common to the whole church" (*Lumen Gentium*, 23).

The bishop of Rome, seen as successor to the chief apostle Peter and head of the apostolic "college" of bishops, serves uniquely as the "supreme teacher of the universal church," discharging "full, supreme, and universal power over the whole church." The pope's infallible teaching office, first proclaimed as an official doctrine at Vatican I, is couched in the context of the general infallibility granted to the entire people of God by virtue of the superintendence of the Holy Spirit. *Lumen Gentium* limits papal infallibility to definitive pronouncements on "doctrine pertaining to faith or morals" declared solemnly *ex cathedra* ("from the chair"). It does not, however, provide any specific examples of such formal pronouncements. Statements made by the pope as a private person and the possibility of new public revelation, it insists, are explicitly excluded from the phenomenon of infallibility (*Lumen Gentium*, 22, 25).

Since the First Vatican Council, Catholic leaders and theologians have been engaged in an ongoing discussion concerning the practical application of papal infallibility, especially as it impinges on issues of intellectual and academic freedom. *Lumen Gentium* captures the tensions of that continuing conversation as it recommends a "religious docility of the will and intellect" in response to even the noninfallible teaching of the magisterium, while also promoting broader collegiality among church officials, advocating the expansion of the lay apostolate, celebrating the "wonderful diversity" within the Catholic community, and honoring the integrity of "the entire people's supernatural sense of the faith" (*Lumen Gentium*, 12, 25, 30). Those tensions are rendered only more evident by the positive treatment given the "lawful freedom of inquiry, of thought, and of expression" in the council's Pastoral Constitution on the Church in the Modern World and the Declaration on Religious Liberty's sanction of the primacy of conscience— what Newman called the "aboriginal Vicar of Christ" (*Gaudium et Spes*, 62; *Dignitatis Humanae*, 3).[19] Postconciliar calls for the recognition of the legitimacy of "loyal dissent" within Catholic intellectual culture, coupled with the infusion of human rights advocacy into contemporary papal discourse, indicate the extent to which the comprehensive implementation of a Vatican II ecclesiology remains unfinished business for the church in the first years of its third millennium.[20]

What is perhaps most striking about *Lumen Gentium*'s ecclesiology is its attempt to balance a high theology of Catholic institutions with a robust commitment to the ideal of unity expressed in Jesus' high priestly prayer: "that they may become completely one" (John 17:23). One of the document's most important passages, expressed in language that has sparked lively discussion for more than four decades, draws attention to the larger horizon of the church's authority rather than the specific order of ecclesiastical positions, duties, or rites. It declares that the one church of Christ,

> which our Saviour, after his resurrection, entrusted to Peter's pastoral care (Jn. 21:17), commissioning him and the other apostles to extend and rule it (see Mt. 28:18, etc.), and which he raised up for all ages as the pillar and mainstay of the truth (see 1 Tim. 3:15) . . . *subsists in the Catholic Church*, which is governed by the successor of Peter and by the bishops in communion with him. (*Lumen Gentium*, 8; italics added)

---

[19]Ian Ker, *Newman on Being a Christian* (Notre Dame IN: University of Notre Dame Press, 1990) 100.
[20]See Charles E. Curran, *Loyal Dissent: Memoir of a Catholic Theologian* (Washington DC: Georgetown University Press, 2006). Hans Kung, *My Struggle for Freedom*, trans. John Bowden (Grand Rapids MI: Eerdmans, 2003).

The ecumenical implications of the council's decision to replace the phrase *est Ecclesia catholica*, as found in the document's original draft, with *subsistit in Ecclesia catholica* have been vigorously explored by a wide variety of scholars.[21] American Jesuit and cardinal Avery Dulles has interpreted the passage to mean that the "Church of Jesus Christ is not exclusively identified with the Roman Catholic Church."[22] The willingness to examine the unique authority of the Catholic church without neglecting the common authority shared by all Christian communions professing the basics of baptism, faith, and canon represents one of the singular achievements of the Second Vatican Council. Combined with the church's positive overtures toward the "separated" Christians of Orthodox and Protestant traditions, the editorial shift from "is" to "subsists in" laid the groundwork for the council's unparalleled commitment to Christian unity articulated in its Decree on Ecumenism, *Unitatis Redintegratio*. *Lumen Gentium* recognizes "many elements of sanctification and of truth" in non-Catholic Christianities and acknowledges the Spirit's desire for the unification of "all of Christ's disciples" (*Lumen Gentium*, 8, 15). Today the spirit of the document continues to fuel Catholic experiments in ecumenical ecclesiology and ecumenical encounter. Arguably the call for ecumenical humility and repentance which became a hallmark of the epic pontificate of John Paul II could never have been possible without the pioneering work of *Lumen Gentium*.[23]

Even more provocative is the document's designation of the church as "the universal sacrament of salvation" (*Lumen Gentium*, 48). Vatican II was the first ecumenical council to exhibit a truly global vision of the church— the first to set its theological sights not only beyond Catholicism but beyond Christianity itself. As it yearns for the restoration of all things, *Lumen Gentium* says, the pilgrim church serves as an emblem of the mysterious unity awaiting the entire human race. Only an ecclesiology set in a global frame of reference, the document suggests, possesses the genuine authority

---

[21]See Peter A. Huff, "Separation Incomplete, Communion Imperfect: Vatican II's Ecumenical Strategy," *One in Christ* 31 (1995): 52-62.

[22]Quoted in Frank Mobbs, "The One True Church according to Vatican II," *Homiletic and Pastoral Review* (July 1985): 58.

[23]See Luigi Accattoli, *Man of the Millennium: John Paul II*, trans. Jordan Aumann (Boston: Pauline Books and Media, 2000).

to advance ventures in the wider ecumenism of interreligious dialogue and encourage the development of a Catholic theology of religions. It declares that Jews and Muslims are incorporated into God's "plan of salvation" and that the truth is not remote from people "who in shadows and images seek the unknown God." In language that has become officially enshrined in the *Catechism*, it affirms the possibility of salvation for individuals "who, through no fault of their own, do not know the Gospel of Christ or his church, but who nevertheless seek God with a sincere heart, and, moved by grace, try in their actions to do his will as they know it through the dictates of their conscience" (*Lumen Gentium*, 16).

One of the extraordinary developments in postconciliar Catholic thought has been the endorsement in official church teaching of a Christo-centric inclusivism that bends toward full solidarity with the religions of the world while continuing to affirm the essential nature of the church's evangelistic task.[24] Perhaps no greater example of this phenomenon can be found than the "living icon" of John Paul II's 1986 World Day of Prayer for Peace, which brought together 160 representatives from all world religions to the Italian hill town of Assisi for an unforgettable moment of shared con-templation on the frontiers of dialogue.[25] In his "exegesis" of the event, delivered to Vatican leaders after the meeting, John Paul, who was often accused of trying to restore the pre-Vatican II monarchial papacy and reverse the reform agenda of the council, drew directly from the council's Dogmatic Constitution on the Church in order to articulate an insight into the link between the authority of the Catholic church and the "hidden but radical unity" of the human community:

In this great design of God for humanity, the Church finds her identity and her task as

> "universal sacrament of salvation" precisely in being "a sign and instrument of intimate union with God and of the unity of the whole human race" (*Lumen Gentium*, 1); this means that the Church is called to work with all her energies (evangelization, prayer, dialogue) so that the wounds and divisions of men— which separate them from their Origin and Goal, and make them hostile to one

---

[24]See Jacques Dupuis, *Toward a Christian Theology of Religious Pluralism* (Maryknoll NY: Orbis Books, 2001).

[25]Michael L. Fitzgerald, "Pope John Paul II and Interreligious Dialogue: A Catholic Assessment," *John Paul II and Interreligious Dialogue*, ed. Byron L. Sherwin and Harold Kasimow (Maryknoll NY: Orbis Books, 1999) 209.

another—may be healed; it means also that the entire human race, in the infinite complexity of its history, with its different cultures, is "called to form the new People of God" (*Lumen Gentium*, 13) in which the blessed union of God with man and the unity of the human family are healed, consolidated, and raised up: "All persons, accordingly, are called to this *catholic unity* of the people of God, which prefigures and promotes universal peace, and to which, in various ways, belong or are orientated both the Catholic faithful and the others who believe in Christ, and finally all who have been called to salvation by the grace of God" (*Lumen Gentium* 8; emphasis added).[26]

Conclusion

John Paul's thoughts on the World Day of Prayer in Assisi tapped the surprisingly centrifugal potential contained within the ecclesiology of Vatican II. His vision of a "civilization of love" embracing both Christians and other believers issued from his conviction that the church's Second Vatican Council played a special part in history's providential design. Before Vatican II, no one—not even the man who would become the "Pope of surprises"[27]—could have imagined an infallible pope exercising his authority to commend the virtues of a new catholicity transcending all religious boundaries.

During the First Vatican Council, when the Catholic hierarchy first asserted the authority of an infallible pope, John Henry Newman spoke for his day's progressive party of Catholic intellectuals, observing that

> a Council's proper office is, when some great heresy or other evil impends, to inspire the faithful with hope and confidence; but now we have the greatest meeting which ever has been, and that at Rome, infusing into us . . . little else than fear and dismay.[28]

Just short of a hundred years later, the Second Vatican Council—Newman's own, as some would have it—inspired a revolution of hope and courage previously unknown in modern Catholic experience. Though called together for a council focused on pastoral, not dogmatic, issues, the bishops and

---

[26]John Paul II, "Address to the Cardinals and to the Roman Curia," *Assisi: World Day of Prayer for Peace* (Rome: Pontifical Commission Justice and Peace, 1987) 139, 142; italics in original.

[27]John Paul II, *Crossing the Threshold of Hope*, vi.

[28]Quoted in Ian Ker, *John Henry Newman: A Biography*, 651.

theologians who participated in the historic event read the "signs of the times" and produced an impressive collection of documents whose influence on Catholic life and thought is only beginning to be fully calculated. The council's documents on revelation and ecclesiology, intentionally addressing issues of Christian faith to a generation of modern readers, attempted to apply the spirit of Pope John's *aggiornamento* to one of the perennial questions in Christian experience: By what authority are you doing these things?

The intra-Christian debate over the issue of authority has engaged many of the best minds within the worldwide Christian community for centuries. Often pitting the text of scripture against the testimony of a living prophet, or the believer's private judgment against the public teaching of an apostolic church, the debate has generated multiple models of authority in Christian thought and practice. At Vatican II, the Roman Catholic community officially reaffirmed its distinctive approach to the question, formulating a modern response in harmony with its classical sacramental view of reality balancing the orders of nature and grace. Emphasizing a dynamic synthesis of sources—including scripture, tradition, the church, and the guidance of the Holy Spirit—the Catholic tradition continues to make a unique contribution to the ongoing conversation about authority in Christianity.

THE AUTHORITY IN QUESTION[1]

Richard John Neuhaus

Among the prominent intellectuals and theologians who have in the last few years entered into full communion with the Catholic Church is R. R. Reno, formerly an Anglican. Each of these thinkers would likely explain the decision to become Catholic in a different way, but I expect that most would be sympathetic to the reasons given by Reno. In *First Things*, he wrote:

> In order to escape the insanity of my slide into self-guidance, I put myself up for reception into the Catholic Church as one might put oneself up for adoption. A man can no more guide his spiritual life by his ideas than a child can raise himself on the strength of his native potential.

Reno quotes Newman, who, while he was still an Anglican, said that, "the Church of Rome preoccupied the ground." Reno understands that to mean:

> She is given, a primary substance within the economy of denominationalism. This one could rightly say that I became a Catholic by default, and that possibility is the simple gift I received from the Catholic Church. She needed neither reasons, nor theories, nor ideas from me.[2]

What stands out is the sheer *isness* of the Catholic Church. To sustain the allegiance of an ecclesial Christian, the Church of the Augsburg Confession needed reasons, theories, and ideas from me and others of like mind. It *was* our idea. To give yourself to your own idea is not to give yourself at all. It is possible that I might make some small contribution to the Catholic Church, also along the lines of reasons, theories, and ideas. But the Catholic Church does not need anything from me for it to be the Catholic Church. The Catholic Church is not about me. The Church is, in her *isness,* grandly and blithely indifferent to the tangle that constitutes my state of *incurvatus est*. Like a mother, she takes me in.

To speak of the Church as a mother or to speak, as Reno does, of putting oneself up for adoption raises a field of red flags for those of a Freudian bent. Is this not an instance of letting oneself be infantilized? And Jesus said, "Unless you become as little children. . . . " It is not a regression to childhood but a progression beyond adulthood falsely defined as the

---

[1]This article is adapted from an expanded version that appears as chap. 3 in Neuhaus's *Catholic Matters: Confusion, Controversy and the Splendor of Truth* (New York: Basic Books, 2006). Used by permission.

[2]R. R. Reno, "Out of the Ruins," *First Things* 150 (February 2005): 11-16.

autonomous self, as the gloriously independent actualization of *me*. It is what the French philosopher Paul Ricoeur describes as "the second naïveté," the rebirth of wonder that had been so long stifled under endless complexifications. It is, on the far side of the notional, to surrender to the real. It is even, I dare to think, to be surprised by the unfamiliar and unexpected experience of something like humility. (A Jewish friend said he would not think of missing my service of ordination: "Just once, I want to see Richard prostrated before somebody.")

The morning after I was received into full communion by Cardinal O'Conner, I woke up and tried to specify just what it was that seemed so different. Then it dawned upon me: for the first time in years I did not begin the day oppressed by the burden of wondering where I was supposed to be and of explaining why I was not there. I was there. The cliché is as banal as it is inevitable: I had come home. I had long resisted the sentimentalized talk about "Rome sweet home." I had cheered when Cardinal Johannes Willebrands, then in charge of the Vatican's office of Christian unity, had declared, "The word 'return' is no longer part of our ecumenical vocabulary." But I knew I had returned; I knew I had come home. More precisely, I knew there was nowhere else to go. And that is something like being home. It was the place that, as a Lutheran, I had left more than four hundred years ago, and now I had returned.

I had no illusions about the problems, confusions, and conflicts within the Catholic Church. As a "separated brother" I had been thinking and speaking and writing about all that for years. I was not sure how my thinking and writing would be received now that it was, so to speak, all in the family. But none of that matters. There was nowhere else to go. Within a few months of my reception, a Catholic publication put me on its cover as "Catholic of the Year." I suggested to the editors that maybe they should have waited until I had been a Catholic for at least a year.

As it turns out, the reception has been mixed. As a Lutheran, I had over the years received dozens of honorary degrees and awards from Catholic colleges and universities—making such awards was the ecumenical thing to do. Now that I am in the family, writing and saying much as I did before, the bestowing of such honors is thought to be a controversial thing to do. Were I a prophet, which I am not, one might recall the maxim that a prophet is not without honor unless he gets too close. As it is, I have not one complaint. My welcome has been far beyond my deserving. And, anyway, there is nowhere else to go.

I am frequently asked whether I had ever considered becoming Orthodox. Eastern Orthodoxy is a real alternative for the ecclesial Christian. The
churches of the East are recognized as "sister church" by Rome. Orthodoxy
possesses so many of the essentials—apostolic ministry and doctrine, a
magnificent richness of liturgy and sacramental life, and a powerful theological tradition of humanity's destined end in the life of God, a fervent
devotion to Mary and the saints. One does have to consider Orthodoxy. But
I am a Western Christian, with all that it entails: Augustine and Thomas
Aquinas on nature and grace, reason and revelation, sin and forgiveness, as
well as the Reformation refractions of those great themes and the continuing
disputes they have occasioned. Moreover, Orthodoxy is powerfully shaped
by ethnic and national identities—Russian, Greek, Romanian, Armenian—
to which I am a stranger.

The late Father Alexander Schmemann, a dear friend, was longtime
dean of St. Vladimir Theological Seminary in New York. He spoke often
of converts, mainly Lutherans and Anglicans, who posed great difficulties
to themselves and to the Orthodox Church by their attempts to become
what, by virtue of their histories, they were not. Much more important,
becoming Orthodox does nothing to remedy the problem of not being in
communion with the Petrine Ministry exercised by the bishop of Rome.
Becoming Orthodox would do nothing to advance a lifelong commitment
to healing the sixteenth-century breach between Rome and the Reformation.
Some might ask whether my becoming Catholic advances that healing, a
fair question to which I hope the answer is in the affirmative. My becoming
Catholic is at least a testimony to that commitment and a personal anticipation of its fulfillment.

But one cannot leave the question of the Orthodox option without
acknowledging the great sadness of continuing division between East and
West. In view of all that is shared between Catholic and Orthodox, it seems
fair to say that the only thing missing for full communion is full communion. One day in a discussion with John Paul II, I asked him what his
greatest hopes for his pontificate were when he was elected in 1978.
Without a moment's hesitation he said that his greatest hope was for
Christian unity. And Christian unity means, first of all, reconciliation with
the Orthodox Church. John Paul repeatedly spoke of the need for the
Church "to breathe again with both lungs, East and West." Despite John
Paul's many conciliatory initiatives, that hope has been delayed, but his
pontificate laid the groundwork for the healing of the thousand-year breach

between East and West. That is a great achievement, and I have no doubt that it is an achievement on which Benedict XVI will build.

Already in the early months of the new pontificate, the Russian Church, which has been among the chief obstacles to rapprochement, seems to be more responsive to initiatives from Rome. History has many ironies in the fire, as it is said, and it may be that the Russians are less uneasy dealing with a German than with a Pole, given the long and bitter history of intra-Slavic conflict.

In becoming a Catholic, one is braced for certain criticisms. Among the most common, usually coming from Protestant sources, is that the person who becomes a Catholic has a "felt need for authority." This is usually said in a somewhat condescending manner by people who say they are able to live with ambiguities and tensions that some of us cannot handle. But to say that I have felt need for authority is no criticism at all. Of course I have, as should we all. The allegedly autonomous self who acknowledges no authority but himself is abjectly captive to the authority of a tradition of Enlightenment rationality that finally collapses into coherence. Whether in matters of science, history, religion, or anything else of consequence, we live amid a storm of different and conflicting ideas claiming to be the truth. Confronted by such truth claims, we necessarily ask, "Sez who?" By what authority, by whose authority, should I credit such claims to truth? Answering the question requires a capacity to distinguish between the authoritative and the authoritarian.

All Christians believe that God has revealed himself in the history of Israel and in the culmination of that history, Jesus Christ, who is the Word of God. All believe, further, that this revelation is authoritatively interpreted by the witness of the apostles, and that over the first centuries this witness was collected and "canonized" by continuing apostolic authority in what came to be called the New Testament, which is the written Word of God. The question is not about the "felt need for authority" but about where that authority is located and how it is exercised. This touches on a familiar dispute between Protestants and Catholics that has been ongoing since the sixteenth century. The dispute is usually framed as the authority of the Bible vs. the authority of the Church, or the authority of the Bible vs. the authority of "tradition." But that way of framing the question is, I believe, deeply coherent.

The Protestant and Catholic positions are rival traditions in conflict. The promise of Jesus that he would send the Holy Spirit to guide his disciples into all truth is a promise made to the Church. That promise is fulfilled, in part, in the fit of the Spirit-inspired writings of the New Testament. But the guidance of the Spirit did not end there. The promise is that the Spirit would guide the Church until the end of time. The Spirit guided the Church in the writing of the inspired texts; guided the Church in recognizing which texts, of the many claiming inspiration at the time, were truly inspired; guided the Church in determining what would be the canon of the New Testament; and guided the Church in declaring the unique authority of the canonical texts for all time. In sum, it is the Spirit guiding the Church from beginning to end, and the end is not yet.

In this understanding, what is crucial is the apostolic foundation and continuing apostolic character of the Church. We Christians confess in the Nicene Creed that we believe in "one, holy, catholic, and apostolic Church"—not in one, holy, catholic, and *biblical* Church. Under the guidance of the Holy Spirit, the Bible is entirely the book of, by, and for the Church, and should never be pitted against the Church. In reaction to the sixteenth-century Protestant rejection of tradition as authoritative, Catholics affirmed a "two sources" theory of revealed truth—the Bible *and* tradition. That way of putting the matter gave rise to numerous misunderstandings, and the formulation was further developed and refined at the Second Vatican Council in the Constitution on Revelation, *Dei Verbum* ("The Word of God").

In a statement of 2002, participants in the ecumenical theological project called Evangelicals and Catholics Together were able to say:

> Together we affirm that Scripture is the divinely inspired and uniquely authoritative written revelation of God; as such it is normative for the teaching and life of the Church. We also affirm that tradition, rightly understood as the proper reflection of biblical teaching, is the faithful transmission of the truth of the gospel from generation to generation through the power of the Holy Spirit. As Evangelicals and Catholics fully committed to our respective heritages, we affirm together the coinherence of Scripture and tradition: tradition is not a second source of revelation alongside the Bible but must ever be corrected and informed by it, and Scripture itself is not understood in a vacuum apart from the historical existence and life of the community of faith.[3]

"The historical existence and life of the community of faith" is another

---

[3]See, e.g., "Your Word Is Truth," *First Things* (August-September 2002).

way of saying tradition. Again, a fair-minded reading of the New Testament
leaves no doubt that Jesus intended a continuing community of discipleship
that is the Church. There is also no doubt that he commissioned the apostles
to shepherd that community under the guidance of the Holy Spirit. From the
beginning, disputes arose over faith and morals. In the New Testament and
in the patristic literature of the first centuries, it is clear that such disputes
were to be resolved by appeal to the authority of the apostles and apostolic
churches. Later, the appeal was to bishops in council, the bishops being
recognized as successors to the apostles. (In the Catholic counting, as noted
earlier, Nicea in 325 was the first council and Vatican II was the twenty-
first. An argument can be made that the first council, or at least the first
exercise of the conciliar principle, is to be found in the fifteenth chapter of
Acts when the apostles addressed the question of what was to be required
of non-Jewish believers.) Admittedly, it is a long and complicated path from
the New Testament to Nicea and on to today's exercise of the Magisterium
in the Catholic Church, but, in logic and in form, the story is one of clear
continuity. It is the story of the apostles gathered by and around Peter.

The division between East and West means that not all the successors
to the apostles are gathered, and then there are the millions of Christians in
nonapostolically ordered communities who are not part of the deliberation.
John Paul II spoke of what might be done about these imperfections in his
1995 encyclical *Ut Unum Sint* ("That They May Be One"). Yet, in this state
of Christianity divided, the Catholic Church makes a uniquely believable
claim to having maintained the form and logic from the beginning. That,
too, is entailed in saying that she is the Church of Jesus Christ most fully
and rightly ordered through time.

When as a young man I was first in Rome, I was Protestant enough to
be inured to much of the splendor and the glory. Was the magnificence of
Michelangelo's basilica of St. Peter, I asked myself, worth the scandal of
the sale of indulgences that paid for it and helped precipitate the schisms of
the sixteenth century? Midst Rome's aesthetic effusion of Catholic sub-
stance, I kept a firm hold on Protestant principle. Until one afternoon—I
remember it now quite clearly—I was struck by the fact that Peter and Paul,
the two chief pillars of the apostolic community, both ended up in Rome
and there they were crowned with martyrdom. I was already aware of that,
of course, but then I recognized the ecclesial logic and form, the rightness
of it, the necessity of it.

"So what?" one may ask. It is a contingent fact, it might have been otherwise. But the whole of Christianity is composed of contingent facts. In the abstract, everything might have been otherwise, but it was not and is not. It is this and that, and thus and so. Abraham, a burning bush, Sinai, exile, mysterious prophecies, a virgin conceiving, water into wine, a cross, a death, his appearance to share a meal of fish (after they had caught exactly 153 of them!) Corinthians speaking in tongues, Peter and Paul in Rome, Constantine and an empire won and lost, Benedict and the monastic anticipation of the new Jerusalem, a papacy divided and a papacy healed, Francis Xavier and the gospel carried to the ends of the earth, and along the way the greatest of minds and souls—Irenaeus and the Gregories and Augustine and Anselm and Catherine and Teresa and Thomas Aquinas and von Balthasar and John Paul II—provide the narrative, stating and restating what it all means. It could have been otherwise, but it wasn't, and it isn't. It is all contingent, which is to say it is all history, the history of a distinct people. And that afternoon, as I contemplated Peter and Paul in Rome, I knew that I had to be, and had to be indisputably, part of that people that was and is the Catholic Church. Sooner or later, I think I knew then, I would have to put myself up for adoption into that people.

Upon becoming a Catholic and then a Catholic priest, I made a solemn profession of faith that included these words: "With firm faith, I also believe everything contained in the Word of God, whether written or handed down in Tradition, which the Church, either by a solemn judgment or by the ordinary and universal Magisterium, sets forth to be believed as divinely revealed." I took a deep breath before saying those words. Am I writing a blank check on my soul? What if the Magisterium, the solemn teaching office of the Church, gets something wrong? May I even admit that question to my mind? By what criterion, by what measure, could I judge a teaching to be wrong? Newman raged against the ravages of "private judgment." Is private the same as personal? Or am I making an intensely personal judgment to believe what the Church believes? Martin Luther spoke derisively of what he called the coal-miner's faith. Asked what he believed, the coal miner answered, "I believe what the Church believes." Asked what the Church believed, he answered, "The Church believes what I believe." Luther insisted that that is no faith at all. I am not quite so sure.

I mentioned earlier the act of faith. For the Protestant, the act of faith is an act of faith in Christ, and only then, if at all, is it an act of faith in the Church. They are two acts of faith. For the Catholic, the act of faith in Christ and his Church is one act of faith. In the Nicene Creed we do not say,

"I believe *that there is* one, holy, catholic, and apostolic Church." We say, "I believe *in* one holy, catholic, and apostolic Church." Because I believe in Christ, I believe in his Church, I entrust myself to her. Christ the head and the Church his body constitute the *totus Christus*, the "total Christ." However it may be that the Church is present in other communities, there is no other community that is prepared to, that would dare to, that should dare to, accept my unqualified trust. I once read an interview with a writer whose name I now forget. He was asked why he went to Mass. "Because I do not know what else I would do with my gratitude," he answered. I am a Catholic because, among many other reasons, I do not know what else I would do with my trust. Trust is risk, trust is faith. Not blind faith but faith with eyes wide open. Christ as true God and true man can, by definition, not betray my trust. But the troubling thought is not easily dismissed: the *totus Christus*, including his very human Church, conceivably could betray by trust. I believe she never will.

But how can I *know* that? How can I know so much that I believe to be true except by believing it to be true? Trust, which is an act of love, is a way of knowing. How can a bride know that the bridegroom will be faithful? Or vice versa? The image is apt, for we are told that the Church is the bride of Christ, and it is no secret that the people who are the Church have, like Israel of old, often gone a-whoring. But also like Israel of old, she is still the people of God. Through Scripture, councils, and the Magisterium she has taught truly, although her children, in positions high and low, have not always been faithful to her teaching. There is development of doctrine, clarification of doctrine, refinement of doctrine, and there will be until the end of time. But there is neither change nor contradiction of doctrine. Where others claim to see change or contradiction, I see development and refinement with a vision transformed by love. I, too, can construe such development as change and contradiction. It is easy to do. I choose to view it as Spirit-guided development and refinement. I accept responsibility for that choice. The apostolic leadership of the Church has been given the authority to judge. I choose to obey.

Ah, now we come to the crunch point: obedience. Nothing is more alien, nothing more offensive, to the autonomous self who judges all and is judged by none. Obedience speaks of a love that obliged, as all love does oblige. From the Latin *obedire*, obedience means to give ear to, to listen responsively. The gift of reason is ordered to truth, and truth commands obedience. Yes, but what if? . . . There are so many *what ifs*. The obstacles on the way to becoming Catholic are typically posed as *what if.* For instance, the Church claims, under certain carefully specified conditions, to teach infallibly. The dogma of infallibility was defined by the First Vatican Council in 1870 and has given rise to many misunderstandings. It means, quite simply, that the Church will never invoke her full authority to require anyone to believe what is false. The Church also teaches infallibly that nothing that she teaches infallibly about faith and morals is incompatible with God's good gift of reason. Yes, but *what if* she did at some time in the future? For instance, *what if* a pope, invoking the fullness of infallible authority, declared that Mary is, along with the Father, Son, and Holy Spirit, the fourth person in the Godhead? What if, indeed?

Once again, to think with the Church (*sentire cum ecclesia*) begins with thinking. *If* a pope were to say that he is infallibly declaring that God is the Holy Quaternity rather than the Holy Trinity, it would pose much the same problem as a pope's declaring that 2+2=5. Under the direction of the Magisterium, the Church can develop and refine doctrine, but she cannot teach anything that contradicts the core truths of the tradition (the "deposit of faith") or that cannot reasonably be believed. Were a pope to say that Mary is God or that 2+2=5, a loving and faithful response might be to say that one has misheard or misunderstood what was said. One might pray that the pope will clarify his statement, or be replaced by a pope who does not cause such confusion. Certainly I would not be bound to believe that Mary is God or that 2+2=5. But this way of thinking is fundamentally wrongheaded. To be obsessed with *what ifs* is to remain captive to fear. The apostle John tells us that "perfect love casts out fear." One finally makes a decision based either on fear and suspicion or on love and trust. It is true that by taking the first way one may avoid a great error; but, if the decision is wrong, one has suffered the loss of an immeasurably greater good. With respect to the big decisions of life, we each choose our own form of risk. Modern agnosticism assumes that our desires are an obstacle to finding the truth. But our desires may also be a guide to truth: They may lead us to the discovery that what we desire is the truth.

Many things are conceivable in the abstract, also things that are contrary to fact. Ask a faithful and loving husband and wife what they would do or think if the other was having an affair on the side. In the abstract, it is conceivable, but what is the point? It is at best a thought experiment, and a marriage is not a thought experiment. So also the Church and one's adherence to her teaching authority is not a thought experiment. It is a living relationship of trust. There may at times be difficulties. But one remembers Newman's maxim: ten thousand difficulties do not add up to a doubt. In this context, a doubt means a decision not to believe. The Church has not invoked and will not invoke her full authority to require anyone to believe what is false. That is a judgment of reason based upon experience. It is also a statement of faith, as in the solemnly undertaken "Profession of Faith."

There is another dimension of magisterial authority that sometimes occasions considerable confusion. I only touch on it here because it will enter the story later. That dimension is "the sense of the faithful," known as the *sensus fidelium*. Newman made much of the claim that in the fourth century most of the bishops subscribed to the Arian heresy, the belief that the Son is not coequally God with the Father. It was the faith of the ordinary believers, the *sensus fidelium*, that preserved the orthodox truth that was later and definitively affirmed by the bishops in council. On certain controverted questions today, some Catholics who describe themselves as progressive appeal to the *sensus fidelium* against the Magisterium. Issues commonly agitated are democracy in the Church, priest celibacy, the ordination of women, homosexuality, contraception, in vitro fertilization, and, much less commonly, the prohibition of abortion.

A brief work on each is in order to clarify our thinking about the *sensus fidelium*. The issues will crop up again in other connections. It is commonly said the Church is not a democracy and that is true—although not sufficient. Political democracy is constituted by the idea of the sovereign will of the people. The Church is constituted by the sovereign will of Christ. It is a matter of doctrine that the responsibility for the leadership of the Church rests with her ordained ministers under the apostolic authority of the bishop exercised "with and under" the bishop of Rome. In a democratic ethos such as ours, however, it is the better part of wisdom for bishops to exercise their authority within a context of accountability and participation that instills confidence in their leadership. (The failure to do that, incidentally, had a great deal to do with the furor of the sex-abuse scandals that erupted in January 2002.)

The requirement that priests be celibate is, it is said, a matter not of doctrine but of discipline, and it could be changed tomorrow. That, too, is true but not sufficient. The celibacy rule is grounded in and formed by a doctrine and spirituality of priesthood that goes back to Christian beginnings. There are a few married priests, mainly married Lutheran and

Episcopal clergy who became Catholics. Were the general rule of celibacy abandoned, it might well, as advocates contend, result in an increase of priestly vocations. (Although I know manly young men whose attraction to the radical vocation of priesthood is, they say, enhanced by the sacrifice involved in celibacy.) Dropping the rule would also bring foreseen and unforeseen consequences for the financial support of clergy, the perception of priests who choose not to marry, and the prospect of marital problems and divorce among priests who do marry. In any event, the ancient tradition of a celibate priesthood—which, contra those who agitate for change, goes back far before the late Middle Ages—has been strongly supported by modern popes and is likely to endure.

The *sensus fidelium* was invoked also for the ordination of women to the priesthood. Apart from a few Gnostic sects in the early centuries, Christianity had never had female priests (or, perhaps more accurately, priestesses). But then, with the feminist surge in the 1970s, Episcopalians, followed by the Church of England, began ordaining women; many thought it only a matter of time before the Catholic Church did the same. Today, the one vigorous agitation for female priests has largely dissipated. The pope solemnly declared that the Church is "not authorized" to ordain women and therefore cannot do it. The Congregation for the Doctrine of the Faith (CDF) has said that the declaration is infallible. Some hardcore progressives have argued that the CDF is itself not infallible and therefore cannot infallibly say whether or not a papal declaration is infallible. It is a nice debating point, but it is almost impossible to envision how the settled doctrine could be unsettled in the future.

Even if there were a possible doubt about whether women could be priests, the Church could not ordain in doubt without throwing the entire sacramental order into question. The theologic is unassailable: A validly ordained minister is essential for a valid Eucharist and the sacramental forgiveness of sins. Dubious ministry means dubious sacraments. Female priests would, in time, mean female bishops doubtfully ordaining other priests, with the result that the entire sacramental life of the Church would be riddled through and through with uncertainty. If one were not convinced by magisterial declarations and the argument from doubt, there is an additional consideration: ordaining women would shatter all hopes of reconciliation with the East because, if one can say never about anything in history, the Orthodox will never ordain women, and reconciliation is impossible without the mutual recognition of ministries. Finally, the Church is universal, but agitation for women's ordination was almost exclusively located in North America and a highly secularized Western Europe. In the Southern Hemisphere, where Catholicism and other Christian movements are growing most rapidly, there is almost no sympathy for such a change and there is powerful opposition against it.

In progressive Catholic circles in this country, the ordination of women had for a couple of decades an air of inevitability about it. It was only a question of time. In support of the claim that the *sensus fidelium* had been heard from, polls were produced showing that a large majority of Catholics in the United States favored ordaining women. In fact, polls on this question, as well as the question of married priests, showed that, *if* the Church were to change her practice, most Catholics would favor the change. Few were *demanding* change. The move for women's ordination is an important case study in the exercise of the Church's teaching authority. For the proponents of the change, it is but another sign of the hopeless recalcitrance of a reactionary Church. For others, it is reassuring evidence of the Church's integrity under powerful pressures of cultural conformity. And, of course, the pressures to conform are not only surrounding the Church but also very much within the Church.

The *sensus fidelium* is not so frequently invoked in the instance of homosexuality, perhaps because the great majority of Americans, Catholic and non-Catholic, essentially agree with the Church's teachings. The teaching is that homosexual acts are "intrinsically disordered," and those who experience homosexual desires are to be lovingly supported in striving to live chaste lives. The Church urges firm resistance to the grim doctrine that homosexuality is simply a matter of fate and to the dehumanizing idea that one's core identity is determined by one's sexual desires. We are more, immeasurably more, than our sexual desires. And morally disordered desires are hardly limited to homosexuality or to sexual desires of any kind. Those who succumb to homosexual desires are, like all sinners, to be loved and assured of the transforming power of God's forgiveness. In law and social practice, they should not be subjected to unjust discrimination, but neither should the practices that define "the gay community" be put on a social or moral par with the union of man and woman in marriage. In sum, the Church's teaching is pretty much the popular intuitive wisdom about the right ordering of human sexuality. Here, too, the appeal is to "natural law." The Church's teaching, one may confidently say, will not change, and the popular wisdom is not likely to change, despite relentless advocacy to the contrary. We will return later to the question of homosexuality, for it is very much part of the sex-abuse scandals that have wracked the Church in this country.

The appeal to the *sensus fidelium* against the teaching authority of the Magisterium is most pronounced on the question of artificial contraception. Herein lies a long and dismal tale of what must be acknowledged as a failure of leadership. In 1968, after several years of apparent uncertainty in which it seemed the question of contraception and of "the pill," in particular, was up for grabs, Pope Paul VI issued the encyclical *Humane Vitae*; in it he affirmed the traditional teaching that sexual intercourse and openness to new life are morally inseparable. This had been the historic teaching of the Church and many observers have argued that the great mistake of Paul VI was in appearing to hesitate before reaffirming it. Defenders of *Humane Vitae* persuasively argue that it was in many ways a prophetic document that accurately foretold what would happen once sex and procreation are separated. What Paul VI said would happen, has happened. When sex asserts its own rights to pleasure and the satisfaction of needs, pleasure and satisfaction are divorced from responsibility, the bond of marriage is loosened, promiscuity is made easier, disordered forms of sexual expression are declared normal, and unintended new life is deemed expendable. Those who contend that there is a logical continuum from artificial contraception to abortion are right, I believe, but they are probably in a distinct minority among Catholics today.

In America and throughout the developed world Catholics practice artificial contraception at about the same rate as the general population. How did this happen? In the years before 1968 and *Humane Vitae*, while Paul VI appeared to hesitate, progressive theologians confidently predicted that the "outdated" teaching on contraception would be modified or abrogated. This expectation was widely disseminated through the media. On the chance that Paul VI would reaffirm the traditional teaching, and in advance of his issuing *Humane Vitae*, some theologians organized a coordinated public rejection of the encyclical. A few bishops, acting in the belief that they are responsible for guarding the Church's teaching, attempted to discipline the dissenting theologians; but they backed off when faced with a firestorm of negative media reaction and, more important, Rome's fear that confrontation might lead to a schism in the Church in the United States. I admit that this is too brief an account of one of the most complex and consequential moments in the history of Catholicism in America.

The result, almost four decades later, is that most Catholics, if they are even aware that the Church once prohibited artificial contraception, assume that the teaching has been effectively nullified. The great majority of Catholics, it is fair to say, have never heard the teaching set forth from the pulpit and they would be quite taken aback by a homily setting forth what, in fact, the Church teaches. But, it is objected, that is to miss the point. The point is that the *sensus fidelium* participates in the teaching authority of the Church and if popular belief and practice reject what is officially taught, then what is officially taught is not authentic teaching.

Well, not quite. On second thought—not at all. The appeal to the *sensus fidelium* depends on what the Church teaches about the *sensus fidelium*. And here is what the Second Vatican Council teaches:

> The whole body of the faithful . . . cannot err in matters of belief. This characteristic is shown in the supernatural appreciation of faith (*sensus fidei*) on the part of the whole people, when "from the bishops to the last of the faithful," they manifest a universal consent in matters of faith and morals.[4]

There is something of a Catch-22 here. If the sense of the faithful (or the supernatural sense of faith—*sensus fidei*) is measured by the belief of those who are faithful, then those who are not faithful to the Church's teaching do not have a voice in defining what is the Church's teaching. One may be forgiven for suspecting an element of circularity in this reasoning. Those who disagree with the official Magisterium are, by definition, not faithful and therefore are not part of the *sensus fidelium* that bears witness of the truth of what the Magisterium teaches. In untangling this knotty question it may be useful to recall Newman's example of how the faithful held out for what would come to be recognized as orthodoxy when most of the bishops were leaning toward the Arian heresy. In the liturgy and devotional life of the Church, the faithful intuited the necessity of affirming that Jesus Christ is at once true God and true man. They knew they *worshiped* Jesus Christ as God and, if he were not God, they would be guilty of idolatry. The bishops assembled in council would in time be led by the Spirit to recognize and ratify what the faithful believed.

Is that comparable, as some progressive Catholics claim, to what is

---

[4]"The Catechism of the Catholic Church," pt. 1, sec. 1, chap. 2, adapted from *Lumen Gentium* 12; the quotation is adapted from Augustine *De praed. sanct.* 14.27: PL 44, 980.

happening today with respect to contraception, in vitro fertilization, and other questions related to human sexuality? I think not. True, there are some Catholic theologians and ethicists who contend that artificial contraception, for instance, is in harmony with Catholic faith; but almost without exception there are writers who challenge the teaching authority of the Magisterium as such, and not just on contraception. They belong to the academic theological guild that orchestrated the rejection of *Humane Vitae* when it appeared and that proposes itself as a "parallel magisterium" to that of the bishops in union with the pope. They frequently claim the support of the *sensus fidelium,* but there is little or no evidence that the many Catholics who contravene church teaching on contraception or in vitro fertilization think that they are bearing witness to a more authentic Catholic teaching. Some who are aware of the Church's teaching feel guilty about what they are doing. Many are unaware of the teaching or have never had it presented to them in a manner intended to be persuasive. Almost all have received the impression, communicated explicitly or by silence, that contravening whatever may be the Church's teaching is no big deal. Anecdotal evidence suggests that in the confessional few Catholics confess the use of artificial contraception and probably a minority of priests tell them that they should. The widespread ignorance or indifference of Catholics on these questions is not an instance in which the *sensus fidelium* is trying to inform the mind of the Church; it is, rather, a moral debacle resulting from a massive failure of pastoral leadership—particularly the failure of bishops—to help the faithful to think with the Church, as in *sentire cum ecclesia.*

Nonetheless, there is and will likely always be a relatively small group of Catholic activists who will continue to agitate for changing the Church's teaching and practice on all the above-mentioned questions. Often, well-meaning people do believe that the *sensus fidelium* mandates something like the democratizing of the Church. There is today, for instance, The Voice of the Faithful, and an older group going back to the 1970s, Call to Action. Groups such as these receive media attention because they fit the decades-long story line that has Catholicism in internal turmoil and crisis and the little people rebelling against an authoritarian hierarchy. There is turmoil and even crisis, as we shall see, but it is usually not along the lines being pressed by these advocacy groups.

A few years ago Call to Action announced that it was embarking on a one-year drive to get a million signatures in support of the changes we have been discussing. In this "mobilization," all stops were pulled in the network of leftward Catholic publications and organizations. At the end of the year, the organizers announced they would need another year to reach their goal. It was pointed out by some that one million signatures from a community of sixty-five million Catholics fell somewhat short of a credible expression of the voice of the faithful. As it happened, the organizers ended up with about 34,000 signatures, which is 0.0005 percent of the Catholics in the country and about 0.0015 percent of regular Mass-goers.

This does not necessarily discredit the causes advocated. After all, sometimes a small minority gets some things right. And no doubt many Catholics are simply indifferent, not caring one way or another about the causes being agitated. But the limp response to the progressive mobilization does discredit the perennially touted notion that there is a major insurrection in the Catholic ranks, portending a revolution in the Church's teaching and governance. In the forty years since Vatican Council II, the progressive networks promoting their interpretation of the Council have not been able to enlist the active support of more than 40,000 Catholics, and their organizations are largely composed of aging refugees from the "post-Vatican II" revolution that was not to be.

That is not to say that their efforts have been without effect. Despite the populist and anticlerical rhetoric, the effective influence of such organizations is mainly through thousands of progressive priests and nuns who have, over the years, understood themselves to be the prophets of the "post-Vatican II Church." In the schools and colleges, and in the chancery offices of dioceses, they have a powerful, though now declining, voice. Because they have the time for it, because matters ecclesiastical constitute their primary, if not exclusive, world of engagement and because they mutually certify one another as experts on a mutually reinforced understanding of "renewal," there is a voice heeded by bishops who are, in many cases, in agreement with them. This is not a conspiracy although some traditionalists claim it is. Unless one wants to get pedantic about it and point out that conspire, from *conspirer*, means to breathe together, which they often do. They certainly tend to think together. It is perhaps best described as an instance of what sociologists call "elective affinity." Like attracts and encourages like. It has little or nothing to do with the much-invoked *sensus fidelium*.

The very idea of authority and of membership in a community by authority is deeply offensive to what is generally thought to be the American spirit. Autonomy, independence, individualism—such are the marks of Americanism. There is a long and understandable tradition of viewing

Catholicism as un-American. A hundred years ago in his classic *The Varieties of Religious Experience* William James defined religion as "the feelings, acts, and experiences of individual men in their solitude, so far as they apprehend themselves to stand in relation to whatever they may consider the divine."[5] James, great man though he was, made no secret of his contempt for Catholicism. More recently, the literary critic Harold Bloom argued in *The American Religion* that the natural religion of almost all Americans, no matter what their religious affiliation, is Gnosticism. In the tradition of Ralph Waldo Emerson, they deem themselves possessed of a "divine spark" by which spiritual truth is discerned by its agreement with their individual aspiration toward the transcendent. Even a brief visit to the sprawling "spirituality" section of your local Borders or Barnes & Noble will confirm the perduring power of what James and Bloom described as the religious culture of America. This is yet another reason why Catholics need to be less concerned about being "American Catholics" than about being "Catholic Americans." Note that the adjective tends to control the noun. I will return to the significance of that later.

Yves Congar was a French Dominican whose thought had a powerful influence on the way the Second Vatican Council addressed the question of Church and authority. "In its different forms," Congar wrote,

> tradition is like the conscience of a community or the principle of identity that links one generation with another; it enables them to remain . . . the same people as they go forward throughout history, which transforms all things. . . . Tradition is memory, and memory enriches experience. If we remembered nothing it would be impossible to advance; the same would be true if we were bound to a slavish imitation of the past. True tradition is not servility but fidelity.[6]

And that explains, in large part, why so many people, wearied of the sophisticated but delusory intellectual games of the autonomous self, have put themselves up for adoption by the Catholic Church.

---

[5]*Varieties of Religious Experience. A Study in Human Nature* (London: Longmans,, 1902) 31; Centenary Edition (London: Routledge, 2002) 29-30.

[6]Yves Congar, *The Meaning of Tradition* (New York: Hawthorn Books, 1964) 2-3.

"AUTHORITY" IN THE EASTERN ORTHODOX TRADITION

Bradley Nassif

In one way or another, most of the theological issues that divide Christians today end up reflecting our different conceptions of authority. Authority lies at the heart of the issues that separate the Eastern Orthodox Church from Roman Catholics and Protestants. In order to understand the meaning of authority in the Eastern Orthodox Church we have to see how it has functioned in relation to the Church's "ecclesial logic" and Christological dogma over the past two thousand years. Such an approach—at once historical and systematic—reveals the Church's belief that Christ, in his trinitarian relations, exercises his authority supremely through holy tradition, that is, the Lord himself working through the life of the Holy Spirit in the Church. The ultimate question any Orthodox theologian who purports to speak on behalf of the Church must answer is, *How* has the voice of the risen Christ been heard through the ongoing life of the Holy Spirit in the Church? Through whom, how, and when does the authoritative voice of the Spirit speak?

My answer to these questions will be given in five parts—arbitrarily divided in form for the purpose of communication, but theologically united in content. In part one I will evaluate the question of authority as a theological category in the history of Orthodox theology. Part two will narrow the question to the authority of Scripture as it relates to the Church's approach to the knowledge of God, the development of the biblical canon, and recent ecumenical dialogue. Part three focuses on the authority of Christ in the Church's eucharistic ecclesiology. Part four centers on the authority of the Ecumenical Councils and the mystery of their reception. Part five focuses on the theological authority of the worshipping community, that is, the Church's liturgy, Fathers, saints, icons, canons, hymnography (the art of composing hymns), and architecture. The conclusion is a brief commentary on how all this is supposed to work in the Church—in theory if not always in practice.

Part 1. Authority as a Theological Category

Eastern Orthodox Christianity generally has not raised the issue of authority in the same way that Catholic and Protestant theology has done. Instead, Orthodoxy understands Scripture and other aspects of the Church's life as expressions of a unified tradition. Orthodoxy's conception of the Church as a whole or "catholic" community results in a more "lived" and much less "defined" understanding of authority. The prophets and apostles, the Church

Fathers, councils, icons, saints, bishops, and laypeople are all understood as being intimately connected with each other. Placing one of these groups in isolation over the others as *the* locus of authority becomes unnecessary and actually destroys the unity of the Church's life. Collectively, all of them are witnesses to the truth in their own particular way with their own particular authority. So "authority" in the Orthodox tradition can best be understood not in legal or external categories, but in relation to the Church's corporate understanding of reality, all of which participates in divine life. This has created a climate in which there is very little developed understanding of theological authority as it has been discussed in the history of Catholic and Protestant theology. However, one cannot conclude that the notion of authority is absent in Orthodoxy. On the contrary, it is more a matter of *how* authority is expressed in the life of the Church than it is a denial of its existence.

It is clear that the question of authority becomes especially important when the Church has had to counter competing pseudo-Christian systems, such as Gnosticism, Arianism, Nestorianism, Iconoclasm, and other heretical challenges to the faith. It is in those contexts that we find the Church rising to defend its "rule of faith" by appealing to the Scriptures and the apostolic faith expressed through the worshipping life of the Church. The dictum of St. Vincent of Lerins sums it up best: "We adhere to that which has been believed everywhere, always and by all." The key question, then, is How does authority manifest itself in the context of the Church's *consensual* tradition? The answer is found through an organic concept of the Church in which Scripture plays a preeminent role.

Part 2. The Authority of Scripture

Orthodox affirmation of biblical authority can be understood best through an understanding of the Church's general approach to the knowledge of God, the formation of the biblical canon, and conciliar statements made by the Church in recent ecumenical dialogue. The limitations of space prevent us from a detailed analysis of patristic texts, liturgical prayers, and the hymnography of the Orthodox tradition—all of which richly communicate the Church's vision of biblical authority.

The Knowledge of God. Orthodoxy's understanding of the Bible and its authority in the life of the Church is personal in its emphasis. The question, "What is the authority of Scripture?" is resolved in the prior answer to "Who is truth?" Unlike certain forms of philosophical apologetics, we do not begin with proofs for the existence of God. Theological inquiry does not start with abstract questions over the possibility of belief in God, arguments for his existence, and the grounds for belief, which are all outside of divine revelation, and then, only after those questions have been answered, proceed to the Christian doctrine of the Bible and its authority. On the contrary, Orthodoxy begins where the New Testament and the Church's liturgy would have us to begin, namely, with the reality of the Father-Son relationship given to us in Christ and into which we are drawn by the Spirit. We embrace by faith the words of the Nicene Creed, "I believe in one God, the Father Almighty . . . and in one Lord Jesus Christ." So the general orientation of the Christian East grounds all genuine knowledge of God in the Person of Jesus Christ. Doctrinal authority, like salvation itself, begins not with a verification of possible belief in God as a hypothesis but with trust in a Person. This approach differs from eighteenth-century European Rationalists and their modern children, but it accords well with the common experience of countless Christians down through the centuries, both East and West. Simply put, faith is based on revealed knowledge.

Church and Canon. Chronologically, the apostolic tradition was anterior to Scripture. The Gospel was first transmitted orally within the liturgical community of the Church as well as in its public preaching and missionary outreach. By the end of the first century that apostolic tradition was enshrined in written texts. The Church later decided which texts constituted the canon of Scripture by "recognizing" their apostolic origins, content, and usage within the worshiping community. Better yet, the Spirit embraced the Church with the Spirit's own canon. This does not mean that Scripture owes its inherent authority to the Church. Authority comes only from the Spirit of God and not a legal institution such as the papacy or a Church council as such. The Church was inseparably united with its sacred texts as the *mediating* authority that simply authenticated what was already there within its own life. Thus when the Church accepted the books of the canon it was also accepting the ongoing, Spirit-led authority of the Church's tradition, which recognized, interpreted, worshipped, and corrected itself by the witness of Holy Scripture.

Here it is important to understand that the Orthodox see themselves as the organic continuation of the same catholic (lower case "c" meaning "whole and adequate") Church that originally produced and recognized the canon of Scripture in antiquity. That tradition is believed to be directly tied to the contemporary Orthodox and Catholic communities, East and West (bracketing for this essay the differences between them). Those Orthodox Churches are now located predominantly in the Middle East, Greece, Russia, Eastern Europe, and now the West. The selection of canonical books originally came from communities in the Greek, Latin, Arabic, Coptic, Georgian, Armenian, and other ancient Christian Churches. Spirit, Bible, (real, identifiable) Churches and tradition were inseparably united, then as now. So, for the Orthodox it appears that whether they are aware of it or not, every time Protestants pick up their Bibles, they are relying on the Church's judgment on the colossal issue of canonicity! Often without acknowledging it, they are validating the authority of the Spirit-led tradition as a norm of canonicity that recognized which books were and were not to be considered as Holy Scripture. It is the Orthodox self-understanding that the same Spirit-led tradition that governed the life of the Orthodox Church over the centuries remains faithful to it in the present. The history of the biblical canon is, of course, much more complicated, but such is the Church's theological conviction about it.

Recent Conciliar Statements. In the area of biblical inspiration and interpretation, the most authoritative documents we can consult are the "Agreed Statements" between Orthodox and non-Orthodox Christians in their ecumenical dialogues over the past thirty years. These statements do not enjoy the same authority as the early Ecumenical Councils, but because of their Pan-Orthodox character they represent the Church's views in the context of contemporary Christian pluralism and are therefore more officially representative of Orthodoxy than are the opinions of any single theologian. An Orthodox theology of biblical inspiration and interpretation is well expressed in the "Common Declaration" of the Anglican-Orthodox Joint Doctrinal Commission adopted in Moscow during the Commission's session in the summer of 1976:

> The Scriptures constitute a coherent whole. They are at once divinely inspired and humanly expressed. They bear authoritative witness to God's revelation of himself in creation, in the incarnation of the Word and in all the history of salvation, and as such they express the Word of God in human language. We know, receive, and interpret Scripture through the church and in the church. Our approach to the Bible is one of obedience so that we may hear the revelation of himself that God gives through it. The books of Scripture contained in the canon are authoritative because they truly convey the authentic revelation of God. . . .
>
> Any disjunction between Scripture and Tradition such as would treat them as two separate "sources of revelation" must be rejected. The two are

correlative. We affirm (1) that Scripture is the main criterion whereby the church tests traditions to determine whether they are truly part of Holy Tradition or not; (2) that Holy Tradition completes Holy Scripture in the sense that it safeguards the integrity of the biblical messages.[1]

In addition to the Moscow Statement, the "Agreed Statements" of the more recent international Lutheran-Orthodox Joint Commission add further points of consensus:

> The function of the holy scriptures is to serve the authenticity of the church's living experience in safeguarding the holy Tradition from all attempts to falsify the true faith (cf. Heb. 4:12, etc.), not to undermine the authority of the church, the body of Christ.
>
> Regarding the relation of scripture and tradition, for centuries there seemed to have been a deep difference between Orthodox and Lutheran teaching. Orthodox hear with satisfaction the affirmation of the Lutheran theologians that the formula *solo Scriptura* was always intended to point to God's revelation, God's saving act through Christ in the power of the Holy Spirit, and therefore to the holy Tradition of the church . . . against human traditions that darken the authentic teaching in the church. . . .
>
> Inspiration is the operation of the Holy Spirit in the authors of the holy scripture so that they may bear witness to the revelation (John 5:39) without erring about God and God's ways and means for the salvation of humankind. . . .
>
> Expressions and concepts of biblical authors about God are inspired because they are unerring *guides* [emphasis theirs] to communion with God. . . .
>
> Authentic interpreters of the holy scripture are persons who have had the same experience of revelation and inspiration within the body of Christ as the biblical writers had. Therefore it is necessary for authentic understanding that anybody who reads or hears the Bible be inspired by the Holy Spirit. The Orthodox believe that such authentic interpretation is the service of the fathers of the church especially expressed in the decisions of the ecumenical councils.[2]

Although few Orthodox seem to be aware of it, the confessional debates within Lutheranism have influenced some of the theological vocabulary of these ecumenical documents, which supports more liberal Lutheran posi-

---

[1] *Anglican-Orthodox Dialogue: The Dublin Agreed Statement 1984* (Crestwood NY: St. Vladimir's Seminary Press, 1985) 50-51.

[2] *Lutheran-Orthodox Dialogue: Agreed Statements 1985–1989* (Geneva: Lutheran World Federation, 1992) 11, 15-17, 26.

tions that may become problematic for some Orthodox in the future. The failure to qualify the distinction between biblical inspiration and contemporary personal inspiration is a case in point. The use of the term "guides" also subtly leads the Orthodox away from accepting any notion of propositional revelation.

Still, these ecumenical documents demonstrate the Church's views on the inspiration, interpretation, and authority of Scripture. The Lutheran-Orthodox agreement maintains,

> Inspiration is the operation of the Holy Spirit in the authors of the holy scripture so that they may bear witness to the revelation (John 5:39) without erring about God and God's ways and means for the salvation of humankind.

It also sees no discord between the Lutheran interpretation of *sola Scriptura* and Orthodoxy's view of the relation between Scripture and tradition. Likewise, the Moscow statement qualifies Scripture as the "main criterion" for testing truth and error in Church tradition.

The ecumenical documents quoted above acknowledge the Church as the final interpreter of the Bible, while Scripture itself is the main criterion of the Church's authority. The Moscow document explains that "Holy Tradition completes Holy Scripture in the sense that it safeguards the integrity of the biblical message." This does not forbid individuals from making personal judgments or discourage them from engaging in critical scholarship, but it does mean that private opinions, as learned as they might be, are not to be preferred to the experience of the saints and the Church's rule of faith down through the centuries. The Church, the Bible, and holy tradition form an unbreakable unity of checks and balances wherein Scripture is given the most authoritative voice on matters of faith and practice.

Part 3. Eucharistic Ecclesiology and the Authority of the Spirit

"Authority" is most fully understood in reference to the Church's *mystical* character. Authority is inseparably united with the Church's understanding of the relation between pneumatology and ecclesiology. The Church is primarily conceived as a mystical communion of the faithful with God and with each other, on earth and in heaven, through the resurrectional life of Christ in his trinitarian relations. That resurrectional life creates a bond of communion (*koinonia*) between God and believers, patterned after the Trinity, through the eschatological irruption of the Kingdom of God that is "already" fulfilled in the Church but "not yet" consummated. The Church is the newly constituted society of the covenant elect, the community of the new age, the mystical body of Christ centered in the proclamation of the Word and celebration of the Eucharist. It is a "mystical community of salvation" more than a sociological reality. That is why Orthodox ecclesiology is marked by a strongly mystical character, in distinction from the more institutional character of the papacy in Roman Catholic ecclesiology.

Communion ecclesiology. The whole of Orthodox ecclesiology is best interpreted under the rubric of "communion ecclesiology." Without going into great detail, in communion ecclesiology, authority in the Church is seen as *relational.* It is not dictatorial or monarchical. This is true on all levels: local, regional, and universal.

On the local level, the authority of the Church lies in the bishop who "teaches aright the word of truth" in an authoritative way. The bishop is also the guardian of truth. The bishop, however, is only an individual. He is interdependent with his community, namely, his presbytery and his lay people. As Christians, all are anointed by the same Spirit who anointed Christ. As the Father exists within the Trinity so the bishop ranks first in his community yet interdependent with his own flock, both clergy and laity. Unless he expresses the faith of his believing community, the bishop may be in error and thus be judged by the faith of the Church, according to established procedures.

Moreover, in communion ecclesiology the Church's understanding of "apostolic succession" is one that passes through the *community* of the local Church. The bishops are not "successors to the apostles" in an equivalent way, since the original apostles were eyewitnesses to the resurrection, and performed itinerant ministries rather than local ones. Bishops are apostolic successors to the extent that they transmit and preserve the original apostolic deposit in the context of their local communities, and to the extent that their ordinations occur within the eucharistic context of a local apostolic Church. Thus apostolic succession is not defined as individualistic, or simply a succession of persons, but a *succession of communities* to which the individual bishops belong and stand in a relation of unity and communion with one another. Each eucharistic community succeeds the previous one and is connected to other communities, thus safeguarding continuity with the Church's apostolic origins, faith, and lifestyle.

On the regional and universal levels, ecclesiastical authority is also *relational and interdependent.* Just as the bishop is part of the community at the local level (not *above* but *within* the community), so he is to be at the regional and universal levels. But how does this relate to authority and the question of Roman primacy over the Eastern Churches? A full answer is impossible here, but it is obvious that the doctrine of the pope's universal jurisdiction is at odds with the Orthodox understanding of communion ecclesiology. In Orthodoxy, every faithful member of the Church has a part in the ministry of Peter as one who proclaims Jesus as the Christ, the Son of the living God. In Catholicism, however, a disjunction has taken place between viewing the authority of episcopal ordinations as coming from their local communities, and seeing their authority as given only from Rome. From an Orthodox perspective, this shift in the bishop's authority from the local community to that of Rome betrays communion ecclesiology.

Much has been said in modern times by Orthodox writers concerning "communion ecclesiology," "eucharistic ecclesiology," "baptismal ecclesiology," and "trinitarian ecclesiology"—all of which affect our understanding of the nature of the Church and its authority.[3] Most recently, John Erickson observed the need for a "baptismal ecclesiology" as both a completion and a corrective of the shortcomings of "eucharistic ecclesiology." He says,

> The Church is a eucharistic organism but only because the Church is a baptismal organism. . . . Modern ecclesiology, like modern church practice, has tended to ignore the significance of baptism. Emphasis has been on eucharistic fellowship, with relatively little concern for the preconditions for this fellowship.[4]

What has not been noticed, however, is that all this discussion about "communion ecclesiology" has been working backwards. It started with Zizioulas's (Metropolitan of Pergamon, b. 1931) retrieval of the Trinitarian foundations of the Church and from there went to the notion of "communion ecclesiology." Then came "eucharistic ecclesiology" followed by

---

[3]John Zizioulas, *Being as Communion* (Crestwood NY: St. Vladimir's Seminary Press, 1981); Maximos Aghiorgoussis, "Some Preliminary Notions of 'Baptismal Ecclesiology': Baptism and Eucharist, Constitutive of the Church as Communion" in *In the Image of God* (Brookline MA, 1999) 75-113. John Erickson, "The Local Churches and Catholicity: An Orthodox Perspective" in *The Jurist* 52 (1992): 490-508.

[4]Erickson, "The Local Churches and Catholicity: An Orthodox Perspective," 505.

Erickson's corrective about the need for "Baptismal ecclesiology" as the underlying reality which makes our experience of the Church as communion possible. Erickson does well to take it back to baptism as a precondition for eucharistic fellowship, but what he fails to discuss are the preconditions for baptism itself. Again, theologians have been working backwards at this. What is needed, therefore, as of first importance in modern ecclesiology is what I would call *kerygmatic ecclesiology*. The Good News of the Kingdom of God is issued in through the Incarnation, life, death, and resurrection of Jesus of Nazareth. That is the fundamental reality that makes the whole of "communion" ecclesiology accessible to the believing community.

Kerygmatic ecclesiology is simply the Church's proclamation of the Gospel and its Spirit-enabled acceptance by all those who believe. This is not to say that the divine life of the three Persons of the Trinity are dependent on the *kerygma*, or that baptismal and eucharistic ecclesiology are unimportant. But it does affirm that the *kerygma* holds a special place of primacy in the Church as the undergirding reality and primary reference point of baptismal and eucharistic ecclesiology. Without the proclaimed Gospel of Jesus Christ—rooted in the apostolic faith, enshrined in the biblical canon, and proclaimed by the faithful—the ecclesiology connected with baptism and Eucharist makes no sense and ultimately falls apart. The historical facts of redemption are proclaimed, transmitted, and received by the enabling power of the Holy Spirit in the ongoing life of the Church. All who believe become members of one another in Christ's body, the Church. The "one baptism" we share through the life of the Trinity, and the "one Eucharist" we partake of in our local communities are rooted in the "one Gospel" we proclaim and embrace. It is that common *kerygma* that makes the Church "one, holy, catholic, and apostolic." In Orthodoxy, kerygmatic unity is expressed in the evangelical dimensions of the liturgical and sacramental life of the local communities that are commonly shared by Orthodox Churches throughout the world. Since Christian existence itself stems from the apostolic *kerygma*, and that *kerygma* is enshrined in the biblical canon of the Church, then the notion of authority is rooted in the apostolic experience that has been interpreted preeminently in the Church's liturgy.

Thus the main ecumenical issue over the meaning of "authority" in this volume centers on answering the question of which Christian community reveals the fullness of catholicity in the totality of its life and interpretation of Scripture as compared to others. It is the humble conviction of the Orthodox Church that authority is to be connected with the original apostolic deposit that has been proclaimed and preserved intact over the centuries in an unbroken succession of truth in the worshipping life of its communities.

Part 4. The Authority of Ecumenical Councils

One might be tempted to generalize that Protestantism locates authority with the Bible alone and Roman Catholicism with the Church hierarchy (principally the pope himself), whereas Orthodoxy locates the authority for determining doctrine with the Ecumenical Councils (325-787 CE). However, this perception would be misleading. The Orthodox do not determine truth by ascribing an inherent authority to the de facto convocation of a Church council. Rather, it is one of the chief responsibilities of bishops to express the truth of the Gospel. Each local bishop has the express responsibility to teach the faith in his own diocese. At the same time, the episcopal authority of local bishops form an indivisible unity because the Church is an organic whole, a living body. It is not merely a collection of individuals. Consequently each hierarch has the responsibility to proclaim the truth and to witness to it not only in his own diocese but in the totality of the Church. Each bishop exercises his episcopal authority in solidarity with every other bishop.

The exercise of this episcopal authority in solidarity becomes a concrete and visible reality primarily when bishops meet as a council of the Church. Christ's promise to abide where two or three gather applies no less to the assembly of the bishops in council. The authority claimed by an episcopal council is none other than the authority of Christ himself, present by the Holy Spirit. This is already apparent in the record of apostolic gatherings in the New Testament. After Christ's Ascension, the Church immediately gathered and asked Christ himself to select a replacement for Judas: "Lord. . . . Show us which one of these two *you* have chosen" (Acts 1:24 NRSV). During their later meeting in Jerusalem they present their decision with these words: "It seemed good to *the Holy Spirit* and to us" (Acts 15:28). It is significant that the decision made by the apostles says "we" and not "I." Collectively, the pastors of the Church—be they the apostles or their appointed elders—speak with an authority which none of them can have individually. In each council that is truly a council of the Church, the totality is superior to the sum of its parts.

The key question to ask of any Church council, then, is this: How do we know if a given council is genuinely voicing the will of God? Are there any external criteria which can guarantee *in advance* that a certain assembly will turn out to be an Ecumenical Council? Can we predict with certainty that a council will be genuinely inspired by the Holy Spirit to manifest the truth of Christ? There are various external criteria we can observe that can indicate the potential presence of the Spirit, but none of them can be guaranteed or taken in isolation. Some of those indicators or signs are as follows, along with their limitations.

(1) The number of bishops who attended a council is no proof of ecumenicity, since some were more numerous than others. Truth cannot be determined merely by a nose-count.

(2) The geographical distribution of the bishops and their representative character requires, in principle, that they represent all the parts of the catholic Church. This does not mean that the bishops have to be from every single geographical quadrant of the world, but simply that those who are in attendance must be in communion with other bishops who themselves may not have been able to attend. Unless it has this representative character, a council cannot be considered as *ecumenical*, even if it is acknowledged that it proclaimed the truth. But this representative character, while being indispensable, is hardly in itself a sufficient criterion for authentic ecumenicity in the deepest sense. Externally, the councils of Rimini-Seleucia and Ferrara-Florence (1438–1439) were as representative as each of the seven Ecumenical Councils, but neither the one nor the other has been recognized as ecumenical by the Orthodox Church because they have not reflected the catholic truth of the great tradition.

(3) The conviction of a council itself is no guarantee of its ecumenicity. Many councils explicitly proclaimed themselves ecumenical which were not, however, recognized as such by the Church. So this criteria is not by itself determinant. On the other hand, a council may in fact be ecumenical even though it did not proclaim itself as such. For example, it is not certain that the council of Constantinople in 381 even considered itself as ecumenical, yet it was subsequently recognized as such by the Church. This criteria, therefore, is not absolute.

(4) Recognition by a later ecumenical council is ecumenically important but it is not sufficient by itself. One of the first tasks done by each ecumenical council was to ratify the decisions of the previous ones. This is an important step in the process of "reception" of a council by the Church in its totality, but once again this is not a sufficient criterion in itself. For as long as the series of ecumenical councils might be, there is necessarily a final

council in the series, which has not as yet been confirmed by a later synod. Consequently, if we rest on this sole criterion, the validity of the entire series is diminished. In any case, we have only pushed the problem back one step. What criteria did the later councils use to measure the previous ones and to distinguish between the true and false councils?

(5) Acknowledgement by the emperor was important in Christian antiquity, but it was not sufficient in the past, nor required for any future council that may be held in our day. Here we enter into the sticky area of "caesaropapism" which asserts that the emperor controlled religious doctrine in the Byzantine Empire. I do not have the space to unpack the complex relationship that existed between the Church and emperor, and the respective spheres of each, but the sum of the matter is simply that it did not exist. To be sure, emperors tried to manipulate the outcome of an ecumenical council, they ratified their decisions and enforced them as law, but they could not impose their beliefs upon the Church. The reception of a council by the emperor was of great importance in the process of "reception" but it did not constitute final and decisive criteria. Moreover, some councils were convoked and confirmed by emperors and yet rejected by the Church, such as the notorious Robber Council of Ephesus (449) and iconoclast Council of Hieria (754). St. John Chrysostom and Maximos the Confessor demonstrated with their lives that the state had no right interfering with the faith of the Church, and that the Church had a mind and a will of its own. The absence of a Christian emperor in the modern world does not render a modern ecumenical council impossible because truth is not determined by a particular time period or a specific political system.

(6) Acknowledgement by the pope is critical so long as the pope is not isolated or exalted above his episcopal brethren. It was of great importance that the bishop of Rome, the pope, accept an ecumenical council simply because he had so often functioned as a theological referee, not to mention the authority of his purported double-apostolic succession and prestigious geographical location in the capital of the Roman Empire. But Orthodox cannot regard the ratification by the pope as decisive by itself, for Orthodox ecclesiology does not wish to isolate the pope from his brothers in the episcopate and from all the body of the Church. Once again, in Orthodox eyes the Council of Ferrara-Florence (1438–1445) is not ecumenical, even though it received the affirmation of both the emperor and of the pope.

So what are we left with? From an Orthodox point of view, there exists *no criterion or collection of criteria which would automatically guarantee the ecumenicity of a council.* The ecumenical councils were not viewed as legal institutions but as *charismatic witnesses* to the unity of the faith accepted by the people of God in communion with their local bishops. There was no formal criteria of reception but rather an organic, Spirit-illumined witness to the truth that was accepted by the faithful. In an illuminating essay on this subject, Georges Florovsky states that the "ultimate authority [of Church councils] was still grounded in their conformity with the 'Apostolic Tradition' . . . It will be no exaggeration to suggest that Councils were never regarded as a canonical institution, but rather as occasional *charismatic events* (emphasis his)." Again, Christ himself is the criterion of truth, not Councils per se:

> The teaching *authority* of the Ecumenical Councils is grounded in the *infallibility* of the Church. The ultimate 'authority' is vested in the Church which is for ever the Pillar and the Foundation of Truth. It is not primarily a canonical authority, in the formal and specific sense of the term, although canonical strictures or sanctions may be appended to conciliar decisions on matters of faith. It is a *charismatic* authority, grounded in the assistance of the Spirit: *for it seemed good to the Holy Spirit, and to us.*[5]

In the final analysis, there is but one decisive indicator of ecumenicity and it is retrospective, namely, "reception." The key question to answer is, Has a given assembly been accepted by the general conscience of the Church? In practice, the one way to determine if a given assembly is or is not authentically ecumenical, and thereby infallible insofar as it accords with apostolic truth, is to discern if the council in question has been later accepted as ecumenical by all the Church. No conciliar decision carries binding force until the communities of faith and their bishops in communion with each other receive that decision.

But even "reception by the faithful" cannot provide automatic proof. One need only study the complicated developments that followed the Council of Chalcedon (451) to see how this is so. To what extent can it be said that this council was in fact "accepted by the faithful?" It was rejected

---

[5]George Florovsky, *Bible, Church, Tradition—An Eastern Orthodox View*, Collected Works of Georges Flovorsky 1 (Vaduz [Liechtenstein], Europa: Bucherevertriebsanstalt; Belmont MA: Notable & Academic Books, 1987) 93, 103. Florovsky says more in this one chapter on the authority of the ancient councils than what has taken a book for others to write.

by the majority of Christians in the Patriarchate of Alexandria and by about half of those of the Patriarchate of Antioch. So these facts merely confirm the point already made, namely, that the truth cannot be established by a mechanical application of formal criteria.

We must also acknowledge that it is difficult to find in the ecclesiastical canons, the dogmatic decrees and the "Acts" preserved from the seven ecumenical councils, any passage where the fathers of the councils speak of the need for a later "reception" of their decisions by all the Church. Nonetheless, this process of "reception" is a fact of history of which there exists abundant witnesses between the years 325 and 1100 CE. How, precisely, does reception take place? There are no rules to follow in which this process is concretely carried out, much to the embarrassment of systematic theologians who are fond of neat categorizations in the theological formulation of the faith. There is no precise number of people required, nor a precise time limit in which the process of recognition must necessarily be finished. Historically, the process of recognition took place in various and sundry times and ways. The "reception" of Nicea (325) as "Ecumenical" was more or less an accomplished fact during the conclusions of the Council of Constantinople (381). But the Council of 381 does not seem to have been counted by Rome among the number of ecumenical councils before 517 CE. And the seventh ecumenical council (Nicea II, 786–787) was not generally received in the West before the eleventh century.

The process of reception is thus not subjected to an external law or referendum. It is simply a historical fact that took place under the guidance of the Holy Spirit. At a true ecumenical council the bishops witnessed to the truth and that witness was then welcomed by the assent of the whole people of God, including laypeople who by virtue of their baptism were to be responsible guardians of tradition. That verification was expressed not formally or explicitly, but simply *lived* in the worshipping community and individual lives of the saints.

Conciliar decisions, therefore, are not true because they have been accepted by the Church, but they have been accepted by the Church because they are true. In this sense, the decrees of an ecumenical council are "authoritative" and "infallible" because they bear witness to the apostolic faith given in Scripture and lived out in the ongoing life of the Church. The truth of the councils are not made true by the external criterion of reception—there was no "confirmation" or "validation" in this process because the faithful do not "render" a council true but merely "recognize" or "receive" its truth. But at the same time this later agreement is the visible manifestation by which we know by faith that a council has in fact been guided by the Holy Spirit. *The definitive authority is the authority of the living truth, Jesus Christ, the Lord of the Church, acting among us and in us by the Holy Spirit.*

As a result, Orthodoxy's view of the Church hierarchy and the councils is quite different from that of Roman Catholicism: Orthodox bishops and councils do not possess any inherent authority in themselves. They are not raised up above the rest of the Church as sources of authoritative teaching. Rather, their function is to recognize the truth that lies within the Church. And that truth is living, dynamic, and communal. It is transmitted not by isolated individuals but by persons in relation, or in communion, with the total ecclesial community, especially when gathered for the celebration of the Eucharist. It is out of that eucharistic unity that the ecumenical councils became true manifestations of the apostolic faith in the life of the Church.

Part 5. Authority and Worship

The remaining sources of theological truth have their own special place of authority in the life of the Orthodox Church. These sources include the liturgy, Fathers and Mothers, lives of the saints, icons, ecclesiastical canons, hymnography, and Church architecture. Together they form a symbiotic relationship that is distinguishable from each other but inseparable from the total life of the Church. Each coinheres in the other. Each has its own reality that testifies in its own way to the truth The late Father Alexander Schmemann had a saying that summarized it best: "The Church is a mystery that has institutions, not an institution that has mysteries."

The Liturgy. The Bible, ecumenical councils and liturgy are the most authoritative voices in the life of the Orthodox Church—in that order.[6] Along with the Bible and ecumenical councils, the Church's liturgy functions as a vital theological authority. It is the function of the liturgy to be the "epiphany" of the Church's faith. The faith of Nicea and Chalcedon is especially evident in its liturgical prayers and hymnography.

Liturgy expresses the beliefs of the believing community. Apostolic truth is liturgical in that it is manifested and communicated in the sacra-

---

[6]Orthodox theologians differ on the precise ranking of theological authorities in the Church. The order I've given above represents a broad consensus.

ments, rites, and prayers of the Church. The old adage applies: *lex orandi lex credendi* ("The rule of prayer is the rule of faith."). Orthodox theology discovers in the liturgy a wholeness of vision that stems from the apostolic faith. The source and goal of all theology is the apostolic experience rooted in the Bible and expressed preeminently in the Church's liturgy. Sometimes, however, the opposite adage has been the case: *lex credendi lex orandi* ("The rule of faith is the rule of prayer."). The victory of icons in the Church is a case in point. After decades of controversy (726–843 CE), icons were finally celebrated in the Feast of Orthodoxy (843) which demonstrates for our purposes how theology impacted the worship of the Church.

When consulting the liturgy as an authoritative source of the Church's theology it is important to note that it is not on the same par as the Bible. The liturgy is an interpretive grid that discerns biblical faith through the eyes of the Church's entire tradition—fathers, councils, creeds, hymns, saints, prophets, martyrs, etc. This is not to say, however, that there are parts of its ancient liturgies which seem to have no biblical justification. The liturgy needs to be read and corrected in light of the total apostolic faith just as every other piece of theology in the Church's mosaic of belief. But it is to be done not on the basis of one's own private interpretation, but on the relational basis of the Church as communion with hierarchy and laity working together.

Church Fathers and Saints. The Church Fathers also enjoy a special place of authority in the Church as reliable teachers of the faith. Most often the Church's liturgy is the product of the "consensus of the Fathers" (*consensus patrum*). No single father, however, has been elevated as "the" theological authority in Orthodoxy, though one had to be in communion with some of them (for example, St. Simeon Stylites—see below) to be considered "orthodox" especially during the great controversies of the early centuries. In other words, there is no Orthodox equivalent to the supreme authority Thomas Aquinas enjoyed in the Catholic Church at Vatican I and elsewhere as the defining doctor of the faith. Orthodoxy has remained committed to the communal character of the faith of the fathers (plural) and not to any one individual among them elevated above the rest. Moreover, it is important to note that no Father is deemed "infallible." One cannot simply quote their writings to settle a dispute. As Serge Verhovskoy, my late professor of Dogmatic Theology at St. Vladimir's Orthodox Seminary once said, "The holy Fathers are not Holy Spirits!" Every one of them can and do err at one time or another. Their authority is a relative one insofar as their teachings must accord with the apostolic faith handed down in the canon of Scripture and worshipping life of the Church.

The lives of the saints also play an authoritative role in testifying to the truth of Orthodoxy. Holy ascetics can be touchstones of Orthodox dogma. In the fifth century, St. Simeon the Stylite was consulted by Emperor Leo I regarding the orthodoxy of Chalcedonian Christology. Simeon's holy life was seen as an embodiment of correct Christological dogma because genuine holiness could not rightly exist without it. Leo decreed that one had to be in communion with Simeon in order to be in communion with the Church's faith. To that extent, great monastic leaders often became (and become) "living texts." Their lives were seen as a living exegesis of the Bible and sacred embodiments of the faith. In fact, some of the strategies employed by the monks for discerning the correct meaning of Scripture included what they called "attaining a text." The way for them to rightly interpret the Bible occurred not simply through "exegesis" but by actually "trying on the text." Once the meaning was correctly lived, it was then correctly understood in the divinely intended sense and vice versa. At no time did the best of the monastic leaders ever diminish the authority of holy Scripture. Important as the liturgy and fathers were, they understood the primacy of Scripture in the life of the Church. This is well illustrated in the fourth century when it was once said that Abba Amoun of Nitria went to visit the great Abba Poemen. While discussing the struggles of the spiritual life, Amoun asked Poemen a question: "When I am obliged to speak to my neighbor, do you prefer me to speak of the Scriptures or of the sayings of the fathers? The old man answered him, 'If you can't be silent, you had better talk about the sayings of the Fathers than about the Scriptures; it is not so dangerous.'"[7]

Icons. Regarding the authority of icons, it is the Church's conviction that images are dogmatic statements of faith in lines and colors. Unlike other useful expressions of Christian art used in the West (such as paintings by Michelangelo), Orthodox icons are fundamentally a witness to the Incarnation. They are artistic affirmations of the Johannine truth that "the Word became flesh and dwelt among us" (John 1:14). As such they are authoritative statements of the Church's theology. The scenes depicted are theological affirmations, and each must be "read" on their own terms. How to inter-

---

[7]*The Sayings of the Desert Fathers*, trans. Benedicta Ward (Kalamazoo MI: Cistercian Publishers) 31-32.

pret the theology of icons is beyond this essay, but suffice it to say that not all icons in the Church are true expressions of the faith. Discernment is needed to sift the wheat from the chaff—to separate what is authentically Christian from what is not. Many centuries of mixture and intermingling between Orthodoxy and Catholicism has sometimes led to Westernized forms of art in the Church (not that "West equals bad" but that the different styles simply communicate different realities, some more adequately than others). In most Byzantine and even Coptic iconography, artistic conventions are used to convey the transfiguration and deification of humans through Christ. The icons are not humanist or pictorial representations of Jesus, but theological affirmations of the union and divine natures and what that means for the deification of humans and the ultimate transfiguration of the cosmos. To the extent that an icon reflects biblical faith, it functions as an authoritative interpretation of and witness to the fullness of Christian experience that is made possible through the Incarnation.

Ecclesiastical Canons. Finally, ecclesiastical canons occupy an authoritative position over the lives of the faithful. Ecclesiastical canons essentially are pronouncements concerning the faith and order of the Church. Often, though not exclusively, they are connected with the proceedings of the ecumenical councils. It is a complicated field of study fraught with the dangers of legalism. Rightly understood, the function of the canons is not to provide salvation, but to delineate the conditions that make salvation possible. They are not codes of law, but guidelines that are to be applied in concrete life situations such as when adultery, murder, or apostasy has occurred as well as less-spectacular offenses regarding marriage, god-children, and a host of others. They also keep the structures of the Church in proper balance so that bishops do not overstep their regional boundaries. The ultimate purpose of the canons is to preserve the rule of faith for the salvation of the faithful. They are to reflect the will of God in each generation with its changing situations. Those known as "dogmatic" canons are the most theologically relevant to the question of authority because they contain official affirmations of the Church's faith and order, which are unchangeable insofar as they reflect biblical faith.

Church Hymns and Architecture. Orthodox hymns have also expressed the faith of the Church. They are not designed to promote aesthetic values. "Dogmatic hymns" (*dogmastika*) are especially authoritative expressions of the Church's faith often reflecting some aspect of Nicene or Chalcedonian Orthodoxy. Very little actually focuses on the spiritual life and struggles of the individual believer. Much more is sung about God, Christ, and the Holy Trinity and what that means for living a life of purity and holiness. The authority of hymns belongs to the wider authority of the liturgy and is subject to correction only in light of the apostolic witness of the Church.

Likewise, Church architecture is designed with the theological purpose of conveying the apostolic faith. For instance, in the Byzantine style one finds a large dome indicating the Incarnation, or Christ looking down in anticipation of the coming Judgment, or (in the Russian tradition) onion domes to convey the fire of the Spirit on the day of Pentecost. These are not on a par with the Bible, councils, or liturgy but they do belong to the larger witness of the Church.

Conclusion

In concluding our analysis of how authority is to operate in the Orthodox Church, one might easily get the impression that Church members know it well and apply it well. However, that is not always the case. The principles of authority do not always match the Church's practice of it. When all is put together, the Orthodox vision of authority may be likened to a Beethoven symphony: The conductor is the Holy Spirit, the baton is the apostolic faith, and the musicians are the diverse sources of the Church's theology. So long as the musicians obey the conductor and take their cues from his baton, their music becomes a rich, varied, and harmonious melody. However, as soon as the musicians take their eyes off the conductor and his baton the result is not a symphony, but a cacophony of discord.

So also is the performance of authority in the Orthodox Church: it is often played with a mixture of sour notes and the sweetness of a Beethoven symphony.

APOSTLES AND BISHOPS.
PUZZLING OVER THE PROBLEM
OF PRIESTHOOD SUCCESSION

Stephen D. Ricks

As a very young man returning from a semester's study in Central Europe by way of Great Britain, I once visited an acquaintance who was a Rhodes Scholar at Oxford. Though a Latter-day Saint, as a part of his cultural experience at Oxford he attended evening services—"chapel," he called them—at an Anglican Church there, and took me with him. That evening we were treated to the preaching of a minister whose sermon consisted of discussing whether Jesus ever actually existed. Finally, with a sigh, the minister finally conceded that, well, Jesus must have existed. (Given his pains to discuss the factual existence of Jesus, we need not ask whether the good reverend accepted Him as the Messiah and Son of God.) All of this suggests widespread uncertainty and confusion about the origins and early history of Christianity. Included in this confusion is the question of the role of apostles, their relationship to bishops, the disappearance of the apostles and the continued existence and functioning of the bishops, and the implications of these facts for our appreciation of earliest Christianity.

In puzzling over the question of apostolic succession from a Latter-day Saint perspective, I will make use of the arguments and evidence of Hugh Nibley in *The World and the Prophets* and *Apostles and Bishops in Early Christianity*, with all of which I agree in principle. The late Prof. Nibley, who died in February 2005 at the very advanced age of nearly ninety-five years, was the supernova of Mormon studies and one of the most brilliantly gifted and prolific scholars in the Church of Jesus Christ of Latter-day Saints. The first of his books that I will use in this discussion, *The World and the Prophets*, was based on a long series of lectures, "Time Vindicates the Prophets," broadcast on the Salt Lake City-based radio station KSL, in 1954, and was republished in 1987 in the Collected Works of Hugh Nibley. His other book, *Apostles and Bishops in Early Christianity*, was the text for a course of the same name he offered, also in 1954 (as a set of "lectures" that reflected its root sense of "readings" from a prepared text); his text was rediscovered among his papers in his garage in 1997, like some lost and priceless symphony or opera, and published for the first time in 2005, more than fifty years after its original presentation.

In what follows I will argue, from the perspective of a Latter-day Saint, that the "church" established by Christ had a fairly sophisticated organization, that the apostleship was on a different plane of authority than that of the bishop, that bishops were subordinate to apostles (with momentary digressions on the question of whether Peter was bishop of Rome and about the anomaly of James the brother of the Lord as bishop of Jerusalem and apostle), that the apostles died out or disappeared by the end of the first Christian century, that the remaining bishops maintained and developed their authority over the centuries, but that the loss of apostolic authority led to a profound sense of loss. I will make this argument based on primary and secondary sources, some older, some more current.

Organization of Earliest Christianity

Though a majority of scholars take the view that Jesus organized an *ekklesia*—a society, congregation, or church—they are in considerable disagreement as to the character of that organization. On the first pages of the premier issue of the *Journal of Ecclesiastical History*, T. W. Manson observed:

> In the Gospels "we begin with the fact that Jesus did gather a community around himself during the course of his ministry; and we may well ask what it was, if it was not the church. . . . It will not do to regard this group merely as the more or less regular disciples of a somewhat unorthodox traveling Rabbi. . . . The more the synagogue evidence is studied, the more clearly the fact emerges that what Jesus created was something more than a new theological school. It was a religious community, of which he was the leader.[1]

Though we see in earliest Christianity a clearly defined local organization, the great German historian Eduard Meyer writes that "the highest authority was held by the Twelve, and at their head was Peter."[2]

" 'At the present time,' says Peter to the youthful Clement in the [*Pseudo-*]*Clementine Recognitions*, 'do not look for any other prophet or apostle except us. There is one true prophet and twelve apostles.' "[3] The discovery of the *Didache* in 1875 led Harnack to announce that, "in

---

[1]T. W. Manson, "The New Testament Basis of the Doctrine of the Church," *Journal of Ecclesiastical History* 1 (1950): 3-4.

[2]Eduard Meyer, *Ursprung und Anfänge des Christentums* (Darmstadt: Wissenschaftliche Buchgesellschaft, 1962) 9.

[3]Hugh W. Nibley, *Apostles and Bishops in Early Christianity*, ed. John F. Hall and John W. Welch (Salt Lake City: Deseret Book and FARMS, 2005) 8; *Recognitiones Clementinae* 4.35; in *Patrologiae cursus completus*, Series Graeca, 218 vols., ed. Jacques-Paul Migne (Paris: Garnier Brothers, 1912) 1:1330.

opposition to everything that had been claimed before," the primitive church was endowed with more than one order of priesthood, a point reiterated by subsequent research, which recognizes different levels of authority between apostles and bishops.[4]

Bishops were Subordinate to Apostles

Were bishops subordinate to apostles? Ignatius, early second-century bishop of Antioch, bishop of the largest and, except for Jerusalem, oldest congregation in Christendom and one of the early "apostolic fathers," recognized the subordination of the bishops to apostles when he noted: "They were apostles; I am but a man."[5] At another time he wrote, "Shall I reach such a pitch of presumption . . . as to issue orders to you as if I were an apostle?"[6] Being "apostolic" certainly did not give him the authority of an apostle.

Jean Reville, reflecting on Ignatius's letters in an early number of the magisterial French journal *Revue de l'Histoire des Religions*, writes significantly:

> It is impossible to dispute that the episcopate as represented in the epistles of Ignatius is essentially a local function, the authority of which is limited to the community in which it was exercised. Never does Ignatius appeal to his title of bishop of Antioch to give more authority to his instructions. . . . One cannot insist too much on the curious fact in the Ignatian literature . . . : the complete absence of any allusion to the apostolic nature of the episcopate, and to any justification of the Episcopal power by the principle of apostolic succession. [There is in Ignatius] not yet the slightest trace of those conferences at which the bishops engaged in struggle, as in the second half of the second century. The bishop . . . does not even have the character of a general authority."[7]

Polycarp, an early second-century bishop of Smyrna, who had sat at the

---

[4]Nibley, *Apostles and Bishops*, 19; Edward J. Kilmartin, "Priesthood," in *Encyclopedia of Early Christianity*, ed. Everett Ferguson (New York: Garland, 1990) 754-55.

[5]Greek: "Ekeinoi apostoloi, ego katakritos," Ignatius of Antioch, *Epistola ad Romanos* 4.3, in *Patrologia Graeca* 5:689 (cf. 5:808).

[6]Ignatius of Antioch, *Epistola ad Phildelphenses* 4, in *Patrologia Graeca* 5:828.

[7]Jean Reville, "Etudes sur les origines de l'episcopat: La valeur du temoinage d'Ignace d'Antioche," *Revue de l'histoire des religions* 21 (1890): 284-85.

feet of the apostle John the Beloved, was equally insistent on the subordination of bishops to the apostles:

> For neither I, nor any other such one, [Polycarp insists,] can come up to the wisdom of the blessed and glorious Paul. He, when among you, accurately and steadfastly taught the word of truth in the absence of those who were then alive. And when absent from you, he wrote you a letter . . . which will build you up in that faith which has been given to you[8]

The letter to which Polycarp refers was the epistle written by Paul to the Philippians, and by all accounts this Epistle to the Philippians to which Polycarp refers is among the weakest letters in the entire Bible—yet the most distinguished bishop of the mid-second century Christian church, "the man whose presence in Rome to settle the Easter controversy was for Irenaeus the surest claim that that church had no apostolic guidance,"[9] views the authority of his own epistle as incomparably below that of a short and rather uninformative letter from an actual apostle.

Clement, bishop of Rome in the final decade of the first century, in making a low-key plea for episcopal authority, modestly declines to mention his own position and his apostolic connections and never dreams of insisting that his will be obeyed, merely giving his opinion about evil men deposing good men and installing themselves in their stead. "Christ came from God," Clement writes, "and the apostles from Christ,"[10] but he resolutely refuses to take the next step and state what in later ages would be automatic, "and the bishops from the apostles." Rather, Clement merely suggests that the apostles set apart bishops and, recognizing that there would be later difficulties about this office, established a special principle (Greek *epinome*, "bylaw, special order") allowing for the proper succession of worthy men as bishops.[11]

Ignatius, Polycarp, Clement, and other early second-century bishops originally ordained by one or another apostle continued to plead with churches in other locations to repent and be obedient. However, they made such appeals only as concerned friends and observers, never presuming to

---

[8]Polycarp, *Epistola ad Philippenses* 3.2, in *PG* 5:1008.

[9]Nibley, *Apostles and Bishops*, 28.

[10]Clement, *Epistola Prima ad Corinthios* 42.2, in *PG* 1:295-96.

[11]Nibley, *Apostles and Bishops*, 28.

issue orders "as an apostle."[12]

Was Peter Bishop of Rome?

Was the apostle Peter the first bishop of Rome? So important was it somehow to connect Peter with the office of bishop that it produced a rich harvest of contradictions and absurd claims. Norbert Brox, the German Catholic scholar of early Christianity, is firm in his assertion that Peter was not the first bishop of Rome (thus providing an apostolic link to the Roman papacy): "The claim that Peter was the first bishop of Rome had its origin in the second century and was dogmatically motivated. We know with a high degree of certainty that Peter was in Rome and was martyred there, but we know nothing about his activities and role in the Christian community in Rome. It is out of the question that he was its first bishop."[13]

So anxious were some individuals to believe that Peter was also bishop of Rome, says Chrysostom, that they claimed that there must have been two Peters![14] *The Gospel of the Twelve Apostles* has Christ ordain Peter an archbishop, though such an office did not exist before the fourth century. And according to the *Apostolic Constitutions*, when the church was being formally organized, Peter suggested first of all ordaining a bishop in the presence of all the apostles, including Paul and James, bishop of Jerusa-lem—pouring all their collective authority into a single individual, and then doing homage to him. This may sound ridiculous, but is it not what the later Christian claim amounts to?

The Jesuit Francis A. Sullivan, who was for several decades professor of Theology at the Gregorian University in Rome, notes in *From Apostles to Bishops* that the argument of a direct line of succession in authority from the apostles to the bishops is historically very difficult: "One conclusion seems obvious," observes Father Sullivan, "neither the New Testament nor early Christian history offer support for a notion of apostolic succession as

---

[12]Ignatius of Antioch, *Epistola ad Philadelphenses*, in *PG* 5:828, p. xvi.

[13]"Die Aussage, dass Petrus der erste Bischof Roms gewesen sei, entstand im 2. Jahrhundert und war damals dogmatisch motiviert. Wir wissen mit grosser Sicherheit, dass Petrus zwar in Rom und dort Märtyrer war, aber über seine Tätigkeit in der Stadt und über seine Rolle in der römischen Gemeinde ist nichts bekannt. Dass er ihr erster Bischof war, ist ausgescholossen," Norbert Brox, *Kirchengeschichte des Altertums* (Düsseldorf: Patmos, 1983) 106.

[14]Nibley, *Apostles and Bishops*, 31.

'an unbroken line of Episcopal ordination from Christ through the apostles down through the centuries to the bishops of today.' "[15]

The difficulties of claiming episcopal succession are true for Rome, Antioch, and Constantinople, which all laid claim to succeeding to the authority of the apostles. Firmilian (AD 230–268), third-century bishop of Caesarea, criticized Stephen, bishop of Rome, because he claimed succession from Peter: "I am justly indignant at this so open and manifest folly of Stephen, . . . who so boasts of the place of his episcopate and contends that he holds the succession from Peter."[16]

Cyprian, in response to Stephen's effort to assert command over the council of bishops in Africa, reflected the general principles of episcopal independence:

> For neither does any of us set himself as a bishop of bishops, . . . since every bishop, according to the allowance of his liberty and power, has his own proper right of judgment, and can no more be judged by another than he himself can judge another.[17]

On another occasion Cyprian observed that the Christian church had become an organization of locally sovereign bishops:

> Thence, through the changes of time and successions, the ordering of bishops and the plan of the church flow onwards; so that the church is founded upon the bishops, and every act of the Church is controlled by these same rulers. Since this, then, is founded upon divine law, I marvel that some, with daring temerity, have chosen to write to me as if they wrote in the name of the church.[18]

This spirit of independence persisted through the fourth century, and even into the succeeding centuries. In 314, at the Council (Synod) of Arles, it was decreed that "no bishop should annoy another bishop."[19] The first

[15]Francis A. Sullivan, *From Apostles to Bishops: The Development of the Episcopacy in the Early Church* (New York: Newman Press, 2001) 15-16.

[16]Firmilian, cited by Cyprian of Carthage, *Epistles* LXXIV.17, in *Ante-Nicene Fathers* (hereafter *ANF*), ed. Alexander Roberts and James Donaldson (1885; repr.: Peabody MA: Hendrickson, 1994) 5:394.

[17]*Seventh Council of Carthage under Cyprian: Concerning the Baptism of Heretics*, in *ANF* 5:565.

[18]Cyprian, *Epistle* XXVI.1, in *ANF* 5:305.

[19]Nibley, *Apostles and Bishops*, 123.

ecumenical council at Nicea (AD 325) was convened at the direction of Constantine. Before the start of the proceedings, Constantine was inundated by denunciations of bishops against each other. It is recorded that, "in a statesmanlike gesture the emperor publicly burned these unopened."[20]

James As an Anomaly

James, the brother of the Lord, may have held two positions of eminence in the earliest church: he was both "bishop" as well as "apostle." Was James a freak, a mistake, a flash in the pan? After all, he had no successors, did he, in his odd and lofty offices? He may have been both bishop (or "presiding bishop," to borrow a term from Latter-day Saint parlance) and apostle, though Hegesippus, quoted by Eusebius, says about him, "James, the brother of the Lord, took over the church along with (GK. *meta* + genitive) the apostles." Yet Jerome renders this passage: *suscepit ecclesiam Hieroso-lymorum post* (= GK. *meta* + accusative) *apostolos frater Domini Jacobus,* "James the brother of the Lord, took over the church at Jerusalem after [this is the meaning of the Latin word "post"] the apostles," suggesting, again, the devout desire of many that bishops be seen as equal to, and successors of, the apostles.

While James may at some time have held the office of bishop, it should be observed that, in the view of my colleague John Hall,

> Paul attributed to James General Authority status as an Apostle. He reported that on the occasion of a visit to Jerusalem when he abode with Peter for fifteen days, 'others of the Apostles saw I none, save James the Lord's brother' (Gal. 1:19). . . . James, the brother of the Lord, whether he served as bishop of Jerusalem, or Presiding Bishop of the Church," very likely "came to receive a calling to join the twelve.[21]

Departure of the Apostles from the Scene and Its Results

No event is more widely agreed upon by scholars of earliest Christianity than that by the end of the first Christian century the apostles had departed the scene. W. H. C. Frend, in his *Rise of Christianity*, observes that "By the

[20]Leo Donald Davis, *The First Seven Ecumenical Councils (325–787): Their History and Theology* (Wilmington DE: Glazier, 1987) 58.

[21]John F. Hall, *New Testament Witnesses of Christ; Peter, John, James, and Paul* (American Fork UT: Covenant Communications, 2002) 180-81.

end of the [first] century, . . . the great men had died; prophecy was not being poured out as expected in the last times."[22] The German Catholic historian of early Christianity, Norbert Brox, notes simply: "The apostles died out."[23] This view is further refined by Father Raymond Brown in his study, *The Churches the Apostles Left Behind* (a position followed by Francis Sullivan in *From Apostles to Bishops*), where he argues that the

> "apostolic period"' closed by the year 67, when Peter, Paul, and James the "brother of the Lord"—the only apostles about whose role in the early Church we have detailed knowledge—had disappeared from the scene. The "subapostolic period," then, would comprise the last third of the first century, during which most of the New Testament (with the exception of the undisputed letters of Paul) was written.[24]

Only at the end of the first Christian century did the "postapostolic period" begin.

The apostles had departed or died, an occurrence that led to a profound sense of loss. On this event Polycarp of Smyrna, who had sat at the feet of the Apostle John and had been ordained to his bishopric by the apostles themselves, gravely pronounced: "In Asia the great lights went out."[25]

The consequences of the departure of the apostles were ominous. Hegesippus, followed by Eusebius in his *Ecclesiastical History*, tellingly observes:

> The Church continued until then as a pure and uncorrupt virgin; whilst if there were any at all that attempted to pervert the sound doctrine of the saving Gospel, they were yet skulking in dark retreats; but when the sacred choir of Apostles became extinct, and the generation of those that had been privileged to hear their inspired wisdom had passed away, then also the combinations of impious error arose by the fraud and delusions of the false teachers. These also, as there were none of the Apostles left, henceforth attempted without shame to preach their false doctrine against the Gospel of truth.

---

[22]W. H. C. Frend, *The Rise of Christianity* (Philadelphia: Fortress Press, 1985) 140.

[23]"Die Apostel starben aus." Norbert Brox, *Kirchengeschichte des Altertums* (Düsseldorf: Patmos-Verlag, 1983) 97.

[24]Raymond Brown, *The Churches the Apostles Left Behind* (New York: Paulist Press, 1984) 1-16; cf. Sullivan, *From Apostles to Bishops*, 54.

[25]"Kai gar kata ten Asian megala stoicheia kekoimetai," Eusebius, *Historia Ecclesicstica* 5.4.2 in *Patrologia graeca* 20:493.

Though Hegesippus's view of the conditions of the era following the death or departure of the apostles may be somewhat overdrawn, it at least underlines his view that "the apostles had a kind of authority that none of their successors had."[26]

The Quandary of the Post-Apostolic Christian

Tertullian is a case study in the quandary of a Christian who was confronted with a church that, according to Henry Chadwick, had become "unspiritual, institutionalized, and compromised by worldlinesss," that is, not motivated by the spirit of prophetic inspiration of the apostolic age.[27] A lawyer by profession, intimately acquainted with the classics of Greek and Roman literature, Terteullian became a Christian as an adult and brilliantly used his learning and insights to defend his newly chosen faith. But for Tertullian "the gift of prophecy was . . . the strongest recommendation of the divinity of the Christian church, and it was only when painful experience had convinced him beyond a doubt that the main church no longer possessed that gift that he did an amazing thing"[28]: Tertullian began to fellowship with the Montanists and became partial to their views (I will grant Sullivan's insistence that "there is no evidence that he ever left the Catholic Church to join or found a schismatic one"),[29] a group that diverged from the main body of Christians in one crucial respect: "they preached that the gift of prophecy must be found in the church if it is the true church."[30] Tertullian, in his tract *De Pudicitia*, straightforwardly challenged his Christian contemporaries: "Show me therefore, you who would be apostolic, some prophetic examples, and I will acknowledge the divinity of your call. . . . The Church is the spirit working through an inspired man; the Church is not a number of bishops. The final decision remains with the Lord, never with the Servant; it belongs to God alone, not to any priest."[31] There were

---

[26]Nibley, *Apostles and Bishops*, 10; Eusebius, *Historia Ecclesiastica* 3.32.8, in *Patrologia Graeca* 20:284.

[27]Henry Chadwick, *The Early Church* (New York: Penguin Group, 1993) 92.

[28]Hugh Nibley, *The World and the Prophets* (Salt Lake City: Deseret Book and FARMS, 1987) 247.

[29]Sullivan, *From Apostles to Bishops*, 154.

[30]Nibley, *World and the Prophets*, 247; see also Dennis E. Groh, "Montanism," in *Encyclopedia of Early Christianity*, 622-23.

[31]Tertullian, *De Pudicitia* 21-22.

already "two factions in the church, those who precluded office by spirit, and those who supplanted spirit by office."[32]

The solution to this quandary was, in Tertullian's view, the presence of prophets and prophecy in the church. In the early eighteenth century, John Kaye, bishop of Lincoln, wrote a compelling study of the gradual loss of prophets and prophecy in the church that was tellingly entitled *The Ecclesiastical History of the Second and Third Centuries Illustrated from the Writings of Tertullian*:

> The miraculous powers conferred upon the Apostles were the credentials by which they were to prove that they were the bearers of a new Revelation from God to man. . . . We might therefore infer from the purpose for which they were conferred that they would on process of time be withdrawn. . . .
>
> . . . The power of working miracles was not extended beyond the disciples, upon whom the Apostles conferred it by the imposition of hands. . . . What, then, would be the effect produced on the minds of the great body of Christians by their gradual desition? Many would not observe, none would be willing to observe it; for all must naturally feel a reluctance to believe that powers, which had contributed so essentially to the rapid diffusion of Christianity, were withdrawn. . . . The silence of ecclesiastical history, respecting the cessation of miraculous gifts in the Church, is to be ascribed . . . to the combined operation of prejudice and policy—of prejudice which made them reluctant to believe, of policy which made them anxious to conceal the truth. . . .
>
> . . . I perceive in the language of the Fathers, who lived in the middle and end of the second century . . . if not a conviction, at least a suspicion, that the power of working miracles was withdrawn, combined with an anxiety to keep up a belief of its continuance in the Church. They affirm in general terms that miracles were performed, but rarely venture to produce an instance of a particular miracle. Those who followed them are less scrupulous, and proceeded to invent miracles.[33]

In Robert Browning's "A Death in the Desert," we see the sense of loss at the departure of the apostles, in the solitary reflections of John, the last of the apostles, who himself is in this poem close to death.

Still, when they scatter, there is left on earth

---

[32]Nibley, *World and the Prophets*, 248.

[33]John Kaye, *The Ecclesiastical History of the Second and Third Centuries Illustrated from the Writings of Tertullian* (London: Rivington, 1825; 2nd ed., Cambridge: J. Smith, 1829) 96-97, 98, 99-102.

No one alive who knew (consider this!)
—Saw with his eyes and handled with his hands
That which was from the first, the Word of Life.
How till it be when none more saith "I saw"?[34]

The Return of Apostles and Prophets?

The second century of the Christian era is critical to our understanding of Christian history and our reflections on apostolic and episcopal authority. Samuel G. F. Brandon compares the second century to a tunnel "from which we emerge to find a situation which is unexpected in terms of the situation which went before."[35] The second Christian century marks the transition from a Christianity that is world-hostile and world-rejecting to a world-conditioned and world-affirming Christianity. Was this due in part to the death and disappearance of the apostles? From a Latter-day Saint perspective, the answer would be powerfully affirmative. What are the implications of this, again, from a Latter-day Saint perspective? We need to look for the return of the apostles and prophets, for miracles and other manifestations of spiritual gifts, of those who could truly say, "I saw!"

---

[34]Robert Browning, "A Death in the Desert" (May 1864) st. 12, ll. 129-33.
[35]S. G. F. Brandon, *Fall of Jerusalem and the Christian Church: A Study of the Jewish Overthrow of A.D. 70 on Christianity* (London: S.P.C.K., 1957) 10.

Is *Sola Scriptura* Really *Sola?*
Edwards, Newman, Bultmann, and Wright
on the Bible as Religious Authority

Gerald R. McDermott

Ever since Martin Luther (1483–1546), Protestants have testified "*Sola Scriptura*" when asked for their understanding of what provides final religious authority—that is, what enables them to know if a particular doctrine or practice is "Christian." Mainline Protestants have tended to qualify *sola scriptura* with creeds and confessions—saying in effect that their theological progenitors have best captured the meaning of *scriptura*, and that therefore *sola* means "the Bible alone" but read through those theological prisms. Therefore Protestants, who historically distinguished themselves from Catholics by rejecting the normative authority of tradition, have (ironically) used their own traditions to enact their own understandings of religious authority.

Evangelicals, on the other hand, have prided themselves on being more Protestant than mainline Protestants by taking *sola* more seriously. They have claimed to recognize the normative value of Scripture more rigorously, by refusing to accept as normative any creed or confession. Many evangelicals have assumed that "their" theologian, Jonathan Edwards (1703–1758), must have thought and done the same. We shall see, however, that while Edwards professed this evangelically standard version of *sola scriptura*, in practice he was a mainline Protestant. In fact, his understanding of the development of theological tradition betrays a curious resemblance to notions of doctrinal development championed by Catholic theologian John Henry Newman (1801–1890).

This chapter explores the meaning of *sola scriptura* by tracing deliberations on related themes by Edwards, Newman, Bultmann (1884–1976) and N. T. Wright (b. 1948). It wrestles with the question of how one uses *sola scriptura* in questions of religious authority—or more sharply, what *sola scriptura* means when using the Bible to decide what is acceptable doctrine or practice for the Christian church. I do not bother to argue *for* the notion of *sola scriptura*; so, for example, I do not argue for a Protestant view of authority against a Catholic view that a *magisterium* should be the Christian's final authority. Instead I assume *sola scriptura* and ask what it means or how it is used. Nor do I want to discuss institutional religious authority per se—so I do not want to discuss which religious leaders or church government or denominational bodies have the best claim to religious authority. Finally, in this chapter I do not try to resolve the question of religious authority as power—or, in other words, what is involved in the use of authority to expel evil spirits or move mountains or bring down empires.

Instead, I focus on what is involved when we say that the Bible has final authority. Can we say, as evangelicals and Mormons often do, that the Bible can and should be interpreted without the interference of tradition? Or that we preach and teach only what the Bible teaches and preaches, without distortions introduced by later tradition? In other words, are Catholics and mainline Protestants wrong when they suggest that tradition plays an important role in our use of the Bible and therefore religious authority? On the other hand, are liberal Protestants right when, following Bultmann, they discount our access to the historical Jesus,[1] and conclude that religious authority has everything to do with the risen Christ and little to do with Jesus of Nazareth because we cannot know the latter? In other words, that the Bible itself demonstrates that it is naïve and impossible to anchor religious authority in history?

I will use my explorations of Edwards, Newman, Bultmann and Wright to argue six propositions that, for brevity's sake, can be summed up as follows: Scripture is inextricably tied to tradition, tradition and Scripture are mutually informing, God reveals himself in ordinary history and continues to illuminate the meaning of Scripture through history, and Scripture presents God and not just the church's thoughts about God.

1. Edwards on Religious Authority: Private Conscience Based on *Sola Scriptura*

While Edwards spent the better part of his career challenging important Enlightenment presuppositions,[2] he was nevertheless influenced by some

---

[1]As we shall see below, Bultmann did not discount *all* access to the Jesus of history, or the possibility of such access. But his concession of access was so minimal, and his neo-Kantian epistemology so pessimistic about knowledge of God, that the effect of his work has been to close the door on knowledge of the historical Jesus.

[2]Such as the deist notions that religion's essence is morality, and its critical standard popular common sense. See McDermott, *Jonathan Edwards Confronts the Gods* (New York: Oxford University Press, 2000) 34-54. See also Josh Moody, *Jonathan Edwards and the Enlightenment: Knowing the Presence of God* (Lanham MD: University Press of America, 2005).

of those same presumptions. For example, he argued, along with most of his
intellectual peers, that the *location* of religious authority is the private
conscience. True religious authority does not belong to a church body or
church leader to tell men and women, for instance, what minister should
preside over them. Instead, "every particular man and every congregation
of men in the world have the same liberty to judge what man is fit to feed
their souls."[3] Edwards made this last statement to support early eighteenth-
century New England congregants who sought to depose ministers they
considered theologically defective.[4] He also insisted that private conscience
is capable of judging every previous theological assertion: "[It is a]
scriptural and Protestant maxim, that we ought to call no man on earth
master, or make the authority of the greatest and holiest of mere men the
ground of our belief of any doctrine in religion."[5] Edwards even went so far
as to charge that Catholics, best known for repudiating the authority of
private conscience, unwittingly appeal to private conscience themselves,
since "they think, in their own private judgment, that they see some reason
why whatever their clergy teaches should be true, to believe that their clergy
are infallible."[6]

In somewhat routine Protestant manner, Edwards held that the *means*
of religious authority was the written text of Scripture, without the help of
anything else. The Bible, he asserted, contains all that is necessary for faith,
worship and practice. "The Scriptures are 'completely sufficient of

---

[3]*Miscellanies* 17. (The *Miscellanies*, Edwards's private notebooks, are
published in vols. 13, 18, 20, and 23 of the Yale edition of the *Works of Jonathan
Edwards*. In this paper, for brevity sake, I will simply refer to Edwards's numbering
system, which is reproduced in the Yale edition.)

[4]David D. Hall, introduction to *Ecclesiastical Writings, Works of Jonathan
Edwards*, vol. 12 (New Haven CT: Yale University Press, 1994) 14-17. He also
used "liberty of conscience" as a principle to support those who wished to break
covenant with a congregation and join separatist churches. *Letters and Personal
Writings*, ed. George S. Claghorn, *Works of Jonathan Edwards*, vol. 16 (New
Haven CT: Yale University Press, 1998) 127-33. Thanks to Ken Minkema for this
reference.

[5]Edwards, "Author's Preface" to *An Humble Inquiry into the Rules of the Word
of God, Concerning The Qualifications Requisite to a Compleat Standing and Full
Communion in the Visible Christian Church*, in *Ecclesiastical Writings*, 167.
Edwards was citing his grandfather Solomon Stoddard's admonition.

[6]*Miscellanies* 70.

themselves' . . . and . . . in all important matters, whether in doctrine or practice, the Scriptures should sufficiently explain themselves."[7] Study of ancient cultures and languages helps us interpret difficult passages, but for the most part the Bible is perspicuous:

> The manifest design of God in the Scripture, is to speak so plainly as that the interpretation should be more independent than that of any other book which is ever to be remembered, and should always be of great weight with us in our interpretation of the Scripture; and so we should chiefly interpret Scripture by Scripture.[8]

To do otherwise—that is, to use anything else as religious authority—is to commit idolatry. In his narrative of the communion controversy, penned sometime after 1750, Edwards cites his grandfather Solomon Stoddard's words approvingly, "He, who believes principles because our forefathers affirm them, makes idols of them."[9] In other words, one should never accept anything as religiously binding simply because Christians in previous times believed them. Edwards goes so far as to raise this precept to the status of "Protestant principle" later in his narrative: "[It is] easily resolved . . . [w]hether, on Protestant principles, the determination of ancestors as to matters of religion and the worship of God, binds future generations without their consent, either express or implied."[10] Edwards implies, in good Enlightenment fashion, that there should be no binding without consent.

This did not mean, however, that tradition is useless. Arguments from "the fathers" and the early church can be helpful in two ways. They can confirm the truth of a doctrine or practice by showing that one's interpretation of the Bible is "more probable." They can also serve heuristically by prodding us to look in the Scriptures for things we had not seen there before.[11]

But Edwards was convinced that no matter how "very rational [and] probable" their arguments may be, God "never designed that the dependence of his church should be *at all* upon them [the Fathers or other traditional authorities]." Edwards argued for this on democratic, fallibilistic,

---

[7] *Miscellanies* 535.
[8] *Miscellanies* 828.
[9] *Ecclesiastical Writings*, 565.
[10] "Narrative of Communion Controversy," in *Ecclesiastical Writings*, 587.
[11] *Miscellanies* 535.

and fiduciary grounds. First, democratic: If traditional authorities outside the Bible were to serve as additional or primary sources of authority, the ordinary Christian would be at a disadvantage. Only "learned men" would have the training and time to master such authorities. But the Bible is "not so large, but that *all* may be well acquainted with them." It is "God's mercy" that His "rule" is "contained within so small a compass . . . that 'tis not beyond the capacity of ordinary Christians to manage it, and become well acquainted with it." With the help of their ministers, humble farmers can see what they need to see for "themselves."[12]

Second, the inherent fallibility of theologians and church leaders makes it unsafe to rely on them. We have no reason to expect that God protected them from "unavoidable mistakes." They might have corrupted the truth, and we cannot expect that "providence" would have always prevented such corruption.[13] Even if they had no intention of changing what they had received, their historical conditions might have caused loss or distortion. For Christians in the first generations were few and scattered, and they could have misunderstood or forgotten what the apostles had told them—"either through a mistake of meaning or through defect of memory." Besides, there were few who heard all of what the apostles taught, and fewer still who understood it properly.

> I suppose it will not be thought by any, that above half of the Christians in the apostles' time ever heard the apostles speak; and not a third of them that did hear any of them speak, ever heard them speak one quarter of the doctrine they taught. There were many even in the apostles' time (if I understand the matter right), that pretended and intended to build their belief upon what the apostles and evangelists taught, that yet believed very erroneous doctrines.[14]

Third, Edwards reasoned that dependence on tradition would detract from dependence on Scripture and God. "The more absolute and entire our dependence on the Word of God is, the greater the respect we shall have to that Word, the more we shall esteem and honor and prize it; and this respect

---

[12]*Miscellanies* 535.

[13]*Miscellanies* 535. Edwards believed, with his Reformed predecessors, that Jesus' promise of the Holy Spirit to "teach you all things, and bring to your remembrance all that I have said to you" (John 14:26 RSV) applied to the apostles and not their successors.

[14]*Miscellanies* 72.

to the Word of God will lead us to have the greater respect to God himself."[15] The temptation, Edwards suggested, would be to pay the Fathers just as much respect as the Bible, which would mean that the Fathers' wisdom would rival that of God's.

The result of dependence on tradition, for Edwards, is dependence on God's providence and hence our ability to discern its meaning. The problem, however, is that "the conduct of divine providence, with its reasons, is too little understood by us, to be improved as our rule. 'God has his way in the sea, his path in the mighty waters, and his footsteps are not known' " (Ps. 77:19).[16] Edwards believed it was inherently problematic to decide with any certainty why God permitted various events in human history, including the events of new developments in theology and biblical interpretation. Thus the wisdom in God's giving us only the Word as our rule.

This pessimism about human ability to interpret providence is surprising, coming from a man who regularly scanned the news for signs of progress in the history of redemption. This was the same man who declared that local events such as drought or pestilence were signs of God's providential judgment.[17] But Edwards's objection to using providence as a rule was in reply to his opponents during the communion controversy, who contended that their (and his grandfather Solomon Stoddard's) open communion policy had been blessed with conversions. Edwards's response was that God blesses those features of pastoral practice "which are very right and excellent" while overlooking and pardoning "their mistakes in opinion or practice."[18] The same of course could be said for the opinions of the Fathers. Many thousands might have been blessed by their theologies and practices, but those theologies and practices may nevertheless have been riddled with errors. We have no guarantee otherwise.

2. Edwards's Practice Was Not Perfect: *Sola Scriptura* Was Not Always *Sola*

But Edwards was inconsistent. Or, to put it another way, the sum total of his thinking on religious authority was more nuanced. *Sola scriptura* was his

---

[15]*Miscellanies* 535.

[16]*Ecclesiastical Writings*, 319.

[17]McDermott, *One Holy and Happy Society: The Public Theology of Jonathan Edwards* (University Park: Penn State University Press, 1992) 43-48, 11-13.

[18]*An Humble Inquiry*, in *Ecclesiastical Writings*, 319-20.

rallying cry, especially when plotting the course of Protestant progress against Catholic persecution,[19] but he also showed in a number of ways that theology and practice must look outside the Bible to know what the Bible means. We can see this pattern in his reflections on the history of revelation, the history of theology, the history of his own theological development, and his remarks on church practice.

In his magisterial *A History of the Work of Redemption*, Edwards noted that before Moses' time God's revelation was transmitted by oral tradition. Adam passed down revelation to Noah (their long lives overlapped), who in turn handed on these revelations to Abraham. The sons of Jacob transmitted what they had learned from Abraham, Isaac and Jacob to their posterity in Egypt. But by this time it was necessary to commit the revelations to writing for three reasons: the distance from the original revelations was so great, "the lives of men [had] become so short" (which would mean presumably that there would be greater chance of corruption with the greater number of transmissions), and to keep his people adequately separated from their pagan neighbors.[20] Edwards also noted that, precisely because redemption proceeded for all those ages *before* Scripture began, God's church has been founded not on Scripture per se but on *revelation*, which has used both oral tradition *and* the written word.[21] The point is that God's church has not always used the Bible for religious authority; for significant periods it used oral tradition, preserved through human teachers invested with authority.

Edwards also observed that the history of theology was driven partly by the "gradual" illumination of the meaning of the Scriptures. God chose not to unfold the sum total of his revelation at once. Just as the Bible was written by degrees and over time, so too God's Spirit imparted understand-

---

[19]See, e.g., *A History of the Work of Redemption*, in vol. 9, *Works of Jonathan Edwards*, ed. John F. Wilson (New Haven CT: Yale University Press, 1989) 414, 421-22.

[20]Ibid., 182-83.

[21]Ibid., 443: "So that the church of God has always been built on the foundation of divine revelation, and always on those revelations that were essentially the same, and which are summarily comprehended in the holy Scriptures, and ever since about Moses' time have been built on the Scriptures themselves." Edwards's emphasis is on the rule of Scripture, but in the process he notes that revelation is even more foundational than Scripture.

ing of the Bible by degrees and over time. The most important parts of revelation have been plain from the very beginning, but God has purposely made other parts "obscure and mysterious," even "difficult." This is because human beings prize something more after they have labored for it. They also find the search and discovery more "delightful."[22]

Edwards considered progressive revelation, and progressive understanding of that revelation, to be evident from the plain text of Scripture.

> There are a multitude of things in the Old Testament which the church then did not understand, but were reserved to be unfolded to the Christian church, such as most of their types and shadows and prophecies, which make up the greatest part of the Old Testament; so I believe *there are many now thus veiled, that remain to [be] discovered* by the church in the coming glorious times.[23]

Therefore Edwards expected more to be illuminated by the Spirit during and after his lifetime. Hence while he would still say that Scripture was his only religious authority, Edwards acknowledged that one could not understand that authority without also attending to the history of theological rumination on Scripture—which, at its best, was directed by the Spirit's gradual unfolding of the meaning of the written Word. This attention to, and following of, the Spirit's hermeneutical leading was, Edwards would have said, what constituted the orthodox *tradition* of theological reflection on Scripture.

Edwards was himself influenced by this tradition. He acknowledged during the communion controversy with his congregation that he changed his mind about the issue, some years after he arrived at Northampton, only after becoming "more studied in divinity" and as he "improved in experience." Theological reading and pastoral experience led him to read the Bible differently, which in turn led him to the change in sacramental practice that got him thrown out of his pulpit. This was not unlike his own description of Martin Luther, whose new views of church and salvation came only after studying the Bible "and the writings of the ancient fathers of the church."[24]

Edwards's theological *magnum opus*, the *Religious Affections*, betrays

---

[22] *Miscellanies* 351; *Miscellanies* 1340.

[23] *Miscellanies* 351; emphasis added.

[24] "Author's Preface" to *An Humble Inquiry*, 169; *A History of the Work of Redemption*, 421.

important influence from theological tradition. Edwards drew explicitly upon sixteen other authors, mostly seventeenth-century English Puritans and dissenting clergy. Although most are well known to students of Puritanism, John E. Smith notes that "their contribution to the formation of Edwards's thought has been underestimated."[25]

Edwards's own creation of tradition has been underestimated. Scholars have recently described the way in which, for Edwards after 1739, his real authority for theological work became not the biblical text per se but his imaginative construal of the story inscribed there, which he called the "work of redemption."[26] This was a master narrative beginning in eternity with the Trinity's plan, proceeding through the "fall of man," the history of Israel, the Incarnation and history of the church and world all the way until "the end of the world." It was centered in the work of Christ but orchestrated by all the members of the Trinity.[27] It could not be read off the face of the biblical text, for central to the plot was the assertion that Christ was the real actor in all of Israel's communication with God—speaking at the burning bush, for example, and camouflaged by every appearance of "the angel of the Lord" in the Old Testament.[28] Only through this story, as told by Edwards, could the true meaning of the biblical text be seen. Hence the waters of the Flood were types of the blood of Christ, and the cultus of the Law that included "all the precepts that relate to building the tabernacle that was set up in the wilderness and all the forms, and circumstances, and utensils of it" were directed by God "to show forth something of Christ.[29]

This Edwardsean version of narrative theology was informed not only by the biblical story as conceived within the canon, but also by its

----

[25]*Religious Affections*, John E. Smith, ed., vol. 2 in *The Works of Jonathan Edwards* (New Haven CT: Yale University Press, 1959) 52.

[26]See, e.g., Harry S. Stout and Nathan O. Hatch, introduction to *Sermons and Discourses 1739–1742*, vol. 22 in *The Works of Jonathan Edwards* (New Haven CT: Yale University Press, 2003) 4-14; and Robert E. Brown, *Jonathan Edwards and the Bible* (Bloomington: Indiana University Press, 2002) 164-96. Many have remarked on Edwards's turn from a rational approach to theology to a historical one, which would require a synthetic narrative; see, e.g., Stout and Hatch, *Sermons and Discourses*, 7.

[27]*History of the Work of Redemption*, 116, 118.

[28]*History of the Work of Redemption*, 131, 196-98.

[29]*History of the Work of Redemption*, 151, 182.

continuation in postbiblical history. The first two-thirds of Edwards's chapters of *A History of the Work of Redemption* tells the biblical story, but the last third, a full ten chapters, traces the work of redemption in later "secular" history and beyond. Edwards describes these sixteen-plus centuries as fulfillment of biblical prophecies, yet at the same time uses the whole history—biblical and later—as the master template through which to read back again the meaning of the Bible itself. All of "the various dispensations of God" related in the Bible are to be understood as simply "successive motions" in this "one work," which proceeds inexorably as "one machine" to its predetermined purpose—which again can be seen only through the lens of Edwards's construal of the master narrative, "a history of the work of redemption."[30]

Finally, Edwards also remarked on how church practice should not always be bound solely by biblical directives. To be sure, he could sound like a traditional Puritan in ruling out anything in Sunday worship that was not explicitly mandated in the biblical text, citing, for example, Nadab and Abihu's executions for instituting service "which was not appointed."[31] But at the same time, he left room for innovation, at least for worshipping in ways that were neither forbidden nor anticipated by Scripture.[32] He also introduced an aesthetic criterion that is extrabiblical: ceremonies should be abolished, he suggested, that "have no intrinsic direct *loveliness*, nor agreeableness to the *lovely* God, or tendency to happiness."[33] On these grounds, one could presumably introduce new elements in worship that are not explicitly warranted in the Bible but are nonetheless recommended by this extrabiblical norm.

Edwards's preference for Presbyterian polity also points in this direction. Long before the conflict with the leaders of his own congregation, he had argued that whole congregations should not be left alone to decide by private judgment but ought instead to respect the judgment of a "convention of churches."[34] But his own falling out with the Northampton leadership convinced him afresh in 1750 that the private judgment of a single congregation is risky:

---

[30]*History of the Work of Redemption*, 119 and passim.

[31]*Miscellanies* 1088.

[32]*Miscellanies* 76.

[33]*Miscellanies* 79; emphasis added.

[34]*Miscellanies* 90, 349.

In so great an affair as the separation of a pastor and a people, it is by no means proper for a people, *whatever their private thoughts may be,* to proceed to declare their judgment in public votes until they have had the voice of a council to lead and conduct them.[35]

It is dangerous, he argued, "for the church to set itself up in a sort of supremacy and self-sufficiency, as above all control and advice."[36] Edwards never seems to have reconciled publicly his pessimism about corporate private judgment with his early celebration of individual private judgment, but it is unlikely that in his later years, especially after his humiliation in Northampton, he would not have questioned his earlier confidence in the supremacy of private judgment.

The third kind of church practice in which Edwards posited religious authority outside of the biblical text was church admission. God commits the keys of the kingdom to "officers of the church" to whose judgments God accommodates himself, so that their judgments become his judgments. "So that when they act regularly. God concurs with them in admitting, and what they do is done in heaven." In this process, God "doesn't act as the searcher of hearts, but admits and receives persons to be his people, as it were, on presumption of their sincerity and faithfulness." In other words, God admits to his church all those whom church officers admit, but provisionally. Only if they are truly regenerate (which church officers can never know for sure) and persevere in the faith, are they admitted to God's eternal kingdom.[37] Yet in the meantime they are justified, if only presumptively and temporarily.[38] For the purpose of this chapter, the important point

---

[35]"Narrative of Communion Controversy," 526; emphasis added.

[36]"Narrative of Communion Controversy," 529.

[37]*Miscellanies* 689.

[38]In *Miscellanies* 689, Edwards wrote that the church receives the baptized into God's family as His children and Christ receives them as His spouse, and they are "as it were" redeemed and justified. Infants, e.g., are baptized on the presumption of their parents' faith, and are received by God on the presumption of their own (future, but in God's eternal present) faith. It can be said, *provisionally,* that Christ's blood cleanses them from sin and they have the benefits of the body and blood of Jesus in the Lord's Supper. They are *presumptively* justified and cleared of guilt by the blood of Christ. That is why Peter can speak, he says, of those who "denied the Lord who bought them" (2 Pet 2:1): Christ bought them as presumptive members of His church, but they eventually showed they were never among the

is that religious authority is said by Edwards to be given by God to human beings, through whose judgments, even if they are only proximate, God acts. God speaks through the Bible, but God also acts authoritatively through certain religious leaders. I am not concerned in this chapter with the qualifications of persons to hold this kind of authority, but merely with the fact that Edwards recognizes authority outside the Bible that is then used to help interpret the Bible—in this case, the use of church practice to interpret what the Bible means by justification when someone is admitted to a church.[39]

Let's recap. Edwards professed repeatedly that our only authority in religion is the written text of the Scriptures. But in practice he seemed to operate with the tacit recognition that the Bible can be read only through and with tradition. And that ultimate religious authority is mediated by God through a story of divine redemption, which is known by theological reflection and transmitted through a theological tradition. Therefore tradition, whose importance he explicitly downplayed, proved to be more significant in actual practice.

Which Edwards was right? The theorist who seemed nervous about attributing any formal role to tradition in religious authority? Or the theological practitioner who used tradition in significant ways, albeit tacitly, both by appropriating others' and creating his own? To help answer that question, we will turn first to John Henry Newman and his treatment of tradition.

-----

elect by denying Him. Hence eternal benefits are *presumptively* promised to the baptized on the condition of (the perseverance of) faith. Not all of those baptized will respond or persevere, just as circumcised Israel repeatedly apostasized. According to Edwards, Christ said that He would spit out of his mouth baptized Christians (Rev 3:16). Those who have professed but later are false to Christ, shall be rejected and cast out (Matt 10:37). The final "casting out" will be at the Final Judgment, one of whose purposes is to show why some professing church members were cast out though baptized. It will also show unbelievers that they, not God, have removed themselves from His grace.

[39]Edwards also advocated and established an oversight committee at Northampton of ten men "of distinguished ability." See his sermon on Deut 1:13-18. " 'Tis the mind of God that not a mixed multitude but only select persons of distinguished ability and integrity are fit for the business of judging causes" (June 1748). Edwards Papers, Beinecke Rare Book and Manuscript Library, Yale University. Thanks to Ken Minkema for this reference.

3. John Henry Newman and the Development of Doctrine

According to Acts 8:31, the Ethiopian eunuch asks Philip, "How can I [understand the Bible] unless some one guides me?" John Henry Newman spent a good portion of his career asking, with the Ethiopian eunuch, how one can understand the Bible without guidance from church tradition. He argued that understanding the Bible *must* involve tradition because of the nature of the human mind, the nature of language, and the character of the Bible.

Newman believed that the church's understanding of revelation grows, like the Kingdom of God itself, like a mustard seed—gradually.[40] This is because the human mind cannot reflect on the greatness of God "except piecemeal." Human beings "know, not by a direct and simple vision, not at a glance, but as it were, by piecemeal and accumulation, by a mental process, by going around an object, by the comparison, the combination, the mutual correction, the continual adaptation of many partial notions."[41]

Therefore it takes time for a great idea to be understood in all its aspects by human minds. Great ideas "need elbow room and open air, the large field of history for germination and maturation." Only opposition to an idea teases out the fuller implications of the idea, and it takes time both for opposition to arise and for proper responses to be made. Therefore all great ideas change as they are developed in response to respectful challenges and hostile parries. In Newman's oft-quoted words, "In a higher world it is otherwise, but here below to live is to change, and to be perfect is to have changed often."[42] Some changes in a great idea distort the idea, but other changes are necessary to develop the full meaning of the idea and its application to new situations.

This is why Newman could say that the Church does not know more than what the apostles knew—despite the Church's professing doctrines such as the Trinity that the apostles never articulated. For the apostolic

---

[40]John Henry Newman, *An Essay on the Development of Christian Doctrine* (Notre Dame IN: University of Notre Dame Press, 1989) 73.

[41]"The Theory of Developments in Religious Doctrine," in *Fifteen Sermons Preached before the University of Oxford between A.D. 1826 and A.D. 1843*, ed. Mary Katherine Tillman (Notre Dame IN: University of Notre Dame Press, 1998) 331, xxii.

[42]Tillman, introduction to *Fifteen Sermons*, xxii; Newman, *Essay*, 40, 151.

church had an "implicit" knowledge of later doctrines: it could possess an idea without being conscious of it, by possessing the seeds that germinated and flowered later. The apostles "would without words know all the truths concerning the high doctrines of theology, which controversialists after them have . . . reduced to formulae, and developed through argument."[43]

If the nature of ideas requires time for them to be fleshed out, the nature of language makes time all the more necessary. Language, even that of Sacred Scripture, is fallible and proximate, because it uses earthly concepts and words "to give color and shape to realities that exceed and reach beyond it." God has "condescended to speak to us so far as human language and thought will admit, [but only] by approximations." As Paul reminds us, even with Scripture we still "see as in a glass darkly."[44] Because of this broken and limited nature of language, it takes time for language to portray its referent.

All human thinking about an object is a matter of "circling." Newman recalled Cicero's description of the orator's method of verbally walking around his subject, describing it from all angles, as one might circle a great sculpture in order to better grasp its integral form and beauty.[45] Scripture, Newman would remind us, shows us the object, God and His Kingdom. Only through the church's circling of the object over the centuries, repeatedly taking snapshots from ever-new angles, will we get a fuller vision of the whole.[46]

Newman taught that Scripture itself displays the gradual unfolding of revelation. Old Testament types point to antitypes later in time. The whole truth is never revealed at once, but only in glimpses, and ever so gradually as the course of revelation proceeds. Jesus said he was teaching his disciples a new commandment, and yet one that was in continuity with the old. He said He had come not to destroy but to fulfill.[47]

The concept of sacrifice in Scripture shows development. First Moses commanded Israel to perform sacrifices. Then Samuel said, "To obey is better than sacrifice." Later God told Hosea, "I will have mercy, not

---

[43]Newman, *Essay*, xxiii.

[44]Tillman, in *Fifteen Sermons*, xxi; Newman, *Essay*, xxiii; "The Theory of Developments in Religious Doctrine," 340.

[45]Tillman, *Fifteen Sermons*, xxi-xxii.

[46]Newman, *Essay*, 29.

[47]Newman, *Essay*, 64.

sacrifice." Later still God said through Isaiah, "Your sacrifices are an abomination to me." Malachi prophesied the pure sacrifices and offerings that were to come, and Jesus finally spoke of worship in spirit and in truth.[48]

If Scripture itself shows development, it also points to the need for later development after the closure of the canon by asking questions which it does not answer. Or, in other words, it "begins a series of developments which it does not finish." Great questions exist in the subject matter of the Bible that are not answered by the Bible. But they must be answered because they are so practical and real, and they can be answered only by development in understanding of the revelation that we do possess. For example, the church of the second century and beyond needed to know what happened to the soul after death and before the final judgment. That could be resolved only by developing new doctrines not stated but implied by the Bible.[49]

If development in Scripture, and questions raised by Scripture, point to the inherent necessity of development in tradition, Newman warned that inattention to tradition will make heresy more likely. Orthodoxy, he proposed, is seeing all the aspects of God and His Kingdom as unified by one vision. Separating Scripture from tradition will tend to treat the Bible as an accumulation of discrete events and statements. Only a living tradition that flows organically from the apostles to the present can transmit the vision with integrity. The nature of heresy is to take one aspect and make it stand for the whole, rejecting everything else. Or it thrives on bits and pieces, tacking them together in ways that suit the spirit of the age. Orthodoxy, on the other hand, receives the vision of the whole, developed uninterruptedly from the beginning.[50]

Heresy, Newman also cautioned, is often more externally like original doctrine than orthodoxy. Faithful development is often more externally unlike original doctrine than heretical development. What is critical, he suggested, is not whether the development uses the same language or formula of the original doctrine or biblical text, but whether it employs the same *principle*. Doctrines therefore are less important than principles. Eternal principles include such things as the principle of dogma (that some supernatural truths are irrevocably committed to human language,

---

[48]Newman, *Essay*, 65-66.
[49]Newman, "Theory of Developments," 335; Newman, *Essay*, 60.
[50]Newman, "Theory of Developments," 336-67 and passim.

imperfectly expressed but pointing to indispensable truths), the principle of faith (one must give absolute acceptance to the divine Word with internal assent), the sacramental principle (divine gifts are conveyed in a material and visible medium), the spiritual or secondary sense of Scripture (that there is a mystical meaning for most texts), the principle of grace (that our Lord makes us what he is in himself), and the principle of asceticism (God changes us by mortifying our lower nature).[51]

Newman's project, then, would warn Edwards and all his tribe that religious authority founded on *sola scriptura* cannot be *sola* in the sense that one can make any sense of Scripture without the help of tradition. The nature of thinking, of ideas, and of the Bible itself all make it inevitable that when we go to Scripture for authority, we are already interpreting it through tradition, which presupposes the development of tradition necessitated by the Bible itself.

Therefore the question for those seeking religious authority can no longer be whether or not tradition plays any integral role. The more important question becomes, Which tradition? Most traditions, even those that appeal to tradition as authoritative, argue that their rendering of *biblical* history is the best. The twentieth century's most influential New Testament scholar, however, insisted that the search for the historical Jesus is both futile and wrongheaded.

4. Rudolf Bultmann on Faith and History

Jonathan Edwards's appeal to *sola scriptura* for religious authority meant, among other things, that we can know what is true religiously by looking to what God has done and spoken in history, both in Israel and Jesus Christ. This is more important for Edwards than for others who appeal to *sola scriptura*, for Edwards's ultimate authority was the *history* of all the work of redemption, which started even before the creation and continued long after the biblical history closed. Edwards was conversant with early biblical criticism and its skepticism toward historical claims in the sacred narratives, and spent considerable energy responding to those claims. As Robert E. Brown has shown, "No less than one-fifth of the 'Notes on Scripture' are taken up with critical historical problems, and hardly a page in the 'Blank Bible' lacks such entries." Brown notes that Edwards acknowledged "the

---

[51]Newman, *Essay*, 176, 325, 346.

historical limitations of the biblical accounts," recognizing that "they did not finally present the comprehensive and pristine narrative of human history that had been assumed."[52] While assuming the basic authenticity of historical accounts in the Bible, he conceded the importance of critical historical research and its influence on hermeneutics.

But what if the historian concludes, as Bultmann did, that it is impossible to conclude much of anything about the life and teachings of the historical Jesus? And that in fact it is theologically illegitimate to search for the historical Jesus? Edwards did not claim that faith rests directly on a knowledge of the historical Jesus, for he defined regenerate faith as the *gift* of seeing the beauty of God's work in redemption—especially as it is demonstrated in Christ. Yet no one sees the beauty of the history without also seeing the history:

> A man cannot see the wonderful excellency [for Edwards, this was a synonym for "beauty"] and love of Christ in doing such and such things for sinners, unless his understanding be first informed how those things were done. He cannot have a taste of the sweetness and divine excellency of such and such things in divinity, unless he first have a notion that there are such and such things.[53]

These include knowledge of "Jesus Christ, and his mediation, his incarnation, his life and death, his resurrection and ascension . . . [which] infinitely concern common people as well as divines."[54]

The German repudiation of the quest for the historical Jesus reached its "zenith" in Bultmann.[55] Bultmann believed the New Testament's presentation of the gospel was based on Palestinian Judaism, the Hellenistic *Kyrios* cult of mystery religions and Gnosticism, with the essential story line coming from the Iranian myth of the Primal Man or Heavenly Redeemer.[56]

---

[52]Brown, *Jonathan Edwards and the Bible*, 114, 97.

[53]Edwards, "The Importance and Advantage of a Thorough Knowledge of Divine Truth," in *Sermons and Discourses*, vol. 22 in *The Works of Jonathan Edwards*, ed. Harry S. Stout and Nathan O. Hatch (New Haven CT: Yale University Press, 2003) 2:158.

[54]Edwards, "The Importance and Advantage of a Thorough Knowledge of Divine Truth," 92.

[55]Alister E. McGrath, *The Making of Modern German Christology, 1750–1990*, 2nd ed. (Grand Rapids MI: Zondervan, 1994) 171.

[56]James F. Kay, *Christus Praesens: A Reconsideration of Rudolf Bultmann's*

Therefore the four gospels contain less the Jesus of history and far more the Christ myth created by Hellenistic congregations, for "there is no historical-biographical interest in the Gospels."[57] They present little of the Jesus as he really spoke and acted in Palestine, but for the most part the risen Christ who is present in the preached Word—the *kerygma*. "We can now know almost nothing concerning the life and personality of Jesus, since the early Christian sources show no interest in either, are moreover fragmentary and often legendary; and other sources about Jesus do not exist."[58]

It is impossible to know much of anything about the historical Jesus because the New Testament gives us access to the early church, not Jesus himself. According to Bultmann, form criticism has shown that the gospels are responses to the *Sitz im Leben* (life setting) of the early church. Since the writers adapted what they had heard of Jesus to the new problems in the postresurrection church, listeners/readers can have little confidence that they are reading what Jesus really said or did. "[T]hat clearly does not exclude the possibility that now and again there was also outer historical truth, i.e., that this or that scripture which the Church used, was also used by Jesus in his struggle; *only that is something it is no longer possible to establish*."[59]

It is not that Bultmann discounted *any* knowledge of the historical Jesus. In his *History of the Synoptic Tradition*, for example, he sifted in painstaking detail the evidence for and against the authenticity of various *logia* or sayings of Jesus in the gospels. Some are "more likely" than others. But only "in very few cases" can "one of the logia be ascribed to Jesus with any measure of confidence." In the vast majority of cases the historian must conclude that whatever was originally from Jesus was so transformed by the

Christology (Grand Rapids: Eerdmans, 1994) 27-28. Bultmann says: "The mythology of the New Testament is in essence that of Jewish apocalyptic and the Gnostic redemption myths." Bultmann, "New Testament and Mythology," in *Kerygma and Myth: A Theological Debate*, ed. Hans Werrner Bartsch (New York: Harper Torchbooks, 1961) 15.

[57]Bultmann, *History of the Synoptic Tradition*, trans. John Marsh (New York: Harper & Row, 1963) 372.

[58]Bultmann, *Jesus and the Word*, trans. Louise Pettibone Smith and Erminie Huntress Lantero (New York: Scribner's, 1934; orig. 1926) 8.

[59]Bultmann, *History of the Synoptic Tradition*, trans. John Marsh (Oxford: Blackwell; New York: Harper, 1963; orig. 1921) 49; emphasis added.

early church, in order to make it apply "to a concrete situation," that "it failed in so doing to preserve anything characteristic of him." In sum, "It is frequently impossible to do more than pass a subjective judgment."[60] So the historian must conclude that the historical Jesus, now for the most part lost in the sifting sands of history, was transformed by the early church into the divine Christ of faith.

Therefore the intent of the gospel writers was not to present historical fact but to show their hearers their need to make a decision. The judgment that was once thought to be at the end of the world was moved to the present, through the proclamation of the gospel: "The *kerygma* is neither a vehicle for timeless ideas nor the mediator of historical information: what is of decisive importance is that the *kerygma* is Christ's 'that', his 'here and now,' a 'here and now' which becomes present in the address itself."[61]

Bultmann found confirmation for his approach in both John and Paul. John believed the *parousia* had already occurred in Christ's resurrection and Pentecost;[62] hence the eschatological event had moved to the present in the *kerygma*. Paul showed that knowledge of the historical Jesus is unimportant and even misleading when he wrote in 2 Cor. 5:16, *hēmeis apo tou nun oudena oidamen kata sarka. Ei kai egnōkamen kata sarka Christov, alla nun ouketi ginōskomen* ("From now on we regard no one according to the flesh. Even though we once knew Christ according to the flesh, we do so no longer"). For Bultmann, *kata sarka* means facts present within natural life and verifiable by everyone. *Kata sarka Christon* therefore is Christ as he could be encountered in the world before his death and resurrection, apart from his destiny as eschatological salvation event—hence Christ as miracle worker or servant, rather than in his present divine glory. Paul is not concerned with the earthly Jesus in his personality or even divine nature on earth but only his salvific role as Messiah. In fact, "to portray his personality is to betray his eschatological significance."[63]

Another reason why we should not regard the gospels as history is that

---

[60]*History of the Synoptic Tradition*, 101, 105, 104, 104, 102.

[61]Bultmann, "Significance of the Historical Jesus for the Theology of Paul," in *Faith and Understanding,* ed. R. W. Funk (London: SCM Press, 1966) 241.

[62]"For John the resurrection of Jesus, Petecost, and the *parousia* . . . are one and the same event." Bultmann, *Jesus Christ and Mythology* (London: SCM,1960) 33.

[63]Kay, *Christrus Praesens*, 41-44; quotation is from 44.

its worldview is unintelligible to moderns.

> It is impossible to use electric light and the wireless and to avail ourselves of modern medical and surgical discoveries, and at the same time to believe in the New Testament world of spirits and miracles. We may think we can manage it in our own lives, but to expect others to do so is to make the Christian faith unintelligible and unacceptable to the modern world.[64]

In other words, since we know that spirits do not cause things to happen and miracles do not take place, and that the gospels are set within a mythical framework that assumes both, we have all the more reason to be skeptical of the historicity of much of what is presented there. We should regard as mythical

> the belief that God guides and inspires men; the notion that supernatural powers influence the course of history; the belief that the Son was sent in the fullness of time; the resurrection of Christ regarded as an event beyond and different from the rise of the Easter faith in the disciples; and the belief in the Holy Spirit, if that Spirit be regarded as more than "the factual possibility of a new life realized in faith."[65]

What are we to make of the Bultmannian challenge to the historicity of the gospels, and therefore to the notion that faith should be based at least indirectly on history? Let's look at some of Bultmann's critics. Wolfhart Pannenberg argued early on that, since God's revelation was intended to be universal and publicly accessible, and God's revelation was in history, therefore Christian faith is indeed to be based on history. Not all will have eyes to see the divine character of what happened in history, but the revelatory events are there nonetheless, open to "historical verification." The meaning of those events will be declared for all to see and understand at the end of history, but humanity was given a sneak preview, as it were, in the history of Jesus Christ.[66]

Then, mainly in the 1970s, New Testament scholars attacked Bultmann's interpretation of the 2 Corinthians passage about "Christ according

---

[64]Bultmann, "New Testament and Mythology," 5.

[65]David Cairns, *A Gospel without Myth? Bultmann's Challenge to the Preacher* (London: SCM, 1960) 83.

[66]Wolfhart Pannenberg, "Redemptive Event and History," in *Basic Questions in Theology*, vol. 1 (Philadelphia: Westminster, 1983) 15-80. This chapter is based on a 1959 lecture.

to the flesh."[67] Recently N. T. Wright has joined the fray, arguing that the context and the verse itself undermine Bultmann's interpretation.[68] Wright explains that the larger argument in 2:14 to 6:13 is about the new covenant in which we see the light of the knowledge of the glory of God in the *face* of Jesus Christ (4:6; emphasis added). The passage goes on to discuss the disciples of Jesus, who bear in their bodies the death of Jesus, so that the life of Jesus might also be manifest in their bodies. "Jesus" refers unambiguously to the human Jesus, and specifically his death. In the long paragraph that follows (4:7-15), Paul never uses the word "Christ"; his point is that the pattern of ministry in Jesus' *life*, which led to his death, is to be reproduced in the apostles.

Wright then asserts that when Paul said he did not know "Christ according to the flesh," he was rejecting not knowledge of the historical Jesus but a certain way of knowing the Messiah (Christ). *Kata sarka* was a "regular Pauline phrase denoting, among other things, the status, attitudes, and theology of Jews and/or some Jewish Christians. The sort of Messiah they had wanted would be one who would affirm and underwrite their national aspirations."[69] Paul was saying that the true Messiah would be different, and he said this on the basis of what he knew of the historical Jesus in his life as a servant. Paul makes this explicit in Romans 15:1-9, where he says Christ "did not please himself" and "became a servant," so that we might learn from his example.

Wright agrees with Bultmann that the gospels contain mythological language that we can decode in light of other apocalyptic writings of the time. But he adds that they have these features precisely because of their Jewishness, and Jewish monotheism demanded that history be the sphere in which Israel's God was to make himself known. Some gospel language was mythological

not because it describes events which did not happen, but *because it shows that*

---

[67]Charles F. D. Moule, "Jesus in New Testament Kerygma," in *Verborum Veritas*, ed. O. Böcher and K. Haaker (Wuppertal: Brockhaus, 1970) 15-26; C. K. Barrett, *A Commentary on the Second Epistle to the Corinthians* (London: A. C. Black, 1973) 171; Ben F. Meyer, *The Aims of Jesus* (London: SCM, 1979) 73-75; Victor P. Furnish, *II Corinthians* (New York: Doubleday, 1984) 330-33.

[68]N. T. Wright, *The New Testament and the People of God* (Minneapolis: Fortress, 1992) 408.

[69]Wright, *The New Testament and the People of God*, 408.

actual events are not separated from ultimate significance by an ugly ditch, as the whole movement of Deist and Enlightenment thought would suggest, but on the contrary carry their significance within them.[70]

Bultmann accepted the *religionsgeshichtliche Schule*'s claim that New Testament soteriology derived from Gnostic redeemer myths. He was also influenced by F. C. Bauer's thesis of separate Jewish and Hellenistic Christianities that were then resolved in Hegelian fashion by early Catholicism. Like Conzelmann and Käsemann, and now Koester, Mack, and Crossan, Bultmann saw early Christianity moving away from Judaism and toward Hellenism by its incorporation of Gnosticism. This view of early Christianity sees the essence of Christianity as only marginally Jewish and more indebted to Gnostic, Cynic, and various other "Wisdom" traditions.[71] But Wright and others contend that Gnosticism was not a major influence on the early church until the second century, and that early Christianity was far more Jewish than Bultmann and these other scholars imagined.[72] They argue that Bultmann's attitude toward history was shaped by neo-Kantian philosophy, mediated by Hermann Cohen and Paul Natorp, who stressed that "objects" (replacing the Kantian "thing") are not "given" but formed by consciousness. Bultmann's liberal teacher Wilhelm Herrman taught him that therefore theological statements cannot be made about God in himself, but only about how he relates to us. Then Bultmann's contact with nineteenth-century Lutheranism persuaded him that "knowledge" is part of what characterizes the human realm of works and law by which human

---

[70]Wright, *The New Testament and the People of God*, 426-27; Wright's emphasis. Bultmann rejected the "mythical eschatology" of the New Testament in part because "the parousia of Christ never took place as the New Testament expected." Wright insists Bultmann misinterpreted the eschatological hope, confusing the end of the physical world for the end of their world as the early Jewish Christians knew it (destruction of Jerusalem). Bultmann, "New Testament and Mythology," 5. See Wright, *The New Testament and the People of God*, 116-17, 352, 373-74, 395-96, 167-68; Wright, *Jesus and the Victory of God* (Minneapolis: Fortress, 1996) 341-42, 345-56, 360-67, 470, 659-61.

[71]Anthony C. Thiselton, *The Two Horizons: New Testament Hermeneutics and Philosophical Description* (Grand Rapids MI: Eerdmans, 1980) 218-23, 273, 281, 320-22.

[72]Wright, *The New Testament and the People of God*, 343.

beings attempt to justify themselves.[73] Thus Bultmann could say that his demythologization was the application of Luther's doctrine of justification by faith alone to epistemology.[74]

According to Anthony Thiselton, Bultmann's more radical claim is not epistemological but theological—

> that acts of God belong to one realm, and this-worldly phenomena belong to a different realm. . . . he tends to assume that statements, for example, about the cosmic Lordship of Christ, or the acts of God in Israelite history, are mere objectifications which can be reduced to existential evaluations without loss.[75]

What Thiselton means is that what finally undermines Bultmann's approach to history is not his pessimism about our ability to know the historical Jesus (after all, as we have seen, Bultmann believed he could know something, though not very much), but his neo-Kantian dualism.

> Justification by works stands in contrast to justification by faith; nature stands in contrast to grace; the indicative, and the realm of facts, stand in contrast to the imperative, and the realm of will; information is set over against address; objectification is set over against encounter.[76]

All objectifying knowledge, whereby the human mind regards an object as distinct from itself, belongs to the phenomenal realm. But faith and God belong to another, transcendent realm, completely removed from the phenomenal realm. This is the realm of address and event, of "wonder" and not objective thought. The New Testament "only *appears* to describe objective events, and insofar as it does so, this obscures and impedes its intention."[77] The reality of God therefore appears in worship, faith, and response to the *kerygma*, not in ideas about God.[78]

Hence it is sinful to speak about God in an objective sense, since God is Wholly Other and cannot be objectified. "Bultmann asserts, 'It is clear that if a man will speak of God, he must evidently speak of himself.'"[79]

[73]Thiselton, *The Two Horizons*, 210-17.
[74]Bultmann, *Kerygma und Myth*, 2 vols., ed. H. W. Bartsch (London: S.P.C.K., 1964) 1:210-11; cited in Thistelton, *The Two Horizons*, 263.
[75]Thiselton, *The Two Horizons*, 284.
[76]Thiselton, *The Two Horizons*, 217.
[77]Thiselton, *The Two Horizons*, 262.
[78]Thiselton, *The Two Horizons*, 232.
[79]Thiselton, *The Two Horizons*, 224. The reference is to *Faith and Understand-*

This is sinful because all objective knowledge is in the realm of the human, with its laws and works. Faith based on knowledge then becomes a work that provides false security. It is false because it places confidence in this world rather than God who is utterly beyond this world.[80]

In reply, Wright maintains that history-based faith becomes a work only if Christian faith is indeed a Gnostic flight from history, "and finding salvation in a realm completely outside it."[81] Such a disjunction between faith and knowledge of history runs the risk, adds Pannenberg, of "blind credulity toward the authority-claim of the preached message. . . . Paul speaks the reverse, of the grounding of faith upon a knowledge (Rom. 6:8-9; 2 Cor. 4:13-14)."[82] To insist that faith cannot or should not be based on knowledge of history, or to place God and his saving acts in a realm removed from ordinary history, is to see the early church through Gnostic rather than Jewish eyes. Jews and early Christians would be amazed, and would consider such a thought to have come from a suburb of Athens not Jerusalem.

Besides, Wright points out, the biblical story itself grounds faith in knowledge of history.

> The Israelites retold the story of creation and fall. Jesus retold, in parable and symbol, the story of Israel. The evangelists retold, in complex and multifaceted ways, the story of Jesus. This may suggest, from a new angle, that the task of history, including historical theology and theological history, is itself mandated upon the followers of Jesus from within the biblical story itself.[83]

Wright goes on to declare that the Enlightenment was right to appeal to history in the context of eighteenth-century dogmatic theology. Paul himself suggested that if Jesus' resurrection is not grounded in real-time history, we are of all humans the most to be pitied.[84]

Not that the Enlightenment's epistemological confidence was warranted. There is no neutral or purely objective history possible. These are

---

ing (London: SCM, 1969) 1:55.

[80]Thiselton, *The Two Horizons*, 210, 285, 224.

[81]Wright, *The New Testament and the People of God*, 94.

[82]Pannenberg, "Insight and Faith," in *Basic Questions in Theology*, vol. 2 (Philadelphia: Westminster, 1983) 28, 31-32.

[83]Pannenberg, "Insight and Faith," 142.

[84]Pannenberg, "Insight and Faith," 136.

the fruit of "positivist fantasy." But it is possible to conduct "genuine historical reconstruction of actual events in the past, of the 'inside' of events as well as the 'outside.' Christianity has nothing to fear from the appeal to history. It makes the same appeal itself."[85]

The implication for our search for religious authority is that Edwards was right to appeal to *sola scriptura* insofar as it was an appeal to God's revelation through His acts in history. Bultmann called into question Edwards's confidence that Scripture gets us to the Jesus of history, suggesting that (for the most part) all we know is the experience of the post-Resurrection church. But if Wright and other critics of Bultmann are right, we can and should appeal to the New Testament for a knowledge, albeit imperfect, of the historical Jesus. Faith is never a direct result of that knowledge, since faith is a gift. But faith requires knowledge of the historical Jesus if it is to have any confidence that it is not faith in faith, faith in a Christ abstracted from Jesus of Nazareth, or Gnostic diversion from the Jewish God of history.

5. The Religious Authority of *Sola Scriptura*: Six Propositions

In this last section I will gather up the threads of argument about the religious authority of *sola scriptura* which we have traced in Edwards, Newman, Bultmann, and Wright. I will try to organize them by teasing out six propositions that should guide our thinking about the religious authority of the Bible. At the end I will return to Edwards and his ambiguous position.

1. *The authority of the Bible is really the authority of the Triune God.* As Wright has recently observed, the risen Jesus does not say, "All authority in heaven and on earth is given to the books you all are going to write," but "All authority in heaven and on earth is given to *me*."[86] We are told in numerous places in Scripture that all authority is God's, and he has delegated that authority to His Son.[87] John says that in the beginning was the Word, and that the Word was not written down but became flesh. The

---

[85]Pannenberg, "Insight and Faith," 137.

[86]Wright, *The Last Word: Beyond the Bible Wars to a New Understanding of the Authority of Scripture* (San Francisco: HarperSanFrancisco, 2005) xi.

[87]Rom. 13:1; Phil. 2:9-11; Isa. chaps. 40–55; Rev. chaps. 4 and 5. All of these are cited by Wright, *The Last Word*, 23.

first chapter of Hebrews declares that God spoke through Scripture in the past but now has spoken through the Son.[88] Jesus' authority was a distinctive feature of his ministry: the crowds marveled at the way he spoke with authority, not like the scribes (Mark 1:22), and he himself proclaimed that he was greater than the Temple, Jonah, and Solomon (Matt. 12:6, 41-42).

2. *Therefore Sola Scriptura means, among other things, God speaking and acting through Scripture.* Since Scripture itself points us away from itself, the true meaning of the authority of the Word is the authority of God working through his Word. Scripture is therefore a means of God's action in and through us, exercising his power to not only save but renew the world. As Wright puts it, " 'Authority of scripture' can make Christian sense only if it is a shorthand for 'the authority of the triune God, exercised somehow *through* scripture.' "[89] This in turn means that in our search for how to interpret the Bible, and whether we use tradition for that interpretation, we are talking about whether God speaks and acts through tradition as we interpret the Bible.

3. *Using the Bible for religious authority means extending the biblical drama into new acts.* Wright uses the analogy of a Shakespearian play to explain what it would mean for something or someone to be (or do) faithful interpretation of the Bible. We would say this analogy explains equally well what it means to use the Bible as religious authority.

Wright hypothesizes that there is a five-act Shakespearian play, whose last act has been lost. Rather than writing a fifth act for all time, it is thought more appropriate to the unfinished state of the play to assign the performance of the last act to experienced Shakespearian actors who have immersed themselves in the meaning and trajectory of the first four acts, and who then perform the fifth act in a way that faithfully follows the direction and spirit of the first four. "A good fifth act will show a proper final development, not merely a repetition, of what went before. Nevertheless, there will be a rightness, a fittingness, about certain actions and speeches, about certain final moves in the drama, which will in one sense be self-authenticating, and in another gain authentication from their coherence with, their making sense of, the 'authoritative' previous text."[90]

According to Wright, the biblical story consists of five acts, the first

[88]Wright, *The Last Word*, 23-24.
[89]Wright, *The Last Word*, 23.
[90]Wright, *The New Testament and the People of God*, 141.

four of which are Creation, Fall, Israel, and Jesus. The first scene in the fifth act is the writing of the New Testament, which gives hints (in Romans 8, 1 Corinthians 15, parts of Revelation) of how the play is supposed to end. The history of the church is to be the completion of the final act, with the previous acts and scenes providing authority for the remaining scenes.[91]

Using this analogy, we would say that the authenticity of our enactment of the last act depends on our faithfulness to the pattern of all the preceding scenes. This is what it means for Edwards's principle of *sola scriptura*, which in reality used the whole history of redemption as a norm, to serve as a principle of religious authority. *Sola Scriptura* would have proper authority only if it shows fidelity to the pattern found in this history.

4. *Sola Scriptura means, among other things, that the story of God's history of redemption guides and corrects tradition.* One implication of *sola scriptura* is that church tradition cannot be permitted to serve in lieu of the redemptive story itself. Ignatius of Loyola therefore did not get it quite right when he swore, "I will believe that the white I see is black, if the hierarchical church so defines it."[92] As Wright puts it, to assert the primacy of the church over the Bible because the church produced the Bible "makes a rather obvious logical mistake analogous to that of a soldier who, receiving orders through the mail, concludes that the letter carrier is his commanding officer."[93] Those who collect and distribute the message do not have the same authority as those who composed the message in the first place.

The Bible itself demonstrates this principle. When Peter refused to eat with Gentile Christians, Paul publicly rebuked him on the basis of the gospel: "When I saw that their conduct was not in step with the truth of the gospel, I said to Cephas before them all . . ." (Gal. 2:14). Paul assumed both apostles (he and Peter) stood under the judgment of the gospel, thereby suggesting the limits of church tradition. This is comparable to Newman's teaching that while our understanding of scripture must develop, that development must be held accountable to gospel "principle." These principles are derived from what Edwards called the history of redemption, which history is truly the history of God's acts within history—not, as Bultmann would have it, simply the church's mythical rendition of

---

[91]Wright, *The New Testament and the People of God*, 141.
[92]Ignatius Loyola, "Rules for Thinking, no. 13, in *The Spiritual Exercise of St. Ignatius* (New York: Doubleday, 1989) 141.
[93]Wright, *The Last Word*, 63.

existential experience.

Even churches that historically prize the authority of tradition have affirmed this principle. ARCIC, the Anglican-Roman Catholic International Commission, declared in 1999 that the Scriptures "require the Church constantly to measure its teaching, preaching and action against them."[94] Catholic theologian Avery Dulles notes that the *episkopoi* (lit., "overseers") in the early church were subordinate to the apostles.[95] George Lindbeck writes that both sides in the Lutheran-Catholic dialogues on papal primacy agreed that the authority of the church cannot be master of the Word but must serve the Word, and that the church stands under the gospel.[96]

If a proper reading of the pattern of God's work in redemption is critical to reading the Bible aright, at the same time one needs the guidance of tradition to see the pattern aright. Hence,

5. *Sola Scriptura requires good tradition to read the pattern properly.* Here is where evangelicals need to be reminded that, as Newman suggested and Edwards himself demonstrated, if unwittingly, the Bible is not, strictly speaking, self-interpreting. As countless commentators have observed, there is no "pure" reading of the biblical text.[97] Every Protestant (which of course includes evangelicals) uses tradition when she reads the Bible, whether she knows it or not. She is influenced by the Protestant tradition in which she finds herself.

Of course, in the abstract the Bible does interpret itself, and the best way to interpret the Bible is to follow the Bible's own statements about and clues to its own meaning. But my point here is that in real human experi-

---

[94]ARCIC, *The Gift of Authority: Authority in the Church III: An Agreed Statement by the Anglican-Roman Catholic International Commission* (Toronto: Catholic Truth Society; Toronto: Anglican Book Center; New York: Church Publishing, 1999) 19.

[95]Avery Dulles, "Doctrinal Authority for a Pilgrim Church," in *The Magisterium and Morality, Readings in Moral Theology No. 3*, ed. Charles E. Curran and Richard A. McCormick (New York: Paulist Press, 1982) 254.

[96]George Lindbeck, "Papacy and *Ius Divinum*," in *Papal Primacy and the Universal Church*, ed. Paul Empie and T. Austin Murphy, Lutherans and Catholics in Dialogue V (Minneapolis: Augsburg, 1974) 197.

[97]See, e.g., John R. Francke, "Scripture, Tradition and Authority: Reconstructing the Evangelical Conception of *Sola Scriptura*," in *Evangelicals and Scripture: Tradition, Authority and Heremeneutics* (Downers Grove IL: InterVarsity, 2004).

ence our acts of reading the Bible are always already influenced by our prior reception of some tradition about the Bible's meaning. Avery Dulles has observed that every attempt to gather up the meaning of the whole Bible is necessarily an act of creative interpretation, because such acts impart to the whole Bible words or concepts which the Bible typically does not ascribe in just those ways to itself. Besides, Dulles adds, it is unbiblical to deny any interpretive authority beyond Scripture because Scripture itself asserts that individuals in the church will speak by the Holy Spirit.[98] Therefore,

6. *Scripture and church tradition cannot be separated; they are co-inherent.* When we read Scripture, we use tradition, knowingly or not. And when we seek true religious authority from tradition, we must use Scripture as an always-correcting norm. The question of which comes first is a false dichotomy, just as stereotypical Protestant-Catholic argument over religious authority has seemed irresolvable. Catholics have said that the church gave us the Bible, while Protestants have countered that the gospel produced the church. Perhaps a way forward is to follow Wright's lead in recognizing religious authority, ultimately, in the Triune God, Who called the church into being through the gospel, and continually uses Scripture to sanctify the church, which in turn seeks the Spirit to understand better that Scripture. The result is a developing tradition which faithfully enacts the last act of the cosmic drama, guided by a reading of all the previous acts and scenes.

This means that church and Scripture are "joint effects of the working out of the event of Christ," and tradition and Scripture are "co-inherent aspects of the ongoing ministry of the Spirit."[99] This is a serious acknowledgement of the importance of tradition without elevating it to a position of final authority. All such talk of what is the "single final norm" is like asking which is more important for human life—the brain or the heart? Both are indispensable. Each is "finally" critical. We cannot read Scripture without tradition, but must always pay attention to how Scripture clarifies and corrects tradition.

Was Edwards right? The answer depends on which Edwards is meant. The Edwards who answered the catechism question, as it were, about religious authority and replied simply "*Sola Scriptura*," was only half-right.

---

[98]Dulles, "Doctrinal Authority for a Pilgrim Church," 250-52.
[99]Francke, "Scripture, Tradition and Authority," 205, 210.

His insistence on liberty of private conscience and the dangers of leaning on the Fathers was belied—or better, nuanced—by his own practice. *That* Edwards, who showed that tradition is indispensable in understanding the pattern of God's working redemptively in history, and recognized intuitively that tradition must be perpetuated, and *was* perpetuated and advanced by his own contribution to tradition, was right. *That* Edwards recognized that *sola scriptura*, interpreted in positivistic fashion, was insufficient to see the beauty of God in Christ. Scripture is perspicuous, but only to the mind trained by a religious tradition that reads redemptive history aright. Therefore *sola scriptura* is not, strictly speaking, *sola*.

WE SPEAK WHERE THE BIBLE SPEAKS:
RELIGIOUS AUTHORITY IN CHURCHES OF CHRIST

Robert M. Randolph

It is a long way from the West Virginia neighborhood of Alexander Campbell to Southern California where I received my earliest religious training. The Church of Christ I knew growing up was an immigrant community. Most members had come from the South and Southwest during the Great Depression; it was a long time before I knew that members of our church could come from anywhere else. The notion that we were part of a religious movement, the Restoration Movement in American church history, was never something we talked about. We were the first-century church restored and reinvented in the sprawling city that was Los Angeles. So confident were we of our uniqueness that I remember with shock the scene I saw on a rare Sunday morning trip to visit with family. Having missed church ourselves to drive to San Bernardino we passed through Pasadena and I noticed that the people entering the Methodist Church looked just like we did.

I have reflected often on that morning wondering what it would take today to so ingrain religious difference in the mind of a child that they thought others to be so demented that it affected how they looked as well as how they behaved. Religious communities that regard the other as different are not unique and it is a testimony to my isolation that such an idea took root, but that it took root in a movement that prided itself on calling for the end of denominational Christianity makes the phenomenon even more noteworthy. So insular were we that it never occurred to me that other religious people were also deeply committed to the Bible, to the good works that marked Christian ministry, and who believed that they were heaven bound.[1]

Some of the sectarian peculiarities had worn off by the time I reached graduate school, but I was jolted at Yale when a friend and teacher hearing me underline in a sermon that the Church of Christ took the Bible seriously, commented that his church also took the Bible seriously, and I knew they did. Unlike Saul of Tarsus I was not struck blind, but suddenly I could see.

What I would like to do here is to trace in broad strokes how a movement that sought to bring unity to a fragmented Christian world on the American frontier flared like a beacon and then fragmented into three

---

[1] Ayaan Hirsi Ali, *Infidel* (New York: Free Press, 2007). This memoir offers a similar tale from a Muslim perspective.

distinct religious communities. The Christian Church (Disciples of Christ) has maintained a passion for Christian unity. The Churches of Christ place emphasis on the restoration of the New Testament Church. The centrist Christian Churches/Churches of Christ, in many ways currently the most vital segment of the movement, seem destined to slip quietly into the Evangelical revival that is sweeping the country. I will offer my ideas on why this occurred and will conclude with notes about the efforts to reknit the tradition that has taken on new life and urgency in the last few years.

The notion of restoring the ancient church, and thus avoiding the sins that adorned contemporary churches has a long history in the story of Christianity. But it seems that the time and circumstances of the early nineteenth century were ripe for a movement that promised to unify divided Christendom on the American frontier. Called into being around the axis of "No creed but the Bible," the reformation initiated by Alexander Campbell and Barton W. Stone swept across the frontier and became in short order the fastest-growing religious body in the emerging nation.

There were antecedents in the new land. The James O'Kelly Christians in Virginia (1794) sought to be "Christians Only" and broke from the emerging ranks of Methodism. The Christian Connection in New England (1801) led by Abner Jones and Elias Smith began among Freewill Baptists and eventually became one with the O'Kelly churches and a movement away from Presbyerianism led by Barton Stone (1810).[2] At the end of the first decade of the nineteenth century there were 20,000 members in the emerging communion that stretched from New England to Virginia and west to Kentucky. Stone eventually led a significant number of these congregations into what became the Restoration Movement. The remainder of the congregations became a full-fledged denomination after the Civil War and despite the loss of churches to the Restoration Movement and the defection of Elias Smith to the Universalists in 1817, they remained an independent body until well into the twentieth century.

Stone began as a Presbyterian and was known for his Christian character even as he was celebrated for being a "theological

[2]Thomas Olbricht, "Christian Connection," In *The Encyclopedia of the Stone-Campbell Movement*, ed. Douglas A. Foster, Paul M. Blowers, Anthony L. Dunnavant, and D. Newell Williams (Grand Rapids MI: Eerdmans, 2004) 190-91. See also Leroy Garrett, *The Stone-Campbell Movement*, rev. and expanded (Joplin MO: College Press, 1994).

controversialist."[3] Born in Maryland, he moved west with his family and attended David Caldwell's academy in Guilford County, North Carolina in 1793. Converted under the preaching of James McGready, he sought a deeper experience of conversion and was successful under the preaching of William Hodge. In the same year he became a candidate for the ministry. He was licensed to preach in 1796. In 1798 Stone determined that he could not be ordained because of his opposition to the Westminster Confession, but eventually he found a way to reconcile his noncreedal approach with the Confession and the Transylvania Presbytery ordained him.

The Great Revival in the West got his attention in 1801 and his experiences during this period changed his life. In 1803 he broke away from the Synod of Kentucky and in 1804 he was among those publishing "The Last Will and Testament of the Springfield Presbytery." In retrospect it seems clear that Stone felt the millennium was drawing near and the thousand-year reign of Christ about to begin. In such times there was no need for such things as synods and presbyteries. Those who signed the document would take no name but Christian and union with the O'Kelly Christians and the Abner Jones Christians was the logical extension of their way of thinking.

Despite difficult personal circumstances, the death of one wife, and the care of four daughters, Stone continued to teach, preach, and engage in doctrinal disputes. He first met Alexander Campbell in 1824. Campbell was younger, better educated, and had just begun publishing *The Christian Baptist*. In the journal he pled for the end of creedal declarations and the restoration of the New Testament Church. Time spent together, conversations, and sermons laid the groundwork for the union of their respective followers eight years later.

Alexander Campbell (1788–1866) with his father, Thomas Campbell (1763–1854) led the movement to unite Christians on the basis of the restoration of primitive Christianity. Born in Ireland, educated by his father with a few years in academies led by others and an unexpected year at the University of Glasgow, Scotland, the younger Campbell was a man of insatiable interest in books and ideas. Thomas had come to America in 1807 and in 1809 the family and Alexander followed.

---

[3]D. Newell Williams, "Barton Warren Stone" in *The Encyclopedia of the Stone-Campbell Movement*, 701b. See also D. Newell Williams, *Barton Stone: A Spiritual Biography* (St. Louis: Chalice Press, 2000).

While in Glasgow, the younger Campbell was exposed to the reform efforts going on within the Church of Scotland. These included the efforts of John Glas and Robert Sandeman and the Haldane brothers. Both groups gave emphasis to the independence of congregations, the value of individual interpretation of scripture and the restoration of the ancient church. Richard Hughes reminds us that this restorationism had a long and storied history in Europe and exerted great influence on the Presbyterianism of the Scotch-Irish Presbyterians settled in the Middle Colonies, the American South, and in Northern Appalachia.[4]

Leroy Garrett, another of several recent interpreters of the history of the movement, argues that as important as the restorationist ideas of the Scottish reformers were, they did not offer Campbell the notions about Christian unity that became a hallmark of the Restoration Movement. This emphasis became the unique feature of Campbell's plea. While the Scots called for a restoration of primitive Christianity as if it were an end in itself, "the Campbells made it a means to an end—the end being the unity of all believers in Christ."[5]

Arriving in Washington, Pennsylvania in the fall of 1809, Alexander joined his father in the efforts he had begun to promote religious reformation. Thomas had begun the Christian Association of Washington with twenty-one people. It was in one of their meetings that he coined the phrase "Where the Bible speaks, we speak. Where the Bible is silent, we are silent." The charter for this effort was the Declaration and Address published in 1811. In it the Elder Thomas Campbell suggested as well that "The Church of Jesus Christ on earth is essentially, intentionally, and con-stitutionally one." The younger Campbell's time in Glasgow had opened him to the new ideas his father was promoting and with a new wife, the younger Campbell settled in Bethany, now West Virginia in 1812 and there he remained for the rest of his life. He was ordained to the Christian ministry the same year.

Uncomfortable for some years, the break with the Presbyterians also took place in 1812 when the birth of the first Campbell daughter forced the

---

[4]Richard Hughes, "Two Restoration Traditions", in *The Stone-Campbell Movement: An International Religious Tradition*, ed. Michael W. Casey and Douglas A. Foster (Knoxville: University of Tennessee Press, 2002) 351-53.

[5]Leroy Garrett, "Alexander Campbell", in *The Encyclopedia of the Stone-Campbell Movement*, 118.

fledgling reformation to rethink baptism. Concluding that baptism was by immersion and was for believing adults, Campbell, his father and much of the Brush Run church were immersed upon profession of faith in Christ. There were no accounts of conversion experiences and some wondered if they had dechristianized themselves by being baptized as adults when they had already been baptized as infants. More importantly, Alexander Campbell emerged after this decision as the leader of the Reformation. His father stepped into the background.

Upon leaving the Presbyterians, the Baptists accepted them despite misgivings and for the next few years they remained in the Baptist orbit on the frontier. The relationship was not one made in heaven and by the 1820s the Campbells and their congregations were forced out of Baptist associations because of their unwillingness to give up individual interpretation of Scripture for the acceptance of creedal statements. Campbell seems to have regretted his separation from the Baptists despite his differences with them. He had always cautioned the Baptists who made him their hero for his debates with pedobaptists that he had as many differences with them as he did with the Presbyterians. He never joined the Baptist church although his early congregations were part of the Redstone Baptist Association.

Alexander Campbell was after 1812 the leading voice in the emerging reformation movement but he also occupied himself with his growing family and farming. His efforts would bring rewards and at the end of his life he was a wealthy man. Like Stone he was a controversialist learning early that debates won more converts than sermons. He was also an educator with both secondary and postsecondary schools under his leadership. After 1823 he was an editor first of *The Christian Baptist* (1823–1830) and later of *The Millennial Harbinger* (1830–1866). In Virginia he was a larger-than-life figure and for the growing movement to unify Christendom he was an important force, holding steady the wavering and encouraging the weak. His intellect offered legitimacy for a movement often dominated by the frontier evangelist with more zeal than learning and for as long as he was alive the movement would hold together valuing individuals more than a party line. A good example is what happened in 1832.

By the end of the 1820s, those following Alexander Campbell, derisively called Campbellites, and the followers of Stone sometimes called Stoneites, but more often simply Christians, had become well aware of one another. Stone and Campbell had worked together and their churches recognized their similarities. They were called by different names, Stone's people were part of the Christian Church; Campbell's churches preferred the name Disciples. The movements overlapped in many places and with a shared desire for Christian unity, the effort to bring the groups together was not surprising. But union came with a willingness to overlook differences on several important topics.

For example, Campbell had proclaimed a carefully worked out notion that baptism was an especially significant rite. One historian has noted that his view was almost sacramental. "He insisted on a serious attitude toward baptism because he could not, on the basis of what the Bible said, disassociate this act of faith from the gracious forgiveness of man's sin."[6] Put simply, baptism by immersion was essential to Christian identity and to the salvation of the individual. The Stone people did not see it that way. While immersion was the acceptable form of baptism in most Christian Churches, baptism was not a condition of salvation or a requirement for church membership. Stone regarded Campbell's views on baptism as sectarian, but since Stone's views were not as carefully worked out, Stone eventually moved closer to Campbell's notions and he brought many of his followers with him. Later in the history of the movement the conflicts on baptism would be replayed leading to division between those who believed baptism essential and only valid if administered in a certain way and those who believed in the validity of baptism regardless of mode or circumstance and who argued that the pious unimmersed should be counted as Christian.

The issues related to the Lord's Supper were also significant. The Disciples practiced closed communion while the Christians allowed all to come to the table. In this case the Christians carried the day in part because the relationship of the individual and God was celebrated in the weekly observance of the Supper. The suggestion by Paul (1 Corinthians 11:29) that individuals should examine themselves before appearing at the Lord's Table fit nicely with the frontier individualism that characterized the churches of the new reformation. Baptism related to whether or not one was a Christian; the Eucharist had more to do with an individual's standing before God.

The two groups also differed on how the individual churches should be organized and how ministry should be carried out. The Christians drew on their Presbyterian heritage and operated with conferences binding congregations together. The Disciples were more independent. They continued to

---

[6]Henry E. Webb, *In Search of Christian Unity*, rev. ed. (Abilene TX: ACU Press, 2003) 153.

believe that there were no organizational ties beyond the local church.

Alexander Campbell believed that the autonomy and independence of the Disciples made any form of union unlikely. Despite his views and the differences between the two communions, a union was affected in 1832. The followers of Stone and Campbell met in Georgetown, Kentucky and declared themselves one church. The *Christian Messenger* reported in January 1832: "We are happy to announce to our brethren and to the world, the union of Christians in fact in our country. . . . The spirit of union is spreading like fire in dry stubble."[7]

Richard Hughes sums it up this way:

> It should be emphasized at this point that both the Stone and the Campbell movements were profoundly American in several respects. First, their discomfort over religious pluralism on the American frontier (i.e., the diversity of religious sects and denominations) provided both with their motivation for Christian unity. Second, both addressed the problem of religious pluralism in a way that was common on the American Frontier: they sought to escape pluralism by returning to primitive Christianity. . . . Third, reflecting the democratic impulse so prominent in their time, both Stone and Campbell were driven by a passion for freedom from creeds, clerics, and ecclesiastical control. With so much in common the Stone and Campbell Movements formally united in 1832.[8]

That the union overcame different views on matters such as baptism, communion, ministry, and church is noteworthy. There were also differences in the worldview of Campbell and Stone. Campbell was a rationalist who favored head over heart. Stone was a Spirit-led pietist who held to holiness as the only true means to redemption and Christian union. He also believed the world headed to hell in the proverbial handbasket. Campbell felt that a new order was coming. He called his new paper, begun when he broke with the Baptists in 1830, *The Millennial Harbinger* because it spoke to the evolving order. He saw a positive future and liked what he saw. Stone did not, yet their movements to restore and unify the Christian world united and grew rapidly in the years that followed.

This reality indicates at least two things about the evolving movement. In the first place, there were forums for conversation. Religious newspapers

---

[7]Webb, *In Search of Christian Unity*, 157.
[8]Richard Hughes, *Reviving the Ancient Faith: The Story of the Churches of Christ in America* (Grand Rapids MI: 1996) 12.

abounded. Campbell had one, Stone had one, and every evangelist wannabe had a newspaper. The quality was not uniform, but in a movement that said that what the Bible said was important, a consensus could be reached and it was. Differences were ironed out; compromises were reached on the grounds that what was done was sanctioned by the Book. One commentator said it best: "Some churches have bishops, the Disciples have editors." Secondly, the presence of Alexander Campbell and his journal gave the movement a center around which others might circle, but none could prevail so long as Campbell was alive. With his death in 1866 that center evaporated and the Restoration Movement disintegrated.

The notion of individual interpretation of Scripture found in the Declaration and Address of Thomas Campbell had its roots in Common Sense philosophy and Campbell held that the "intelligent and consecrated minds" of individual Christians can lead to a viable consensus regarding New Testament truth.[9] In the 1840s "intelligent and consecrated minds" included that of John Howard of Tennessee. Howard began to articulate what would become orthodoxy for most in the Churches of Christ. He held that the Church of Christ was of first-century origin; that is why on the cornerstones of many Churches of Christ you will see one date: AD 33. The correct name of the church was the Church of Christ, Churches of Christ, Church of God, and Christian Church. Eventually even the latter was dropped and the notion that the Church of God might be used was abandoned because of denominational competition. This church had no creed but the Bible, it was (small-c) catholic, and one entered the church only through profession of faith, repentance and baptism. Organizationally the church was made up of autonomous congregations with no national or local organization beyond the local church. The offices of the church were elders/bishops, deacons, deaconesses, and evangelists. The church met each Lord's Day for worship and the observance of the Lord's Supper. John Howard promoted these marks of orthodoxy in his paper *The Bible Advocate* and this summary found its way into print in 1848. When asked if his description of the church did not exalt his church and damn all other churches to perdition, he

---

[9]Paul M. Blowers and William J. Richardson, "Declaration and Address," *The Encyclopedia of the Stone-Campbell Movement*, 264. See also Thomas H. Olbricht and Hans Rollman, *The Quest for Christian Unity, Peace, and Purity in Thomas Campbell's Declaration and Address* (Lanham MD and London: Scarecrow Press, 2000).

replied: "It is not me who has done it, but it has been done by the New Testament—by the word of God."[10] Contrast Howard's ideas to the spirit of compromise that made unity possible in 1832.

Howard effectively describes the church I knew as a child. There were no deaconesses because the emerging consensus had had enough trouble with women teaching Sunday school. There was a creed in all senses except that it was not written down and formally subscribed to upon joining the church. It is important to note that fifteen years after the union of two diverse strands of American Christianity, you can see the impact of a radical individualism that shaped a sectarian outlook. Editors of religious journals largely forgotten today promoted this orthodoxy and I think you can trace patterns of belief in Churches of Christ, indeed patterns of belief in the wider movement, according to the influence and readership of journals scattered across the nation in the years shortly before and after the death of Alexander Campbell.

I have found the story of Arthur Crihfield (1802–1852) instructive. Crihfield saw as his task the advancement of the orthodoxy outlined by Howard and took as his approach the detection of heretics. In his journal, *The Heretic Detector* (1837–1843), and in other publications thereafter, he sought to identify those who had abandoned the "Jerusalem Gospel" as the ancient order was called. He even took on Alexander Campbell and Bethany College, charging that

> they may turn out a great many white-fingered and pretty dapper preachers whose voices will be cultivated to the most scientific squeak, whose sentences will be framed with the most punctilious regard to both rhetoric and logic, and whose gestures will be most gracefully mechanical; but such lads will be found unfit for pioneers in this wilderness of sin.[11]

Campbell responded with scorn to such notions, but when he was no longer on the scene, the freewheeling nature of the movement grounded on individual interpretation and goaded by editors and evangelists shattered the fragile unity of the Movement.

Two other factors in addition to the reality of human nature must be taken into account as we describe the nature of the emerging Church of Christ. The first is the devastation caused by the Civil War in the South.

[10]Richard Hughes, *Reviving the Ancient Faith*, 56-58.
[11]Richard Hughes, *Reviving the Ancient Faith*, 60.

David Lipscomb whose paper, The *Gospel Advocate*, pleaded with his brethren in the North to aid the devastated Southern churches. The aid was not forthcoming. To add to the insult, the American Christian Missionary Society, disliked already by conservatives as an extrabiblical organization, met in Cincinnati in 1861 and passed a statement of loyalty to the Union. Two years later the Society passed an even stronger statement calling Southerners traitors. For those who were already concerned about changes in their churches these resolutions and the introduction of other departures created great unease. The introduction of instrumental music into churches only allowed some to lump together the diverse insults; it was "wrote," one wag said, a combination of "niggers and organs."[12]

After the war ended and as the century played out, many would take pride in the fact that the Civil War did not divide the Restoration Movement, unlike the Baptists and the Methodists. As historians began to look at the division that was documented in 1906 by the census when Churches of Christ emerged as a full-blown religious body, it was soon noted that the strength of the Churches of Christ was below the Mason/Dixon line and in those areas where Southerners moved during economic dislocation, for example, Detroit. The Movement had in fact divided.

A second factor was the growth of urban wealth and the increased sophistication real and imagined that marked segments of the church during the Gilded Age. Many Disciples saw their lives in terms of the course the life of Alexander Campbell took. Campbell died a rich man surrounded by the values of virtues of being an American in a turbulent time. As had Campbell they placed emphasis on wealth, ecumenicity, and postmillennial progress. Disciples in many Northern cities built lavish churches with fine organs while their less-affluent brethren struggled to survive and remembered when their church met in a log cabin. Central Christian Church in the border city of Cincinnati became in 1872 an illustration of what was wrong. Benjamin Franklin, editor of the *American Christian Review* at the time, was highly critical of the building and his response illustrates the growing social divide. Franklin, wrote the minister of First Christian Church, had not learned "the first lesson of progress—namely that 'the world moves.' This fact is so apparent that . . . even you ought to understand it."[13]

These evolving socioeconomic tensions became even clearer when in

---

[12]Leroy Garrett, *The Stone-Campbell Movement*, 342.
[13]Richard Hughes, *Reviving the Ancient Faith*, 83.

1889 Daniel Sommer issued his Address and Declaration (a play on Thomas Campbell's earlier Declaration and Address) at Sand Creek, Illinois. Six thousand Disciples gathered to hear Sommer lash out at those who have brought innovations into the Church. There are those who would not honor speaking where the Bible speaks. Sommer wrote:

> In closing this address and declaration, we state that we are impelled from a sense of duty to say that all such innovations and corruptions to which we have referred, that after being admonished, and having had sufficient time for reflection, if they do not turn away from such abominations, that we cannot and will not regard them as brethren."[14]

Sommer by then was the editor of the *American Christian Review*. North of Dixie, his influence was great, but his views were not endorsed by the Southern opinion shapers such as David Lipscomb. He felt "Sommers views . . . are not law and gospel. We shall dissent from then when we deem their influence dangerous."[15] By the end of the century, Lipscomb had come to share many of Sommer's positions, but not his views on ministry or his criticism of church-related colleges. As David Lipscomb shifted so did the Southern churches following his lead. In 1906 the Church of Christ appeared for the first time on the census list. This church was poor, modest in number, and on the wrong side of the tracks. It was ridiculed for being backward, but took comfort in its slogans and identity. It alone was the true church restored from the first century. Over the course of the century it grew rapidly, moved across the tracks and identified with mainstream American values, putting off, for example, the pacifism that led to its being identified as a "peace church" in the earlier years of the century. Colleges were founded almost immediately to train ministers and the sending of missionaries to far fields honored the great commission. In the years following World War II Churches of Christ were among the fastest-growing denominational organizations in the nation. This growth has now ceased, but they remain the largest segment of those churches associated with the Restoration Movement. Disciples of Christ have lost numbers in recent years as they have moved into the mainstream of American denominational-ism; Christian Churches/Churches of Christ, another division of the movement shaped by the fundamentalist mentality of the early twentieth

---

[14]Leroy Garrett, *The Stone-Campbell Movement*, 382.
[15]David Lipscomb, in *The Gospel Advocate*, 7 Nov. 1882.

century, have now emerged as one of the most rapidly growing segments of American religious life.

But go back to the church I knew as a child, a church so insular that one could think those in other churches looked different. It was a church made up of migrants from the South and Southwest. Few had been born in California, not all would stay in the state. A consensus had been reached about the marks of the church. They were the basic doctrines spelled out by John Howard with a few additions endorsed by denominational consensus. For example, we had a Sunday school. (This had caused a division and I was aware of another church near our home that wore the same name but had no Sunday school.) Within a five-mile radius there were congregations of all the branches of the Restoration Movement, but we had nothing to do with each other. Our creed was the Bible but clearly we were shaped by personalities and forces we did not remember nor recognize as extrabiblical.

Refreshingly, of late, a movement has begun to fashion a new synthesis that would reknit the fractured heirs of Campbell and Stone. A cooperative effort has resulted in a volume called *The Encyclopedia of the Stone-Campbell Movement*, which tells the story of the movement. I have purposely cited the volume often in this presentation. Recently there were news reports of meetings in Oklahoma and Texas where members of the larger movement reconciled and agreed to count past differences as of opinion rather than doctrine. These meetings represent a growing wave that has been building for forty years. If any substantial reunion occurs I would submit that it would be as noteworthy as the original union in 1832 but like Alexander Campbell I have my reservations, given the independent nature of those involved.

I am, however, aware that Holy Spirit may well be working in ways that we only dimly perceive. Such a reunion would be without precedent in American religious history. Organizations can reknit with relative ease. To heal a fractured fellowship without and sometimes in spite of organizational expressions is more difficult. That is what is happening now. Like an extended family, there are those who recognize in the practice of others long separated that they are of the same family. This is a hopeful sign for which I give thanks.

JOSEPH SMITH, THE *BOOK OF MORMON*, AND THE LEGAL ADMINISTRATOR

Robert L. Millet

In January 1843, Joseph Smith declared that

> Whenever men can find out the will of God and find an administrator legally authorized from God, there is the kingdom of God; but where these are not, the kingdom of God is not. All the ordinances, systems, and administrations on the earth are of no use to the children of men, unless they are ordained and authorized of God; for nothing will save a man but a legal administrator.[1]

One of the distinguishing features of The Church of Jesus Christ of Latter-day Saints is its organization—its priesthood hierarchy from the most recently ordained deacon in Recife, Brazil to the president of the Church in Salt Lake City; its lay ministry but intricate organizational structure with callings, assignments, and officers; and its powers to communicate, spread the word, and mobilize in a matter of moments or hours in times of natural disaster, the offering of humanitarian aid, and efforts to attend carefully, stand up and speak out on moral issues in society.

This is not accomplished solely because of a kind of spontaneous, service-oriented Mormon propensity that just takes shape naturally, but rather because of a systematic form of governance that the Latter-day Saints know as the *priesthood*. For Mormons the priesthood is the power of God, delegated to man on earth, to act in all things pertaining to the salvation of men and women. It is not a person or a group of people, particularly male people or male administration;[2] rather, it is what Latter-day Saints believe to be the divine authorization and organizing principle that must be in place if the Church and Kingdom of God are to move forward on the earth to accomplish its foreordained purposes.

Clearly today's organization did not exist in the earliest days of Mormonism. The growing complexity of the priesthood organization during the past 176 years simply mirrors the complexity of life and the mutation and proliferation of spiritual challenges posed by a world fixated on toys

---

[1]Joseph Smith, *Teachings of the Prophet Joseph Smith*, selected by Joseph Fielding Smith (Salt Lake City: Deseret Book, 1976) 319.

[2]See James E. Faust, "Official Report, General Conference of the Church of Jesus Christ of Latter-day Saints, April 1993," 45; Dallin H. Oaks, "Official Report, General Conference of the Church of Jesus Christ of Latter-day Saints, October 2005," 25-26.

and temporalities. But how did we get here? How did it all get started? How did a young Joseph Smith, who would have had much more immediate contact with and exposure to a world of Protestantism (there is little evidence that Joseph had much contact with Roman Catholics in his area), a society of people whose break with Roman Catholicism had resulted in a "priesthood of all believers"—how did Joseph Smith come to establish a church that was so very different in organization than the Methodists, the Baptists, the Presbyterians? In this chapter I will suggest at least one source of the young Mormon prophet-leader's views on church government, one early avenue for information and impetus that would have helped to formalize his thinking on religious authority.

A Priesthood Primer

My thesis is that Joseph Smith's encounter with the *Book of Mormon* had a profound effect upon his theological mindset and, in particular, his ecclesiology. Before diving into the specific sections of the *Book of Mormon*, let me, for the benefit of those who have not read or even perused the book, speak of what it is and what it is not.

1. The *Book of Mormon* does not detail the life or work of Joseph Smith.
2. It is not a history of the LDS Church.
3. It is not a systematic theology of Mormonism, nor does it contain some of the most singularly distinctive LDS teachings.

On the other hand,

1. The *Book of Mormon* is a narrative that purports to be history, dating from approximately 2200 BC to AD 421.
2. The *Book of Mormon* is a preexilic and postexilic account of God's dealings with a branch of the house of Israel.
3. It is a document that deals directly with anthropology (the fallen nature of man) and Christology (the nature of and vital need for redemption in Christ). In fact, it speaks at great length of a people in ancient America who believed in and worshipped Jesus Christ hundreds of years before He was born in Bethlehem.
4. It describes the religious beliefs and governance of a people organized under a patriarchal theocracy for some fifty years, under a theocratic monarchy for more than 450 years, the operation of a church or ecclesiastical order for about six centuries, and a system of judges for a little less than a century.
5. The *Book of Mormon* speaks of a people who receive authority to

establish a church known variously as the Church of God, the Church of Christ, and the Church of Jesus Christ. The members are called saints and come to be known by their enemies as Christians. Some of the offices called and ordained in the church include deacons, teachers, priests, elders, high priests, and apostles.[3]

6. It chronicles the struggles of the people of God against those who have chosen to reject the true Messiah and the tenets of His gospel.

7. Finally, the *Book of Mormon* contains several references to the necessity of ordinances (sacraments) and the designated power needed to perform them. This authority was frequently referred to as the "holy order of God."

As early as the first chapter of the *Book of Mormon*, Lehi—a resident of Jerusalem in 600 BC and presumably a contemporary of such notable prophets as Jeremiah, Ezekiel, Obadiah, Zephaniah, and Habakkuk—receives his mission and commission to call the people of his surroundings to repentance through a kind of "throne theophany"—he is caught up to the throne of God; sees the heavenly hosts worshiping Deity; is given a book to read in which he learns of the coming destruction of Jerusalem at the hands of the Babylonians; and becomes privy to the prophetic word affirming the coming of the Promised Messiah in six centuries. Although there is no mention of Lehi receiving his prophetic mantle and authority by the laying on of hands, his becomes a prophetic role and, as Joseph Smith explained, "All the prophets [of the Old Testament era] had the Melchizedek [or higher] priesthood and were ordained by God himself."[4]

Some forty years later, Lehi's son and prophetic successor, Nephi, observes: "And it came to pass that I, Nephi, did consecrate Jacob and Joseph [his younger brothers], that they should be priests and teachers over the land of my people" (2 Nephi 5:26; compare Jacob 1:17-18). After living under a patriarchal theocracy and a monarchy for approximately 450 years, a young man named Alma responded to the prophetic warnings of one Abinadi, separated himself from the wayward majority, and established a

---

[3]The twelve special disciples in America called by Jesus to lead this American branch of Hebrews were, in all respects, Apostles. See Moroni 2:2; *History of The Church of Jesus Christ of Latter-day Saints*, 7 vols., ed. B. H. Roberts (Salt Lake City: Deseret Book, 1957) 4:538; Parley P. Pratt, *Key to the Science of Theology*, classics ed. (Salt Lake City, UT: Deseret Book, 1978) 15, 42, 69.

[4]Smith, *Teachings*, 181.

"church in the wilderness." He initially taught and baptized more than two hundred in a relatively hidden part of the wilderness called Mormon.

At the waters of Mormon, his baptismal prayer to the first initiate into the faith began with these words:

> Helam, I baptize thee, *having authority from the Almighty God*, as a testimony that ye have entered into a covenant to serve him until you are dead as to the mortal body; and may the Spirit of the Lord be poured out upon you; and may he grant unto you eternal life, through the redemption of Christ, whom he has prepared from the foundation of the world. (Mosiah 18:13; emphasis added)

Later Jesus instructed the one performing the baptism to use the following words: Calling the person by name, "Having authority given me of Jesus Christ, I baptize you in the name of the Father, and of the Son, and of the Holy Ghost. Amen" (3 Nephi 11:24-25).

The narrator of the record, Mormon, having himself been given authority from God (Moroni 8:16), wrote that the people were called a church and denominated themselves as the church of God or the church of Christ and then adds: "Alma, having authority from God, ordained priests, even one priest to every fifty of their number." Further, Alma instructed those priests that "they should teach nothing save it were the things which he had taught, and which had been spoken by the mouth of the holy prophets" (Mosiah 18:17-19). Later in the story, however, another group of people had been taught the gospel and desired to enter the church through baptism, "but there was none in the land that had authority from God" (Mosiah 21:33).

Eventually Alma and his followers joined with a larger group of believers who were governed by a king named Mosiah. Mosiah, who served as both king and priest over the people, was impressed with what Alma had accomplished and asked that Alma implement his ecclesiastical system among the entire population of believers. He delegated to him the office of high priest or president of the church (Mosiah 26:8; Alma 5:3).

> And it came to pass that King Mosiah granted unto Alma that he might establish churches throughout all the land . . . and gave him power to ordain priests and teachers over every church. . . . And thus, notwithstanding there being many churches, they were all one church, yea, even the church of God; for there was nothing preached in all the churches except it were repentance and faith in God. (Mosiah 25:19, 22)

In fact

> none received authority to preach or to teach except it were by [Alma, the high

priest] from God. Therefore he consecrated all their priests and all their teachers; and none were consecrated except they were just men. Therefore they did watch over their people, and did nourish them with things pertaining to righteousness. (Mosiah 23:16-18)

Nephi, son of Lehi, had earlier made it clear that baptism was an essential ordinance—one necessary for entrance into the church and kingdom of God. In speaking of the baptism of Jesus at the hands of John the Baptist (which he had seen in vision), Nephi wrote:

And now, if the Lamb of God, he being holy, should have need to be baptized by water, to fulfil all righteousness, O then, how much more need have we, being unholy, to be baptized, yea, even by water! . . . Know ye not that he was holy? But notwithstanding he being holy, he showeth unto the children of men that, according to the flesh he humbleth himself before the Father, and witnesseth unto the Father that he would be obedient unto him in keeping his commandments. (2 Nephi 31:5, 7; see also vv. 9-12)

While we have touched on this before, it is important to note the number of times the *Book of Mormon* speaks of the necessity of persons being properly ordained (2 Nephi 6:2; Alma 5:44; 6:8; 43:2; Helaman 8:18; Ether 12:10), and that such ordination came through the laying on of hands. Mormon recorded that Alma "ordained priests and elders, *by laying on his hands, according to the order of God*, to preside and watch over the church" (Alma 6:1; emphasis added). When the resurrected Lord appeared to the Nephites, "he touched with his hand the [apostles] whom he had chosen, one by one, even until he had touched them all, and spake unto them as he touched them." These later affirmed "that he gave them power to give the Holy Ghost" (3 Nephi 18:36-37). Later in the account, Mormon writes of this occasion:

And [Jesus] called them by name, saying: Ye shall call on the Father in my name, in mighty prayer; and after ye have done this ye shall have power that to him upon whom ye shall lay your hands, ye shall give the Holy Ghost; and in my name shall ye give it; for thus do mine apostles." (Moroni 2:2)[5]

---

[5]We do have one account of a lengthy preaching ministry that began as follows: "Now it came to pass that when Alma had said these words [had offered a prayer in behalf of those to whom they were called to preach], that *he clapped his hands upon all them who were with him*. And behold, as he clapped his hands upon them, they were filled with the Holy Spirit" (Alma 31:36; emphasis added). Latter-

Twenty years before the coming of Jesus to the Old World, a prophet named Nephi in the New World taught the gospel with great power, warned the people of coming destruction if they did not repent, and even demonstrated signs and wonders among them. But the majority of his listeners remained unconverted and rebellious. While pondering sadly upon the plight of his world, a voice came to him, saying:

> Blessed art thou, Nephi, for those things which thou hast done; for I have beheld how thou hast with unwearyingness declared the word . . . And now . . . I will make thee mighty in word and in deed, in faith and in works; yea, even that all things shall be done unto thee according to thy word, for thou shalt not ask that which is contrary to my will. Behold, thou art Nephi, and I am God. Behold . . . ye shall have power over this people. . . . I give unto you power, that *whatsoever ye shall seal on earth shall be sealed in heaven; and whatsoever ye shall loose on earth shall be loosed in heaven*; and thus shall ye have power among this people. (Helaman 10:4-5, 7, emphasis added)

This latter statement should be of especial interest to Christians who are familiar with Matthew's account of Peter's confession at Caesarea Philippi and Jesus' commendation to Peter that follows. It appears that Nephi is here granted the same power that Peter and the early apostles received to govern the church, what Mormons would call the "sealing power," the power to perform a sacrament or an ordinance on earth and rest assured that the ordinance will be recognized and acceptable in heaven. Linked with that idea is the fact that in the *Book of Mormon*, after the Nephite Twelve had passed away, "other disciples [were] ordained in their stead" (4 Nephi 1:14), thus setting up, at least for a season, apostolic succession in the New World, just as it had operated in the Old World when Matthias was chosen to succeed Judas Iscariot (Acts 1:15-26).

Without question, the most detailed description of priesthood in the *Book of Mormon* is found in Alma 13, right in the middle of a series of fiery sermons directed to an extremely wicked and rebellious group of people. This chapter speaks at some length of people who bear the priesthood in this life being foreordained to the same in a premortal existence. The speaker, Alma, referred to the ancients who had been ordained to the "holy order of

---

day Saints have generally presumed that "clapped his hands upon them" implies that he laid his hands upon them, set them apart for their assignment, and thereby empowered them for the ministry.

God," and who, through the purifying work of the Atonement and through the priesthood of God,

> were sanctified, and their garments were washed white through the blood of the Lamb. Now they, after being sanctified by the Holy Ghost, having their garments made white, being pure and spotless before God, could not look upon sin save it were with abhorrence; and there were many, exceedingly great many, who were made pure and entered into the rest of the Lord their God. (Alma 13:11-12)

Alma went on to use as a specific example of one who attained unto this level of holiness—the man Melchizedek, the king of Salem and contemporary of Abraham.

> Now this Melchizedek was a king over the land of Salem; and his people had waxed strong in iniquity and abomination. . . . But Melchizedek having exercised mighty faith, and received the office of the high priesthood according to the holy order of God, did preach repentance unto his people. And behold, they did repent; and Melchizedek did establish peace in the land in his days. . . . Now, there were many before him, and also there were many afterwards, but none were greater; therefore, of him they have more particularly made mention. (Alma 13:17-19)

Building on the Foundation

In his 1838 history of the Church, Joseph Smith indicated that on 5 April 1829 he first met Oliver Cowdery in Harmony, Pennsylvania. Two days later, Oliver began to serve as scribe in the translation of the *Book of Mormon*, a work Joseph had begun many months earlier. "We still continued the work of translation," Joseph stated,

> when, in the ensuing month (May 1829), we on a certain day went into the woods to pray and inquire of the Lord respecting *baptism for the remission of sins, that we found mentioned in the translation of the plates.* While we were thus employed, praying and calling upon the Lord, a messenger from heaven descended in a cloud of light, and having laid his hands upon us, he ordained us to the Aaronic or Lesser Priesthood.[6]

The messenger identified himself as John the Baptist and explained that he acted under the direction of Peter, James, and John, the ancient apostles,

---

[6]Joseph Smith et al., *History* 1:68.

who would come shortly to restore the Melchizedek or Higher Priesthood, including the holy apostleship, which contained the power to confer the gift of the Holy Ghost and perform sacred, saving ordinances. Within a matter of weeks, Joseph reported, the higher priesthood was indeed conferred upon them.[7]

In October 1834 Oliver Cowdery described the coming of John the Baptist in much more colorful detail in the church newspaper in Kirtland, Ohio, the *Messenger and Advocate*. In speaking of the work of translation, of which he proved to be the principal scribe, Cowdery stated: "These were days never to be forgotten—to sit under the sound of a voice dictated by the inspiration of heaven, awakened the utmost gratitude of this bosom!" Then he wrote of the specific portion of the *Book of Mormon* narrative that elicited the greatest curiosity concerning ordinances and power to perform the same:

> After writing the account given of the Savior's ministry to the remnant of the seed of Jacob, upon this continent, it was easy to be seen, as the prophet said it would be, that darkness covered the earth and gross darkness the minds of the people. On reflecting further it was as easy to be seen that amid the great strife and noise concerning religion, none had authority from God to administer the ordinances of the Gospel. For the question might be asked, have men authority to administer in the name of Christ, who deny revelations, when His testimony is no less than the spirit of prophecy, and His religion based, built, and sustained by immediate revelations, in all ages of the world when He has had a people on earth?

Oliver then went on to describe hearing the voice of Jesus Christ and feeling thereafter the hands of an angel, a heavenly messenger—John the Baptist, upon their heads.

> The assurance that we were in the presence of an angel, the certainty that we heard the voice of Jesus, and the truth unsullied as it flowed from a pure personage, dictated by the will of God, is to me past description, and I shall

---

[7]Joseph Smith, *The Doctrine and Covenants of the Church of Jesus Christ of Latter-Day Saints: Containing Revelations Given to Joseph Smith, the Prophet: For the Building Up of the Kingdom of God in the Last Days* (Salt Lake City: Deseret, 1911) 18:9; 27:12. See also Smith, *The Doctrine and Covenants of the Church of Jesus Christ of Latter-Day Saints: Containing Revelations Given to Joseph Smith, the Prophet, with Some Additions by His Successors in the Presidency of the Church* (Salt Lake City: Deseret, 1971).

ever look upon this expression of the Savior's goodness with wonder and thanksgiving while I am permitted to tarry; and in those mansions where perfection dwells and sin never comes, I hope to adore in that day which shall never cease.[8]

In the years that followed until the death of Joseph Smith in 1844, the Church and its organization came into place "precept upon precept; line upon line . . . here a little, and there a little" (Isaiah 28:10). At the formal organization of the Church at Fayette, New York on 6 April 1830, Joseph Smith was named as the first elder and Oliver Cowdery as the second elder; in June 1831 the first high priests were ordained; in March 1832 the First Presidency was organized (the president of the Church and his two counselors); in February 1835 the Quorum of the Twelve Apostles and the Quorums of the Seventy were put in place. In May 1842 Joseph began to deliver to the Church covenants and ordinances associated with the temple and, in conjunction with the rites of the temple, began in the fall of 1843 to confer the fullness of the blessings of the priesthood upon men and women.

With the growing complexity of the organization, Joseph the Prophet began to teach principles of priesthood government, tenets that clearly grew out of his work with the *Book of Mormon*, concepts that addressed current needs of the nineteenth century, directives that still form a foundation for the operation of the Church of Jesus Christ of Latter-day Saints today. Some of these include:

1. "The Priesthood is an everlasting principle, and existed with God from eternity, and will to eternity, without beginning of days or end of years. The keys [the right of presidency, the directing power] have to be brought from heaven whenever the Gospel is sent." This Priesthood was first given to Adam, and the kingdom of God was set up in that earliest age.[9] The priesthood is "a perfect law of theocracy."[10]

2. "There are two Priesthoods spoken of in the Scriptures, namely, the Melchizedek and the Aaronic or Levitical. Although there are two Priesthoods, yet the Melchizedek Priesthood comprehends the Aaronic or Levitical Priesthood, and is the grand head, and holds the highest authority which pertains to the priesthood, and the keys of the Kingdom of God in all ages of the world to the latest posterity on the earth; and is the channel

[8]Oliver Cowdery, *Messenger and Advocate* 1 (October 1834): 14-16.
[9]Smith, *Teachings*, 157, 166-67, 319.
[10]Smith, *Teachings*, 322.

through which all knowledge, doctrine, the plan of salvation and every important matter is revealed from heaven. Its institution was prior to 'the foundation of the earth.' "[11]

3. John the Baptist held the keys of the Aaronic Priesthood and was what Joseph Smith called a "legal administrator."[12] John taught the same gospel and performed the same ordinances as those who followed him—Christ and the apostles.[13] "The Savior said unto John, I must be baptized by you. Who so? To fulfil all righteousness. John refuses at first, but afterwards obeyed by administering the ordinance of baptism unto him, Jesus having no other legal administrator to apply to."[14]

4. Jesus Christ held the keys of the Melchizedek Priesthood and was also a legal administrator.[15] He conferred the keys of the kingdom upon Peter, James, and John on the Mount of Transfiguration.[16]

5. While the Bible is the word of God and may be relied upon as a guide for our lives, "There is no salvation between the two lids of the Bible without a legal administrator."[17] In other words, while the accounts of miracles and signs and wonders and the performance of ordinances in the Old and New Testaments are historical and real, they do not convey the necessary authority to us to act in the name of the Almighty.

6. There has been no change in the ordinances (either in the necessity or the mode) since the beginning of time. Adam and Eve were earth's first Christians. By extension, Christian prophets have taught Christian doctrine and administered Christian ordinances since the dawn of time. "Ordinances instituted in the heavens before the foundation of the world, in the priesthood, for the salvation of men, are not to be altered or changed. All must be saved on the same principles."[18] "It is said that Abel himself obtained witness that he was righteous [Hebrews 11:4]. Then certainly God spoke to him: indeed, it is said that God talked with him; and if He did, would He not, seeing that Abel was righteous, deliver to him the whole plan

[11]Smith, *Teachings*, 166-67; see also 112.
[12]Smith, *Teachings*, 272-73, 276, 318, 319.
[13]Smith, *Teachings*, 274.
[14]Smith, *Teachings*, 319.
[15]Smith, *Teachings*, 274, 319.
[16]Smith, *Teachings*, 158.
[17]Smith, *Teachings*, 319.
[18]Smith, *Teachings*, 308.

of the Gospel? And is not the Gospel the news of redemption? How could Abel offer a sacrifice and look forward with faith on the Son of God for a remission of his sins, and not understand the Gospel? . . . And if Abel was taught of the coming of the Son of God, was he not taught also of His ordinances? We all admit that the Gospel has ordinances, and if so, had it not always ordinances, and were not its ordinances always the same?"[19] Even as pertaining to the temple, "The order of the house of God has been, and ever will be, the same, even after Christ comes; and after the termination of the thousand years it will be the same; and we shall finally enter into the celestial kingdom of God, and enjoy it forever."[20]

In speaking of Noah, Joseph Smith observed:

> Now taking it for granted that the scriptures say what they mean, and mean what they say, we have sufficient grounds to go on and prove from the Bible that the gospel has always been the same; the ordinances to fulfil its requirements, the same; and the officers to officiate, the same: therefore, as Noah was a preacher of righteousness he must have been baptized and ordained to the priesthood by the laying on of the hands, etc. For no man taketh this honor unto himself except he be called of God as was Aaron. (Hebrews 5:4)[21]

7. Though salvation is in Christ and His is the only name by which eternal life comes to us, the ordinances of the gospel are not optional; they are required. "All men who become heirs of God and joint heirs of Jesus Christ," Joseph stated, "will have to receive the fullness of the ordinances of his kingdom; and those who will not receive all the ordinances will come short of the fullness of that glory, if they do not lose the whole."[22] "The question is frequently asked," Joseph later declared, 'Can we not be saved without going through with all those ordinances?' I would answer, No, not the fullness of salvation."[23]

8. God works through his legal administrators on earth. He will seldom if ever become personally involved in the performance of a priesthood ordinance or sacrament or send an angel if someone on earth can do so. "No wonder the angel told good old Cornelius that he must send for Peter to

[19]Smith, *Teachings*, 59.
[20]Smith, *Teachings*, 91.
[21]Smith, *Teachings*, 264.
[22]Smith, *Teachings*, 309.
[23]Smith, *Teachings*, 331; see also 362.

learn how to be saved: Peter could baptize, and angels could not, *so long as there were legal officers in the flesh holding the keys of the kingdom, or the authority of the priesthood.* There is one evidence still further on this point, and that is that Jesus himself when he appeared to Paul on his way to Damascus, did not inform him how he could be saved. He had set in the church first Apostles, and secondarily prophets, for the work of the ministry . . . so Paul could not learn so much from the Lord relative to his duty in the common salvation of man, as he could from one of Christ's ambassadors called from the same heavenly calling of the Lord, and endowed with the same power from on high."[24]

9. It matters very much that an ordinance be performed and even be performed properly, but it must be done by one who is duly authorized. In speaking briefly of the Protestant and Catholic claims to their own form of authority, he said: "I will illustrate it [the situation in the Christian world in regard to divine authority] by an old apple tree. Here jumps off a branch and says, I am the true tree, and you are corrupt. If the whole tree is corrupt, are not its branches corrupt? If the Catholic religion is a false religion, how can any true religion come out of it?"[25] Joseph Smith was especially drawn to the story in Acts 19 of the Apostle Paul encountering certain disciples at Ephesus who claimed to be Christians but had not so much as heard anything concerning the bestowal of the Holy Spirit. They indicated that they had been baptized "unto John's baptism. Then said Paul, John verily baptized with the baptism of repentance, saying unto the people, that they should believe on him which should come after him, that is, on Christ Jesus. When they heard this, they were baptized in the name of the Lord Jesus. And when Paul had laid his hands upon them, the Holy Ghost came on them; and they spake with tongues and prophesied" (Acts 19:2-6).

Joseph explained that these disciples at Ephesus were called upon "to repent and be baptized for the remission of sins, *by those who have legal authority,* and under their hands you shall receive the Holy Ghost, according to the Scriptures."[26] On another occasion the Mormon leader taught that "some sectarian Jew had been baptizing like John, but had forgotten to inform them that there was one to follow by the name of Jesus Christ, to baptize with fire and the Holy Ghost—*which showed these*

---

[24]Smith, *Teachings*, 265; emphasis added.

[25]Smith, *Teachings*, 375.

[26]Smith, *Teachings*, 99; emphasis added.

converts that their first baptism was illegal, and when they heard this they were gladly baptized."[27] From the journal of Wilford Woodruff under the date of 10 March 1844, Joseph took the part of Paul and said: "No, John did not baptize you, for he did his work right. And so Paul went and baptized them, for he knew what the true doctrine was and he knew that John had not baptized them."[28] Or, my favorite recitation of this story by the Prophet is as follows: "Unto what were you baptized? And they said, Unto John's baptism. Not so, not so my friends; if you had, you would have heard of the Holy Ghost. But you have been duped by some designing knave who has come in the name of John, an imposter. . . . John's baptism stood good, but these had been baptized by some imposter."[29]

10. The powers of the priesthood span the veil of death and continue into the world to come. Joseph faced head-on one of the vexing issues of Christian history and theology: If indeed Jesus Christ is the only name by which salvation comes (Acts 4:12), then what of the untold billions of souls who come to earth and die without so much as ever hearing of Him, much less having the opportunity to receive his message of salvation? "What has become of our fathers?" Joseph asked. "Will they be damned for not obeying the Gospel, when they never heard it? Certainly not. But they will possess the same privilege that we here enjoy, through the medium of the everlasting Priesthood, which not only administers on earth, but also in heaven, and the wise dispensations of the great Jehovah; hence those characters referred to by Isaiah [61:1] will be visited by the Priesthood, and come out of their prison upon the same principle as those who were disobedient in the days of Noah were visited by our Savior and had the Gospel preached to them by Him in prison [1 Peter 3:18-20; 4:6]; and in order that they might fulfill all the requisitions of God, living friends were baptized for their dead friends, and thus fulfilled the requirement of God, which says, 'Except a man be born of water and of he Spirit, he cannot enter into the kingdom of God" [John 3:5], they were baptized of course, not for

---

[27]Smith, *Teachings*, 263; emphasis added; see also 336.

[28]*The Words of Joseph Smith*, ed. Andrew F. Ehat and Lyndon W. Cook (Provo UT: Brigham Young University Religious Studies Center, 1980) 328; spelling and punctuation corrected.

[29]*The Words of Joseph Smith*, ed. Ehat and Cook, 333; spelling and punctuation corrected.

themselves, but for their dead."[30]

I should add that, just prior to his death; Joseph Smith began to hold lengthy meetings with members of the Quorum of the Twelve Apostles, to teach and instruct them, to prepare them against the time when his life would be taken. On one occasion he said to the Apostles: "I have sealed upon your heads all the keys of the kingdom of God. I have sealed upon you every key, power, [and] principle that the God of heaven has revealed to me. Now, no matter where I may go or what I may do, the kingdom rests upon you. But, ye apostles of the Lamb of God, my brethren, upon your shoulders this kingdom rests; now you have got to round up your shoulders and bear off the kingdom. If you do not do it you will be damned."[31]

Conclusion

Outside Catholicism's reach and claims, there seemed to be little discussion in Joseph Smith's area and time of the need for a formal priesthood or an unbroken priesthood line. "Respecting the Melchizedek Priesthood," Joseph stated in 1843, "the sectarians never professed to have it. . . . There was an Episcopal priest who said he had the priesthood of Aaron, but had not the priesthood of Melchizedek: and I bear testimony that I never have found the man who claimed the priesthood of Melchizedek."[32]

Indeed, the quest for religious authority was alive and well in the eighteenth century and especially in the spirit of primitivism and restorationism of the nineteenth century. Roger Williams, later in his life, renounced the views of the Baptists and "turned seeker, i.e., to wait for new apostles to restore Christianity." He felt the need "of a special commission, to restore the modes of positive worship, according to the original institution." Williams concluded that the Protestants were "not . . . able to derive the authority . . . from the apostles . . . [and] conceived God would raise up some apostolic power." In short, Williams held that there was "no regularly constituted church of Christ, on earth, nor any person authorized to administer any church ordinance, nor can there be until new apostles are sent by the great head of the Church, for whose coming I am seeking."[33]

---

[30]Smith, *Teachings*, 221-22.

[31]Wilford Woodruff, *Discourses of Wilford Woodruff*, selected by G. Homer Durham (Salt Lake City: Bookcraft, 1946) 72.

[32]Smith, *Teachings*, 322.

[33]Roger Williams, in *Magnalia Christi Americana* (1853) 2:498; cited in

John Wesley was a magnificent preacher and religious leader in the eighteenth century and became essentially the father of Methodism. His brother Charles, probably less well known, is responsible for many of the magnificent hymns sung in Christianity today. Though they were very close as brothers, on one occasion Charles criticized his brother John when the latter ordained a man to an office without authority to do so. Charles wrote:

> How easily are bishops made
> By man or woman's whim:
> Wesley his hands on Coke hath laid,
> But who laid hands on him?[34]

There is little reference to any priesthood in the Old Testament except for the consecration of the tribe of Levi and the descendants of Aaron, brother of Moses. We know there were prophets and holy men in the Old Testament; that they stood as covenant spokesmen and mouthpieces for Deity to the people; and presumably that they were called by God and empowered by him. But as to how and in what manner they were ordained, set apart, commissioned, or how they related to one another—such as in the days of Jeremiah when there were many prophets in the land—the biblical record is silent. The *Book of Mormon* purports to be a record of God's dealings with his children in ancient America, the greater portion of which takes place during a period that roughly parallels the time from Jeremiah to Malachi, as well as the first four centuries of the Christian era. In it priesthood and authority and covenants and ordinances (sacraments) are found throughout the text and one sees, in fact, a seamless narrative running between the biblical Testaments.

The *Book of Mormon* contains either direct mention of principles associated with divine authority or passing allusions to the same throughout the record.[35] It was inevitable that Joseph Smith and the Latter-day Saints

---

Jeffrey R. Holland, "Official Report, General Conference of the Church of Jesus Christ of Latter-day Saints, October 2004," 6.

[34]Cited in LeGrand Richards, *A Marvelous Work and a Wonder* (Salt Lake City: Deseret Book, 1950) 29. See also Milton V. Backman, Jr., *Christian Churches of America*, rev. ed. (New York: Scribner's, 1983) 180-81.

[35]Rose Ann Benson has suggested that "the *Book of Mormon* acts as a primer for priesthood leadership by illustrating how the spirit can teach receptive individuals to lead like Christ." See Benson, "The *Book of Mormon*: A Primer for Priesthood Leadership," *The Religious Educator: Perspectives on the Restored*

should begin to view biblical history and teachings and practices through the lenses of the *Book of Mormon*, and that many of these teachings should stand in stark contrast to a nineteenth century religious world made up largely of "a priesthood of all believers." In addition, further revelations through Joseph Smith, as found in the *Doctrine and Covenants* and in a surprising number of sermons, expanded upon the *Book of Mormon* foundation of priesthood government. To the outsider, therefore, Mormonism partook of the spiritual trust of Protestantism with an emphasis on the fallenness of man; our need for redemption and renewal in Christ; and the salvation that comes as a free gift, through grace and acceptance of the atoning blood of Jesus. At the same time, Mormonism spoke of priesthood, a priesthood hierarchy, of councils and quorums, of essential sacraments, and of apostolic succession, thereby resembling the conversation and thrust of Roman Catholics. An enigma, to be sure. A religious conundrum, a movement that defied categorization or even valid explanation.

Unless. Unless one recognizes that the Latter-day Saints believed themselves to be living in what they called the "dispensation of the fullness of times," a period, an era, an epoch when the God of heaven would restore truths from ages past and bring all things to consummation in Christ (Ephesians 1:10). In their minds, all of the streams and rivers of the past were now flowing into the ocean of revealed truth and divine power. At the end of August 1842 Joseph reflected upon his own mission and the work that lay ahead. He observed that

> My feelings at the present time are that, inasmuch as the Lord Almighty has preserved me until today, He will continue to preserve me, by the united faith and prayers of the Saints, until I have fully accomplished my mission in this life, and *so firmly established the dispensation of the fullness of the priesthood* in the last days, that all the powers of earth and hell can never prevail against it.[36]

Gospel 4/2 (2003): 66.

[36]Smith, *Teachings*, 258; emphasis added.

ANGELS IN THE AGE OF RAILWAYS

Steven C. Harper

It may seem to some to be a very bold doctrine that we talk of.
—Joseph Smith, September 1842

For nearly two millennia, meetings have convened to discuss authority in Christian traditions. For nearly two centuries such meetings have involved Latter-day Saints. One of these took place in Burslem, England in 1842 at the behest of Brabazon Ellis, incumbent of St Paul's Episcopal Church. He invited Alfred Cordon, a lay Mormon minister, to discuss authority in Christian traditions. Each man brought a companion, "and after the usual compliments" they all knelt as Ellis prayed that the Lord would enlighten each of them. Cordon voiced a heartfelt amen and fielded Ellis's first question:

> He asked me who ordained me in the Church of Latter Day Saints. I told him Wm Clayton. I then said and Sir, Who ordained you. He answered the Bishop. He then asked me who ordained Wm Clayton. I answered Heber C Kimball. I then asked him who ordained the Bishop. He answered: Another Bishop. He then asked me who ordained Heber C. Kimball; I answered Joseph Smith and said I: Joseph Smith was ordained by Holy Angels that were sent by commandment from the Most High God. I asked him from what source the Ministers of the Church of England obtained authority. He answered from the Apostles.

Ellis offered Cordon a book to establish his claim to apostolic succession. Cordon accepted and promised to read it diligently. Ellis asked Cordon to "work him a miracle." Cordon "asked him whether he was a believer and a Minister of Christ. He answer[ed] that he was." "Show me a miracle and then I will believe it," Cordon replied. From there the conversation touched on several controversies of Christian history and doctrine. Each man asserted authority for his positions. Each arrived at his assumptions and conclusions through different epistemologies. Cordon wrote that afterwards "we wished him good night and walked to our own homes, more confirmed in the faith of Latter Day Saints than ever we were."[1]

I approach the question of authority in Christian traditions with the same assumptions as Alfred Cordon took to his encounter with Brabazon

---

[1]Alfred Cordon Journal, LDS Church History Library, Salt Lake City. For a discussion of the Episcopal views on authority that informed Brabazon Ellis, see E. Brooks Hollifield, *Theology in America: Christian Thought from the Age of the Puritans to the Civil War* (New Haven CT: Yale University Press, 2003) 245-47.

Ellis. I approach my task as a historian who believes that divine authority is vested in the Church of Jesus Christ of Latter-day Saints, and one willing to openly investigate all other claims with diligence. I recognize—as Joseph Smith put it—that "it may seem to some to be a very bold doctrine that we talk of."[2] Given that bold doctrine, my words may sound apologetic or combative to some. That is not my intention. My desire is to quite personally explicate Mormonism's historical claims to divine authority along with a particularly Mormon epistemology. I will put my faith on display for examination, leaving readers to judge its merits or weaknesses.

Long before he was a Mormon invited to meet with Brabazon Ellis, Alfred Cordon avidly read the Bible. He was brought up in the Church of England and "in the fear of God." As a young apprentice in the Stafford-shire potteries, Cordon went from one post to another, married in 1836, but "led a desolate life." "I was troubled again and again on account of my sins," he wrote, "but I would not begin to serve God." Then his infant daughter "took very ill with convulsions" and died in agony in early 1837, spurring Alfred to "pray to the Lord to direct me and to have mercy upon me." He did. Shortly after the Cordons buried their daughter, members of Robert Aitken's short-lived Christian Society visited and discussed religion. "I was quite willing to give up my sins and do anything to find salvation," Cordon wrote. A bit shocked by what he called the "terrible noise" of an enthusiastic prayer meeting, Cordon nevertheless "came home rejoicing in God my Savior and my Redeemer." He devoted himself to the Christian Society and became a class leader; his wife "yielded and was made happy" also.[3]

"About this time" a Mormon woman named Mary Powel told Cordon that "the Lord had set his hand again the Second Time to recover the remnant of his people according to" Isaiah 11 "and that the Angel spoken of in" Revelation 14 had come, bringing "the Everlasting Gospel once more

---

[2]Joseph Smith, *The Doctrine and Covenants of the Church of Jesus Christ of Latter-Day Saints: Containing Revelations Given to Joseph Smith, the Prophet: For the Building Up of the Kingdom of God in the Last Days* (Salt Lake City: Deseret, 1911) 128:8. See also Smith, *The Doctrine and Covenants of the Church of Jesus Christ of Latter-Day Saints: Containing Revelations Given to Joseph Smith, the Prophet, with Some Additions by His Successors in the Presidency of the Church* (Salt Lake City: Deseret, 1971). Hereafter cited as D&C.

[3]Cordon, Journal.

unto lost man." Cordon rejoiced, for, as he wrote,

> I had many times prayed for this time to come. We began to talk about the Ordinances of the Gospel and I found that I was standing upon the Precepts of Men and not on the pure word of God. Away I went to my Bible and to prayer. The Spirit of God bore testimony to the truth of what she said. We conversed about the Baptism of Christ. I saw plainly it was by Immersion. Without hesitation I made up my mind in spite of all other things I would obey the Gospel. As soon as the Atkinites heard that I Had been with her they came unto me to try if they could stop me but it was all in vain.

Cordon's friends told him Latter-day Saints were "money diggers, gypsies, fortune tellers, and anything but a good report." But Cordon wanted to talk about baptism. Was it essential for salvation? It was not, Reverend Staley declared.[4]

The next morning Cordon set out on foot for Manchester to be baptized by David Wilding, an elder in the Church of Jesus Christ of Latter-day Saints. Wilding immersed Cordon and soon thereafter laid on hands to confirm Cordon a member of the church and invite him to receive the gift of the Holy Ghost. A few weeks later Mormon leader William Clayton baptized and confirmed several others, Cordon noted, and "he ordained me to be a Priest" by the laying on of hands. "I commenced preaching," Cordon wrote, and he never stopped but "went on laboring in the cause of God preaching and baptizing."[5]

What does this mean? What in the teachings of the Mormon woman Mary Powel was so compelling to Alfred Cordon, and how did he come to know it for himself? Why would he walk to Manchester to be baptized and confirmed by a Mormon elder? What was it about William Clayton's ordination of Alfred Cordon that turned him from a teacher whose authority was grounded in knowledge of the Bible into a minister with authority to baptize others by immersion for the remission of their sins, an ordinance in which he would pronounce the words, "having been commissioned of Jesus Christ, I baptize you in the name of the Father, and of the Son, and of the Holy Ghost?" (D&C 20:73).

Latter-day Saints believe "that a man must be called of God, by prophecy, and by the laying on of hands by those who are in authority, to

---

[4]Cordon, Journal.
[5]Cordon, Journal.

preach the Gospel and administer in the ordinances thereof."[6] "By what authority?" one may justifiably ask, as the chief priests and elders did of Jesus (Matthew 21:23 NIV). By priesthood authority, Mormonism answers, meaning an unmediated divine commission, direct authorization from God to preach and administer gospel ordinances like baptism, communion, confirmation, and, for Mormons, temple ordinances that represent the ultimate in our theology.[7] Joseph Smith wrote, "we believe that no man can administer salvation through the gospel, to the souls of men, in the name of Jesus Christ, except he is authorized from God, by revelation, or [in other words] by being ordained by some one whom God hath sent by revelation."[8] Mormonism's modern apostles call this "divine authority by direct revelation" the faith's "most distinguishing feature."[9]

"And who gave you this authority?" the elders asked of Christ (Matthew 21:23 NIV). Joseph Smith answers frankly, boldly, thus: "The reception of the holy Priesthood [came] by the ministering of Angels."[10] In his now-canonized history, Joseph Smith remembered the events of May 1829 as he and scribe Oliver Cowdery were translating the *Book of Mormon* from ancient metal plates revealed by an angel. "We . . . went into the woods to pray and inquire of the Lord respecting baptism for the remission of sins, that we found mentioned in the translation of the plates. While we were thus employed, praying and calling upon the Lord, a messenger from heaven descended in a cloud of light, and having laid his hands upon us, he ordained us"[11]

---

[6]Joseph Smith, "The Articles of Faith of the Church of Jesus Christ of Latter-day Saints" (1842) no. 5: "We believe that a man must be called of God, by prophecy, and by the laying on of hands by those who are in authority, to preach the Gospel and administer in the ordinances thereof."

[7]Gordon B. Hinckley, *Ensign* (November 1995): 53.

[8]Joseph Smith to Isaac Galland, 22 March 1839, in *The Personal Writings of Joseph Smith*, rev. ed., Dean C. Jessee, ed. and comp. (Salt Lake City: Deseret, 2002) 459.

[9]Jeffrey R. Holland, "Our Most Distinguishing Feature," *Ensign* (May 2005): 43. Also Dallin H. Oaks, "Joseph Smith in a Personal World," *BYU Studies* 44/4 (2005): 154.

[10]"A History of the Life of Joseph Smith, Jr.," Joseph Smith Letterbook 1, pp. 1-6, LDS Church History Library, Salt Lake City.

[11]Joseph Smith, *History of the Church of Jesus Christ of Latter-day Saints*, 7 vols., ed. B. H. Roberts (Salt Lake City: Deseret Book, 1957) 1:68-69.

Joseph continued his matter-of-fact narrative, noting how the angel "said this Aaronic Priesthood had not the power of laying on hands for the gift of the Holy Ghost, but that this should be conferred on us hereafter; and he commanded us to go and be baptized, and gave us directions that I should baptize Oliver Cowdery, and that afterwards he should baptize me. . . ." Only late in the account, almost as an afterthought, does Joseph reveal the identity of the ministering angel. He

> said that his name was John, the same that is called John the Baptist in the New Testament, and that he acted under the direction of Peter, James and John, who held the keys of the Priesthood of Melchizedek, which Priesthood, he said, would in due time be conferred upon us, and that I should be the first Elder of the Church, and he (Oliver Cowdery) the second.[12]

Joseph Smith combines nonchalance and historicity. He remembered that "it was on the fifteenth day of May, 1829, that we were ordained under the hand of this messenger, and baptized." Oliver Cowdery, by contrast, could hardly contain himself when he sat down to pen the good news:

> The angel of God came down clothed with glory, and delivered the anxiously looked-for message, and the keys of the Gospel of repentance. What joy! what wonder! what amazement! . . . our eyes beheld, our ears heard, as in the "blaze of day"; yes, more—above the glitter of the May sunbeam. . . . Then his voice, though mild, pierced to the center, and his words, "I am thy fellow-servant," dispelled every fear. We listened, we gazed, we admired! 'Twas the voice of an angel from glory, 'twas a message from the Most High! . . . But, dear brother, think, further think for a moment, what joy filled our hearts, and with what surprise we must have bowed . . . when we received under his hand the Holy Priesthood as he said, "Upon you my fellow-servants I confer this Priesthood and this authority. . . ."[13]

But Cowdery, too, in other statements, reported the events with striking straightforwardness. This example makes the point well: Joseph "was ordained by the angel John, unto the . . . Aaronic priesthood, in company with myself, in the town of Harmony, Susquehannah County, Pennsylvania, on Fryday, the 15th day of May, 1829. . . . After this we received the high and holy priesthood."[14]

[12]Smith, *History* 1:68-72.
[13]*Messenger and Advocate* 1 (October 1834): 14-16.
[14]Patriarchal Blessings, book 1 (1835): 8-9, "Oliver Cowdery, Clerk and

The understated nature of these claims to overtly historical ordinations by corporeal angels becomes more striking. For neither Joseph Smith nor Oliver Cowdery composed a narrative of their ordination to the high or Melchizedek priesthood by no less worthies than apostles Peter, James, and John. All we have are passing reminiscences: a revelation to Joseph in which the Lord describes "Peter, and James, and John, whom I have sent unto you, by whom I have ordained you and confirmed you to be apostles" (D&C 27:12); an 1842 musing about the time, it must have been in either 1829 or 1830, when Smith met "Peter, James, and John in the wilderness" near the Susquehannah River and they declared "themselves as possessing the keys of the kingdom." They, along with a veritable who's who of angels, transmitted to Joseph Smith and Oliver Cowdery "the power of their priesthood" (D&C 128:21). Smith and Cowdery in turn ordained new apostles. Cowdery told them: "You have been ordained to the Holy Priesthood. You have received it from those who had their power and authority from an angel."[15]

The climactic event in this history came as Smith and Cowdery prayed together in the Mormon temple at Kirtland, Ohio. No account was published until 1852, but Smith's journal entry for 3 April 1836 says that they "saw the Lord standing upon . . . the pulpit before them."[16] He was followed in succession by Moses, Elias, and Elijah, each authorizing some aspect of the gospel, the gathering of Israel, or the preparation of the world for the impending millennium. Feeling self-important, Cowdery became disaffected from Smith shortly thereafter. He confessed later to being hypersensitive but defended his character on the grounds that he had "stood in the presence of John . . . to receive the Lesser Priesthood—and in the presence of Peter, to receive the Greater, and look[ed] down through time, and witness[ed] the effects these two must produce."[17]

"In the early Spring of 1844," according to Apostle Wilford Woodruff, "Joseph Smith called the twelve apostles together and he delivered unto them the ordinances of the Church and Kingdom of God and all the keys

---

Recorder. Given in Kirtland, December 18, 1833, and recorded September 1835."
    [15]Kirtland High Council Minutes, 21 February 1835, 159.
    [16]Jessee, ed., *Papers of Joseph Smith* 2:210. *Doctrine and Covenantss* 110.
    [17]Oliver Cowdery to Phineas Young, 23 March 1846, LDS Church History Library, Salt Lake City.

and power that God had bestowed upon him."[18] Smith's commission of the apostles, Brigham Young chief among them, is crucial to Latter-day Saint claims to continuing priesthood authority. An early statement by the apostles is thus celebrated. It says that a quorum of apostles were "confirmed by the holy anointing under the hands of Joseph," after which he declared "that he had conferred upon the Twelve every key and every power that he ever held himself."[19]

Spencer W. Kimball, president of the LDS Church during my youth, stood with apostle Boyd K. Packer and others in the Church of Our Lady in Copenhagen, Denmark, admiring Thorvaldsen's *Christus* and his sculptures of the twelve apostles. "I stood with President Kimball before the statue of Peter," Packer said. "In his hand, depicted in marble, is a heavy set of keys. President Kimball pointed to them and explained what they symbolized." Kimball then charged Copenhagen stake president Johan Bentine, the Mormon equivalent of a Catholic bishop, to "tell every prelate in Denmark that they do not hold the keys. I hold the keys!" As the party left the church, President Kimball shook hands with the caretaker, "expressed his appreciation, and explained earnestly, 'These statues are of dead apostles,' " then, pointing to Apostles Tanner, Monson, and Packer, added, "You are in the presence of living apostles."[20] Terryl Givens wrote that "Mormonism's radicalism can thus be seen as its refusal to endow its own origins with mythic transcendence, while endowing those origins with universal import since they represent the implementation of the fullest gospel dispensation ever. The *effect* of this unflinching primitivism, its resurrection of original structures and practices, is nothing short of the demystification of Christianity itself."[21]

Such claims to authority have always been contested. But *how* does one contest such blatantly historical claims of two witnesses that they have been

---

[18]Wilford Woodruff statement, 19 March 1897, LDS Church History Library, Salt Lake City.

[19]Declaration of the Twelve Apostles, Brigham Young Papers, LDS Church History Library, Salt Lake City.

[20]Boyd K. Packer, *The Holy Temple* (Salt Lake City: Bookcraft, 1980) 83. Edward L. Kimball, *Lengthen Your Stride: The Presidency of Spencer W. Kimball* (Salt Lake City: Deseret, 2005) 108, 327.

[21]Terryl L. Givens, *Viper on the Hearth: Mormons, Myth, and the Construction of Heresy* (New York: Oxford University Press, 1997) 93.

"ordained under the hands" of John, Christ's formerly beheaded baptizer?[22] Can one disprove Cowdery's claim that "upon this head have Peter, James, and John laid their hands and confered the Holy Melchesdic Priestood?" "Where was room for doubt?" Cowdery asked. But there was plenty of doubt if not disproof. Joseph Smith was threatened with violence for claiming that "angels appear to men in this enlightened age."His history says that he and Cowdery "were forced to keep secret the circumstances of our having . . . received this priesthood; owing to a spirit of persecution." But the secret was soon out. Cowdery "pretends to have seen Angels," one editor wrote in 1830, and "holds forth that the ordinances of the gospel, have not been regularly administered since the days of the Apostles, till the said Smith and himself commenced the work."[23]

Alexander Campbell contested Mormon claims to authority. Many of the first Mormons in Ohio came from his flock, including Sidney Rigdon, one of Campbell's "leading preachers" until, as Campbell put it, he fell "into the snare of the Devil in joining the Mormonites" and "led away a number of disciples with him."[24] Many of those disciples were looking for God to "again reveal himself to man and confer authority upon some one, or more, before his church could be built up in the last days."[25] Edward Partridge went to New York to be baptized by Joseph Smith and became Mormonism's first bishop shortly thereafter. Parley Pratt liked Campbell's doctrine very much, "but still one great link was wanting to complete the chain of the ancient order of things," Pratt wrote (using one of Campbell's favorite phrases), "and that was the *authority* to minister in holy things—the apostleship, the power which should accompany the form." Pratt began looking for someone like Peter, who "proclaimed this gospel, and baptized for the remission of sins, and promised the gift of the Holy Ghost, because he was commissioned to do so by a crucified and risen Savior." He asked

[22]Stephen Post, Journal, 27 March 1836, Stephen Post Papers, LDS Church History Library, Salt Lake City.

[23]"The Golden Bible," *Painesville* (Ohio) *Telegraph*, 16 November 1830, 3.

[24]J. H. Kennedy, *Early Days of Mormonism* (New York: Scribner's, 1888) 67. In June 1828 Campbell noted how effective Rigdon had lately been: "Bishop's Scott, Rigdon, and Bentley, in Ohio, within the last six months have immersed about eight hundred persons." *Christian Baptist* (2 June 1828): 263.

[25]Edward Partridge Papers, 26 May 1839, LDS Church History Library, Salt Lake City.

of Campbell's ministry, "who ordained them to stand up as Peter?" Pratt subsequently sold his Ohio farm and set out in search of authority. He found it in Manchester, New York at the home of Hyrum Smith, brother of Joseph. The two men talked through the night as Smith unfolded "the commission of his brother Joseph, and others, by revelation and the ministering of angels, by this the apostleship and authority had been again restored to the earth." Pratt said he duly weighed "the whole matter in my mind" and concluded "that myself and the whole world were without baptism, and without the ministry and ordinances of God; and that the whole world had been in this condition since the days that inspiration and revelation had ceased."[26] When Joseph Smith and Oliver Cowdery ordained twelve apostles in 1835, Parley Pratt was one.

Campbell's remaining followers criticized Mormons for "their pretensions to miraculous gifts" and apostolic authority. Campbell dismissed Mormonism as one more group of "superlative fanatics" claiming extrabiblical revelation.[27] A war of words ensued in which Campbell and Smith jabbed at each other by evoking passages from the Acts of the Apostles, each man casting himself implicitly as a modern apostle. Campbell was Paul condemning Elymas the sorcerer.[28] Smith was Peter, calling on a modern son of Sceva to "repent and be baptized . . . in the name of Jesus Christ . . . and ye shall receive the gift of the Holy Ghost" (Acts 2:38).

A December 1830 revelation to Smith pressed this point. Speaking to Rigdon in the first-person voice of Jesus Christ, the revelation called

---

[26]Parley P. Pratt, *Autobiography of Parley P. Pratt*, ed. Scot Facer Proctor and Maurine Jensen Proctor (Salt Lake City: Deseret, 2000) 22, 32.

[27]*Painesville Telegraph*, 15 February 1831. Alexander Campbell, "Mormonism Unvailed," *Millennial Harbinger* 1/6 (January 1835).

[28]In the February 1831 issue of the *Millennial Harbinger*, Campbell's influential article, "Delusions," includes this line: "I have never felt myself so fully authorized to address mortal man in the style in which Paul addressed Elymas the sorcerer as I feel towards this Atheist [Joseph] Smith" (page 96). Campbell refers to Acts 13:6-12. Joseph Smith responds with his own references to the Acts of the Apostles, including Acts 19:2-15. Each man implicitly casts himself as a modern apostle. Joseph Smith develops the argument by drawing on Bible passages to emphasize a doctrinal difference between himself and Campbell. At Acts 2:38 Peter invites his hearers on the day of Pentecost to "Repent, and be baptized, every one of you, in the name of Jesus Christ for the remission of sins, and ye shall receive the gift of the Holy Ghost" (KJV).

Rigdon to "a greater work" than assistant to Campbell. It acknowledged that Rigdon had been baptizing "by water unto repentance, but they received not the Holy Ghost. But now I give unto thee a commandment, that thou shalt baptize by water, and they shall receive the Holy Ghost by the laying on of the hands, even as the *apostles* of old" (D&C 35:5-6). Joseph Smith emphasized the point in subsequent editorial answers to Campbell's critiques, associating himself with apostles while noting that whatever Campbell's gifts, he neither had nor claimed apostolic authority to lay on hands: "With the best of feelings, we would say to him, in the language of Paul to those who said they were John's disciples, but had not so much as heard there was a Holy Ghost, to repent and be baptised for the remission of sins by those who have legal authority, and under their hands you shall receive the Holy Ghost, according to the scriptures."[29]

In 1832 Nancy Towle watched as Joseph Smith turned to some women and children in the room; and lay his hands upon their heads; (that they might be baptized of the Holy Ghost;) when, Oh! cried one, to me, "What blessings, you do lose!—No sooner, his hands fell upon my head, than I felt the Holy Ghost, as warm water, to go over me!" But I was not such a stranger, to the spirit of God, as she imagined; that I did not know its effects, from that of warm water! and I turned to Smith, and said "Are you not ashamed, of such pretensions? You, who are no more, than any ignorant, plough-boy of our land! Oh! blush, at such abominations! and let shame, cover your face!" He only replied, by saying, "The gift, has returned back again, as in former times, to illiterate fishermen."[30]

---

[29]Joseph Smith, Kirtland, Ohio, to the Elders of the Church, *Messenger and Advocate* 2 (December 1835): 225-30. "Then laid they their hands on them, and they received the Holy Ghost.—Acts: ch. 8, v. 17. And, when Paul had laid his hands upon them, the Holy Ghost came on them: and they spake with tongues, and prophesied.—Acts: ch. 19, v. 6. Of the doctrine of baptisms, and of laying on of hands, and of resurrection of the dead, and of eternal judgment.—Heb. ch. 6, v.2. How then shall they call on him in whom they have not believed? and how shall they believe in him of whom they have not heard? and how shall they hear without a preacher? And how shall they preach except they be sent? as it is written, How beautiful are the feet of them that preach the gospel of peace, and bring glad tidings of good things!—Rom. ch. 10, vv. 14-15."

[30]Nancy Towle, *Vicissitudes Illustrated, in the Experience of Nancy Towle, in*

So it went, Joseph Smith claiming that "The Savior, Moses, & Elias—gave the Keys to Peter, James & John . . . and they gave it up" to him, critics citing Joseph's ignorance, low-breeding, credulity, deception, and "pitiable superstitious delusion." Said Charles Dickens, "Joseph Smith, the ignorant rustic, sees visions, lays claim to inspiration, and pretends to communion with angels," all "in the age of railways."[31]

Competing but rarely expressed assumptions underlie these two positions. Mormons assume prima facie the possibility of Peter, James, and John ordaining Joseph Smith. Most people simply do not. Those among the majority who believe in angels at all are confident that they stopped appearing to rustics about the same time the last fisherman was ordained an apostle, certainly before the Enlightenment or the age of railways. This certainty strikes Mormons as presumptuous, much as Mormon certainty of angels in the age of railways sounds to others.

In May 2005, various holders of these two assumptions took the stage at the Library of Congress in a conference on the worlds of Joseph Smith. His claim to apostolic authority by direct revelation was a pervasive theme in their presentations. It was another installment in the long history of discussions about authority in Christian traditions, more polite but otherwise not far removed from the nineteenth-century contest over Joseph Smith's claims. Dallin H. Oaks, former law professor, university president, and state supreme court justice, was the featured speaker, but not primarily on those credentials. He is an apostle, and alongside references to his own research and scholarship, he spoke like one.

Mormon philosopher David Paulsen spoke on the ways Joseph Smith challenges Christian theology, beginning with the premise that theology itself is necessary only in the absence of apostles who are chosen and ordained as the New Testament indicates. "Apostolic authority is not something that can be chosen," Paulsen argued, "it was a divine calling issued by the Lord himself, the fruits of which are evidence of the call's divine origin." Chief among such fruits, says Paulsen, are revelations that

---

Europe and America (Charleston SC: James L. Burges, 1832) 144-45.

[31]Joseph Smith Sermon (ca. 1839), recorded in Willard Richards Pocket Companion, in *The Words of Joseph Smith*, ed. Andrew F. Ehat and Lyndon W. Cook, Religious Studies Monograph series no. 6 (Provo UT: Religious Studies Center, Brigham Young University, 1980) 9. Charles Dickens, "In the Name of the Prophet—Smith!" *Household Words* 69/3 (July 1851): 69.

"enabled the apostles to direct the church's affairs under God's direction." The rise of theology is evidence of the end of apostolic authority, Paulsen contends, and his is no voice in the wilderness. Thus, Joseph Smith's claim to direct revelation from God is his ultimate challenge to theology, "a challenge based on the Bible itself."[32]

Randall Balmer, professor of Religion at Barnard College of Columbia, addressed Paulsen's key points, agreeing that "the issue of authority has been vexing throughout Christian history," but rejecting Paulsen's premise that a loss of apostolic authority necessitated a divine restoration. Instead, Balmer argued, Jesus put authority in Peter in a very Protestant way, so as to "vitiate some of the authoritarianism of the episcopal polity in the Roman Catholic Church." Balmer calls Peter "the apotheosis of fallibility," arguing that Christian authority, God's special revelation, is Jesus, and following him, "of course, is the scriptures." Knowing our next question, Balmer asks it himself. "What counts as scripture?" "How does one know what is and is not scripture.?" The questions unfold. "How do we know anything? What is the basis of our epistemology?"[33] Elder Oaks had the previous evening set forth a distinctive Mormon epistemology, "the principle of independent verification by revelation."[34] Paulsen asserted it again by quoting Joseph Smith:

> Search the revelations which we publish, and ask your Heavenly Father, in the name of His Son Jesus Christ, to manifest truth unto you, and if you do it with an eye single to His glory, nothing doubting, He will answer you by the power of His Holy Spirit. You will then know for yourselves.[35]

I longed to hear Balmer's analysis of this epistemology, which I find so compelling, but he dismissed it as quickly as Alexander Campbell had done, though on different grounds.[36] "Circularity," Balmer called it, caricaturing

---

[32]David Paulsen, "Joseph Smith Challenges the Theological World," *BYU Studies* 44/4 (2005): 177-78.

[33]Randall Balmer, "Speaking of Faith: The Centrality of Epistemology and the Perils of Circularity," *BYU Studies* 44/4 (2005): 224-26. See also Robert Clyde Johnson, *Authority in Protestant Theology* (Philadelphia: Westminster, 1959).

[34]Dallin H. Oaks, "Joseph Smith in a Personal World," *BYU Studies* 44/4 (2005): 167.

[35]David Paulsen, "Joseph Smith Challenges the Theological World," *BYU Studies* 44/4 (2005): 202.

[36]Alexander Campbell, "Delusions," *Millennial Harbinger* (10 February 1831):

Paulsen as saying that we know the *Book of Mormon* is true because it says so, or that Joseph Smith received revelations because he said he did. Balmer did not engage the epistemology of independent verification by personal revelation. And he offered little instead. "The early church settled the issue of canonicity," he says, "through a kind of emerging consensus, codified finally in various church councils." The *kind* of consensus to which Balmer refers is a highly qualified kind, as Arians and Donatists would testify. When has there been any other kind of consensus among Christians about the canon? Balmer concluded with what must have been self-conscious irony. He quoted Karl Barth's "simple Sunday-school ditty: 'Jesus loves me, this I know; for the Bible tells me so.' "[37] The questions he raised went unanswered.

Thus the Library of Congress conference did not resolve Christianity's contested claims to authority. But it was an impressive stage for the ongoing debate. Durham University Professor of Religion Douglas Davies led off the concluding session with a learned analysis of Mormonism's potential to become recognized as a world religion. He predicted the possibility that Mormonism would grow globally by decentralizing and taking on regional identities. "Not and continue to be Mormonism," I thought to myself. Roger Keller, professor of Church History and Doctrine at Brigham Young University and a former Presbyterian minister, offered a penetrating response based on his own deep learning and experience.

> Latter-day Saints have often said to me [Keller stated], "We are so glad that you found the gospel." My response has always been, "I knew the gospel long before I was a Latter-day Saint. What I have found is the fulness of the gospel." The essence of that fulness is that the authority of the priesthood is found only within the Church of Jesus Christ of Latter-day Saints. . . . This understanding of authority is absent from Davies's paper [Keller said], and this absence colors what he has said about the dynamics and constraints of Latter-day Saint Church growth.

96.

[37]Balmer, "Speaking of Faith," 230. On this point also see Kathleen C. Boone's penetrating study, *The Bible Tells Them So: The Discourse of Protestant Fundamentalism* (Albany: State University of New York Press, 1989). See also Randall Balmer, *Growing Pains* (Grand Rapids MI: Brazos, 2001) 61-62; and Balmer's *Mine Eyes Have Seen the Glory: A Journey into the Evangelical Subculture in America*, 3rd ed. (New York: Oxford University Press, 2000) esp. 40-45.

Keller concluded with his own prediction that Mormonism will never take on the decentralized and diverse characteristics Davies prescribed for global religions, precisely "because . . . restored authority to administer the saving ordinances of the gospel through a divinely revealed structure—will not permit us to do so."[38]

Davies rose when it was time to respond and said with obvious frustration, "What are we doing here?" venting some of the tension that always accompanies Mormon claims. Brabazon Ellis vented it by asking Alfred Cordon to work him a miracle. There was none of that at the Library of Congress, but Davies wondered aloud whether we were having an academic conference or proselyting. It is hard and somewhat purposeless for Mormons to separate the two. Because Mormon claims to authority are historical, because they demystify Christianity, merely asserting them, as I have done, sounds like preaching. They have a kind of challenging aspect.

If so, I might as well take another crack at explaining the epistemology of independent verification by personal revelation. It is, first of all, irreducibly historical. As Paulsen put it, "Joseph claimed that God restored divine authority by literal hand to head transfer by the very prophets and apostles whose lives and words are recounted in the Bible."[39] But we misunderstand if we think Mormonism claims to be scientifically provable based on historical documentation or Enlightenment propositions. Rather, the historical record provides Latter-day Saints with something to verify independently by direct revelation. And, to quote Joseph Smith, "whatever we may think of revelation . . . without it we can neither know nor understand anything of God."[40] One does not know that John the Baptist ordained Joseph Smith because Joseph said so, but because God reveals to the individual that Joseph told the truth when he said so. The first and perhaps finest example is furnished by Samuel Smith, Joseph's younger brother. Joseph's history says that a few days after John the Baptist ordained him and Cowdery, Samuel came to visit. Zealous teaching by the

---

[38]Roger R. Keller, "Authority and Worldwide Growth," *BYU Studies* 44/4 (2005): 308-309, 315.

[39]David Paulsen, "Joseph Smith Challenges the Theological World," *BYU Studies* 44/4 (2005): 184.

[40]Joseph Smith, "Try the Spirits," *Times and Seasons*, quoted in Joseph Smith, Jr., et al., *History of the Church of Jesus Christ of Latter-day Saints*, 7 volumes (Salt Lake City: Deseret, 1976) 4:574.

newly ordained missionaries notwithstanding, Samuel

> was not . . . very easily persuaded . . . but after much enquiry and explanation,
> he retired to the woods, in order that by secret and fervent prayer he might
> obtain of a merciful God, wisdom to enable him to judge for himself: The
> result was that he obtained revelation for himself sufficient to convince him of
> the truth of our assertions to him; and . . . Oliver Cowdery baptized him; and
> he returned to his father's house greatly glorifying and praising God, being
> filled with the Holy Spirit.[41]

Joseph Smith was conscious, as I am, of the perils of self-deception and all manner of pseudorevelation. Mormonism certainly runs that risk. But considering the alternatives of agnosticism, or even of strict historicism, or of an epistemology dependent on so-called consensus achieved by emperor-sponsored philosophers, I have chosen to put my faith in independent verification by personal revelation, and have not been disappointed. An inerrant Bible would not even suffice unless we had inerrant interpreters, or, as Mormons claim, an inerrant Christ to guide otherwise fallible interpreters by direct revelation.[42] Still, without revelation, we cannot know anything of God. "God has revealed it to us by his Spirit," Paul taught the Corinthians, based on the premise that "no one knows the thoughts of God except the Spirit of God" (1 Corinthians 2:10-11 NIV).

I find this principle of independent verification by revelation to be liberated from the limitations of Enlightenment or postmodern epistemologies, and unconstrained by what Joseph Smith regarded as the God-muzzling composition of creeds and closure of the canon.[43] Often Joseph turned the Bible on those who regarded themselves as its biggest champions. To the question, "Is there any thing in the Bible which licenses

---

[41]Joseph Smith, History, in *The Papers of Joseph Smith*, vol. 1, ed. Dean C. Jessee (Salt Lake City: Deseret, 1989) 232.

[42]Boone, *The Bible Tells Them So*, 77.

[43]An admirable work limited by Enlightenment rationalism is Hans Von Campenhausen, *Ecclesiastical Authority and Spiritual Power in the Church of the First Three Centuries* (Palo Alto CA: Stanford University Press, 1969). A postmodern approach is Laura Salah Nasrallah, *An Ecstasy of Folly: Prophecy and Authority in Early Christianity* (Cambridge MA: Harvard University Press, 2003). For a Catholic approach shaped by both Enlightenment and postmodern modes, see David J. Stagman, *Authority in the Church* (Collegeville MN: Liturgical Press, 1999).

you to believe in revelation now a days?" He answered, "Is there any thing that does not authorize us to believe so; if there is, we have, as yet, not been able to find it." But "is not the canon of the Scriptures full?" "If it is," he replied, "there is a great defect in the book, or else it would have said so."[44] Holding open the possibility that angels could restore priesthood and that anyone may verify whether they have by direct revelation is liberating and empowering epistemology. It frees the mind to believe that some things can indeed be certainly known, though not by history itself. Rather, this knowledge is gained at the intersection of historically attested events and a kind of pragmatism of personal experience, something similar to what Richard Bushman has called the social meaning of priesthood.

My life is organized by this priesthood authority. I was baptized by my father, who afterward laid his hands on my head and invited me to receive the gift of the Holy Ghost. I share the tangible if incommunicable experience of Samuel Smith and the woman Joseph Smith confirmed in 1832, whose witness Nancy Towle dismissed as the effects of warm water. My father later ordained me to the Aaronic and the Melchizedek priesthoods, giving me a "line of authority" that traces my ordination through him back to Peter, James, and John. He again laid on hands when I was critically ill with encephalitis and I was healed. My grandfather laid his hands on my head for a patriarchal blessing when I was fourteen and fixated on things other than an academic life. He talked much of school and foretold several of my most formative experiences, including pursuit of an endless education. Most personally, my wife and I were sealed in the temple by this priesthood, which transcends death. For us that means our children are bound eternally to us and us to each other. I now bless and baptize and confirm those children in turn by virtue of the holy priesthood Joseph Smith received from ministering angels. It is the single greatest determinant of my life.

Some will surely say, then, that Mormon priesthood is just so much sentimentality. But for me its power is undeniable. And not primarily because it heals bodies or validates binding ordinances. Rather, the power of Mormon priesthood holds the key to knowing God, the key to transcendence and godliness (D&C 84:19-23). One of Joseph Smith's most sublime

---

[44]Editorial, July 1838, Far West, Missouri, *Elders' Journal* 1 (July 1838): 42-44. Richard L. Bushman, *Joseph Smith: Rough Stone Rolling* (New York: Knopf, 2005) 284-85.

revelations declared that "the rights of the priesthood are inseparably connected with the powers of heaven," which cannot be controlled or handled illicitly. Priesthood may be conferred, the revelation says, but "amen to the priesthood or the authority of that man" who exercises control, or dominion, or compulsion on anyone in any degree of unrighteousness. Authoritarianism is not authority. Priesthood is not license. Men exercise authority tyrannically by nature and disposition, the revelation says, but this is apostate priesthood. Priesthood power is as dew that distills upon the soul who self-consciously rejects authoritarianism in favor of persuasion, long-suffering, gentleness and meekness, kindness, unfeigned love, without hypocrisy or guile. Otherwise "no power or authority can or ought to be maintained." Anyone who exercises what the revelation calls "unrighteous dominion" forfeits priesthood and "is left unto himself . . . to fight against God" (D&C 121). God, though sovereign, compels no one. He makes plans and provisions for the salvation of His children but neither elects them to grace unconditionally or saves them contrary to their will. He loves, sacrifices, and ministers. We may be confident in His presence only if we willingly act in the same way.

Nineteenth-century Protestants made no pretensions to "confer any new powers by the acts of ordination," but increasingly democratized authority by locating priesthood in believers generally. Catholic and Mormon priesthood seemed the opposite of this and akin to each other. Ordination in both traditions elevated one nearer to Christ.[45] But the priesthood Joseph Smith conferred actually elevated the ordained even as it maximized their number. His radical priesthood of believers did not mitigate authority by democratizing it, but universally endowed ordained men with "transcendent power which cut against every grain of American, republican culture."[46] Joseph Smith read Hebrews 7 literally. Melchizedek was ordained a priest of the most-high God, and made like the Son of God, and abideth a priest continually. But Joseph Smith added a potent gloss declaring that "*all* who are ordained unto this priesthood are made like unto the Son of God, abiding a priest continually" (Hebrews 7:3 JST[47]). Joseph "wanted to invest

---

[45]David Holland, "Priest, Pastor, and Power: Joseph Smith and the Question of Priesthood," *Archive of Restoration Culture* (Provo UT: Joseph Fielding Smith Institute for Latter-day Saint History, 2000) 11-12.

[46]Holland, "Priest, Pastor, and Power," 14.

[47]That is, the Joseph Smith Translation, Smith's modified translation of por-

all the men among his followers with the powers of heaven descending through the priesthood."[48] Such power rendered God knowable and every man and woman capable of exaltation in the image of God (D&C 84, 132).

A kitschy plaque I received before my ordination summed all this up: "Priesthood," it said, "is not only the power to act in the name of God. It is the power to become like Him." That possibility is blasphemous to most Protestants and Catholics, though not, unless I am mistaken, to Orthodox Christians. It seems therefore safe to say that Joseph Smith's testimony of angels ordaining him to priesthood for the express purpose of exalting men and women as priests and priestesses, kings and queens, will continue to be contested for a long time.[49]

I cannot solve the problem; perhaps only exacerbate it. Randall Balmer asked "Why Smith?" But one can just as legitimately ask, Why not? The documentation evidencing that John the Baptist ordained Joseph Smith is at least as good as that for his baptism of Christ. And if one can independently verify both claims by direct revelation through the Holy Spirit, why not believe? If anyone cannot independently verify the truthfulness of a claim by revelation, why believe either? I wonder whether such an epistemology will appeal to anyone unwilling to grant the premises that angels could have ordained Joseph Smith, or that he might have received extrabiblical revelations, or that anyone can verify these by an unmediated experience with God. But for me to be convinced otherwise would require potent refutation—not merely rejection—of those same premises. The argument would have to explain why God no longer gives special revelation to prophets and apostles, and it seems unlikely that anything short of a special revelation could do that. The Westminster Confession's certainty about the sufficiency of the Bible, "unto which nothing at any time is to be added," not even by "new revelations of the Spirit," sounds presumptuous in Mormon ears—perhaps as presumptuous as St. Peter ordaining a New

---

tions of the King James Version (ca. 1833–1844), first published (posthumously) in 1867: *Great Contrast. A Selection of Texts from King James's Translation of the Bible, Contrasted with the Corresponding Texts in the Inspired Translation of Joseph Smith, the Seer* (Plano IL: True Latter Day Saints' Herald, 1867ff.).

[48]Richard L. Bushman, *Joseph Smith: Rough Stone Rolling* (New York: Knopf, 2005) 160.

[49]Richard J. Mouw, "Joseph Smith's Theological Challenges: From Revelation and Authority to Metaphysics," *BYU Studies* 44/4 (2005). *Doctrine and Covenants.*

York farmer must sound to its adherents. Divine authority by direct revelation is the reason for Mormonism's existence.[50] Moreover, the power to know for oneself that divine authority is vested in the Church of Jesus Christ of Latter-day Saints is that without which Mormonism would cease to be, or at least cease to be compelling to me.[51] This pair of doctrines is simultaneously authoritative and empowering to the individual—truth that makes me free.

Is it possible that angels could appear in this enlightened age, bringing authority to act for Christ again, as in former times, to unsophisticated mortals? As the epigraph for his influential *Millennial Harbinger*, Alexander Campbell chose Revelation 14:6-7, "Then I saw another angel flying in midair, and he had the eternal gospel to proclaim to those who live on the earth" (Revelation 14:6 NIV), though Campbell rendered it as "I saw another messenger flying through the midst of heaven, having everlasting good news to proclaim to the inhabitants of the earth." What Campbell intended by replacing the biblical word *angel* with the less-defined *messenger*, I do not know. But Joseph Smith's literal reading of the same passage is a revealing contrast. He thought John's revelation foresaw actual angelic ministers, one of whom appeared in Joseph's New York bedroom as he prayed in September 1823. Joseph said "he called me by name, and said unto me that he was a *messenger* sent from the presence of God to me, and that his name was Moroni; that God had a work for me to do; and that my name should be had for good and evil among all nations" (JSH 33). Such a claim was foolishness to Alexander Campbell, Nancy Tracy, Charles Dickens, and countless others. It was biblical and thoroughly believable, however, to those who knew Joseph best. And it sounded so to Alfred Cordon on the other side of the Atlantic. But how could he know? He sought independent verification by direct revelation. "Away I went to my Bible and to prayer," he wrote, and "the Spirit of God bore testimony to the

---

[50] Joseph Smith taught that "The Church of Jesus Christ of Latter-day Saints was founded upon direct revelation, as the true church of God has ever been, according to the scriptures." Quoted in I. Daniel Rupp, *He Pasa Ekklesia: An Original History of the Religious Denominations at Present Existing in the United States. Containing Authentic Accounts of Their Rise, Progress, and Doctrines* (Philadelphia: J. Y. Humphreys, 1844).

[51] James E. Faust, "Where Is the Church?" typescript of devotional address, Brigham Young University, 1 March 2005, 8.

truth of" Mary Powel's testimony that the angel of Revelation 14 had indeed proclaimed the eternal gospel in the age of railways.[52]

---

[52]Cordon, Journal, LDS Church History Library, Salt Lake City.

VISIONS AND THE WORD:
THE AUTHORITY OF ELLEN WHITE IN RELATION TO THE AUTHORITY OF SCRIPTURE IN THE SEVENTH-DAY ADVENTIST MOVEMENT

George R. Knight

By what authority? That is always an interesting question. But it is doubly so in a Christian movement that believes in the authority of Scripture but also claims to have had an inspired prophet as one of its founders.

Such is the situation in the Seventh-day Adventist Church, which, according to its current statement of fundamental beliefs, holds that the Word of God in the Bible contains the "knowledge necessary for salvation," is the source of doctrine, and "is the standard by which all teaching and experience must be tested," but also maintains that Ellen G. White (1827–1915) had a valid and "authoritative" prophetic gift.[1]

Such statements may (or may not) sound all right in the abstract, but how does or should a body of believers relate the authority of a modern prophet to the authority of the ancient prophets canonized in the sixty-six books of the Bible? That is the topic of this paper. It is also a topic that has occupied Adventist thinkers across the 160 years of their church's history.

Christian Connection Antecedents

In fact, it is not too much to say that the Seventh-day Adventist movement was formed in the matrix of tension on the subject of visions versus the Word. On the one hand, Millerite Adventism[2] (one of its major historical antecedents) had gone on record in June 1843 that "we have no confidence whatever in any visions, dreams, or private revelations." That sentiment was reaffirmed in May 1845,[3] some seven months after the Millerite disappointment related to the nonadvent of Christ and some five months after young

---

[1]"Fundamental Beliefs of Seventh-day Adventists," *Seventh-day Adventist Church Manual*, 16th ed. (Hagerstown MD: Review and Herald, 2000) 9, 15.

[2]For major discussions of Millerite Adventism, see *The Disappointed: Millerism and Millenarianism in the Nineteenth Century*, ed. Ronald L. Numbers and Jonathan M. Butler (Bloomington: Indiana University Press, 1987); George R. Knight, *Millennial Fever and the End of the World: A Study of Millerite Adventism* (Boise ID: Pacific Press, 1993).

[3]"Declaration of Principles," *Signs of the Times* (7 June 1843): 107; "Conference of Adventists at New York," *Morning Watch* (15 May 1845): 158.

Ellen G. Harmon's (White after August 1846) first vision.[4] Millerite Adventism was a movement of one authoritative book—the Bible.

One of Seventh-day Adventism's other theological roots had the same position on the authority of the Bible. The Christian Connection (or Connexion), a restorationist group related to the Stone-Campbell movement, held to the Bible as the only rule of faith. William Kinkade (b. 1783), who studied under Barton W. Stone and became the "theologian of this group" of seven men who founded the Christian Connection,[5] wrote in 1829 that he had in his early years refused to call himself by "any name but that of *Christian*" and that he would take no book for his "standard but the *Bible*."[6]

Kinkade was certainly clear on the supreme authority of the Bible in religious matters. However, in his extended discussion of the "restoration of the ancient order of things" he claimed that he could not settle for "one inch short" of the New Testament order. And at the center of New Testament order, he argued, were the spiritual gifts, including the gift of prophecy, set forth in such places as 1 Corinthians 12:8-31 and Ephesians 4:11-16. The presence of spiritual gifts in the church "is the *ancient order of things*; every one opposed to this, is opposed to primitive Christianity. To say God caused these gifts to cease, is the same as to say, God has abolished the order of the New Testament church. . . . These gifts constitute the ancient order of things." They were not temporary gifts that ceased with the apostolic age. Rather, "these gifts, as they are laid down in the scripture, compose the gospel ministry" as set forth in the New Testament.[7]

Kinkade's New Testament theology of the perpetuity of spiritual gifts in the context of the Bible as the only source of authority is important for

---

[4]For more on Ellen White's life and ministry, see Arthur L. White, *Ellen White*, 6 vols. (Washington DC: Review and Herald, 1981–1986). For a briefer treatment, see George R. Knight, *Meeting Ellen White: A Fresh Look at Her Life, Writings, and Major Themes* (Hagerstown MD: Review and Herald, 1996).

[5]Milo True Morrill, *A History of the Christian Denomination in America: 1794–1911 A.D.* (Dayton OH: Christian Publishing Assn., 1912) 58-65; Leroy Garrett, *The Stone-Campbell Movement: An Anecdotal History of Three Churches* (Joplin MO: College Press, 1981) 290.

[6]William Kinkade, *The Bible Doctrine of God, Jesus Christ, the Holy Spirit, Atonement, Faith, and Election; to Which Is Prefixed Some Thoughts on Natural Theology and the Truth of Revelation* (New York: H. R. Piercy, 1829) iv.

[7]Kinkade, *The Bible Doctrine of God*, 331-33.

understanding early Seventh-day Adventism because two of the movement's three founders had been active in the Christian Connection—Joseph
Bates as a leading layperson and James White as a Connectionist pastor. In
short, they had come into Adventism from a movement in which the most
influential theologian[8] held to both the Bible and the Bible only as a
determiner of faith and practice and the continuation of spiritual gifts
including prophecy throughout the Christian era as set forth in the New
Testament. Kinkade did not seem to be concerned with possible conflict
between the two realms of authority.

Early Adventists on Authority

The earliest Sabbatarian Adventists were quite clear on the issue of
authority. James White, Ellen's husband, stated the developing denomination's position quite accurately in 1847 when he wrote that "the Bible is a
perfect, and complete revelation. It is our only rule of faith and practice."
But, he added in harmony with Kinkade's line of thought,

> this is no reason, why God may not show the past, present, and future fulfil-
> ment of his word, in these *last days*, by dreams and visions; according to
> Peter's testimony [see Acts 2:17-20; Joel 2:28-31]. True visions are given to
> lead us to God, and his written word; but those that are given for a new rule of
> faith and practice, separate from the Bible, cannot be from God, and should be
> rejected.[9]

In White's statement we see the delicate balance followed by several early
Adventist thought leaders. The central idea is that the Bible is supreme, but
that it indicates that God will send visions and spiritual gifts during the last
days of earth's history to guide His people back to the Bible and through the
shoals of the end-time crisis. Thus White points out that Peter's use of Joel
2:28-31 in his Pentecost sermon of Acts 2 did not exhaust the fulfillment of

---

[8]Morrill, the first historian of the Connexion movement, not only identifies
Kinkade as its major theological voice but indicates that his *Bible Doctrine* book
was still being printed by the denomination's official publishing house in its 4th
rev. ed. 80 years after its first publication. See *A History*, 65, 67.

[9]James White, *A Word to the "Little Flock"* (1847) 13. Reprinted as one of ten
pamphlets in *GTU Historic Pamphlet Collection: Seventh Day Adventist* (N.p.:
trustees of the White Publications, 1907[?]). Online at <http://www.earlysda.com/
flock/lflockcontents.html>.

that prophecy. God would send His Holy Spirit again at the end of time and "your sons and your daughters shall prophesy" and see visions before the Second Advent. White also quoted 1 Thessalonians 5:19-21, where Paul says: "Despise not prophesyings. Prove all things; hold fast that which is good."[10]

James White and the other early leaders of the Seventh-day Adventist Church had no doubt that the Bible taught that God would pour out the prophetic gift during the last days, and that individuals had a responsibility to test by the Bible criteria those who claimed to be prophets. Adventist leaders also had no doubt that any such gifts must be subordinate to the Bible in the life of believers, and that whenever they were not subordinated they were being used wrongly.

Thus James could write in 1851 that "the gifts of the Spirit should all have their proper places. The Bible is an everlasting rock. It is our rule of faith and practice." He went on to assert that if all Christians were as diligent and honest as they should be, they would be able to learn their whole duty from the Bible itself. "But," James noted, "as the reverse exists, and ever has existed, God in much mercy has pitied the weakness of his people, and has set the gifts in the gospel church to correct our errors, and to lead us to his Living Word. Paul says that they are for the 'perfecting of the saints,' 'till we all come in the unity of the faith.' " [Eph. 4:12, 13]— The extreme necessity of the church in its imperfect state is God's opportunity to manifest the gifts of the Spirit.

> Every Christian is therefore in duty bound to take the Bible as a perfect rule of faith and duty. He should pray fervently to be aided by the Holy Spirit in searching the Scriptures for the whole truth, and for his whole duty. He is not at liberty to turn from them to learn his duty through any of the gifts. We say that the very moment he does, he places the gifts in a wrong place, and takes an extremely dangerous position. The Word should be in front, and the eye of the church should be placed upon it, as the rule to walk by, and the fountain of wisdom, from which to learn duty in "all good works." But if a portion of the church err from the truths of the Bible, and become weak, and sickly, and the flock become scattered, so that it seems necessary for God to employ the gifts of the Spirit to correct, revive, and heal the erring, we should let him work.[11]

---

[10]White, *A Word to the "Little Flock,"* 13, 14.

[11]James White, "The Gifts of the Gospel Church," *Review and Herald* (21

In a similar vein in 1868 James White cautioned the believers to

> let the gifts have their proper place in the church. God has never set them in the very front, and commanded us to look to them to lead us in the path of truth, and the way to Heaven. His word he has magnified. The Scriptures of the Old and New Testament are man's lamp to light up his path to the kingdom. Follow that. But if you err from Bible truth, and are in danger of being lost, it may be that God will in the time of his choice correct you [through the gifts], and bring you back to the Bible.[12]

At this juncture it is important to recognize that just because the early Adventist leaders believed that Ellen White's gift of prophecy was subordinate to the authority of the Bible, that did not mean that they held her inspiration to be of a lesser quality than that of the Bible writers. To the contrary, they believed that the same Voice of authority that spoke through the Bible prophets also communicated through her.

We find a careful balance here. Even though early Adventists viewed her inspiration as being equally divine in origin with that of the Bible writers, they did not see her as being the same in authority. Ellen White and her fellow Adventists held that her authority was *derived* from the Bible and thus could not be equal to it.

As a result, her authority was not to transcend or contradict the boundaries of truth set forth in the Bible. As Ellen White so aptly put it in 1871, "the written testimonies are not to give new light, but to impress vividly upon the heart the truths of inspiration already revealed" in the Bible.[13]

Ellen's understanding of the gift harmonized with that of her husband. Thus in 1851 she could write in the conclusion to her first little book, "I recommend to you, dear reader, the Word of God as the rule of your faith and practice. By that Word we are to be judged. God has, in that Word, promised to give visions in the 'LAST DAYS'; not for a new rule of faith, but for the comfort of his people, and to correct those who err from Bible

April 1851): 70.
    [12]James White, "Time to Commence the Sabbath," *Review and Herald* (25 Feb. 1868): 168.
    [13]Ellen G. White, *Testimonies for the Church*, 9 vols. (Mountain View CA: Pacific Press, 1948) 2:605.

truth."[14]

It is important to realize that Ellen White believed that her visions were for the guidance of the Adventist community rather than the Christian church at large. Writing to Adventist believers in 1871 she noted that

> if you had made God's word your study, with a desire to reach the Bible standard . . . , you would not have needed the *Testimonies* [that is, her counsel]. It is because you have neglected to acquaint yourselves with God's inspired Book that He has sought to reach you by simple, direct testimonies, calling your attention to the words of inspiration which you had neglected to obey, and urging you to fashion your lives in accordance with its pure and elevated teachings.[15]

The theoretical statements on the relation of the authority of the Bible to that of Ellen White were quite consistent. But, we need to ask, did the early Adventists practice what they preached on the topic? More specifically, did Ellen White's visions have a significant role in doctrinal formation and how did her writings relate to the interpretation of the Bible?

The second point is the most easily addressed, since in the first decades of Adventism Ellen White's writings were not thought of as interpreting the meaning of scriptural passages. As to doctrinal formation, James White wrote in 1855 that "it should be understood that all these views as held by the body of Sabbath-keepers, were brought out from the Scriptures before Mrs. W. had any view in regard to them. These sentiments are founded upon the Scriptures as their only basis."[16]

That statement is found in the context of a discussion of Seventh-day Adventist doctrine being a "vision view" rather than a "Bible view." That accusation was a popular one among the denomination's detractors. Miles Grant, for example, argued in 1874 in the *World's Crisis* (a leading Advent Christian periodical) that the Sabbatarian's understanding of the heavenly sanctuary doctrine had come through Ellen White's visions.[17]

---

[14]Ellen G. White, *A Sketch of the Christian Experience and Views of Ellen G. White* (Saratoga Springs NY: James White, 1851) 64.

[15]E. G. White, *Testimonies* 2:605.

[16]James White, "A Test," *Review and Herald* (16 Oct. 1855): 61.

[17]Miles Grant, *World's Crisis* (25 Nov. 1874) in *Review and Herald* (22 Dec. 1874): 204.

Uriah Smith vigorously responded to that accusation.

> Hundreds of articles [he stated] have been written upon the subject [of the sanctuary]. But in no one of these are the visions once referred to as any authority on this subject, or the source from whence any view we hold has been derived. Nor does any preacher ever refer to them on this question. The appeal is invariably to the Bible, where there is abundant evidence for the views we hold on this subject."[18]

Of course, it is one thing to make such claims as those cited from Smith and James White, while it is quite another to substantiate them. The interesting thing about Smith's assertion is that any person willing to go back into early Seventh-day Adventist literature can either verify or disprove it. On the subject of the heavenly sanctuary Paul Gordon has done that and has verified Smith's claims in his *The Sanctuary, 1844, and the Pioneers*.[19] On a broader scale, extensive research by Merlin Burt, Rolf J. Pöhler, and George R. Knight has demonstrated that Adventism's various doctrines were originated and fleshed out by several individuals, none of whom became Seventh-day Adventists.[20] The Adventist contribution was in integrating the various doctrines they had accepted through Bible study into an apocalyptic theology. But even that was a contribution by Joseph Bates rather than Ellen White.[21] Her early visions tended to be visions of confirmation of Bible study or related to building unity in matters of detail.[22]

Early Seventh-day Adventists appear to have been a people of the

---

[18]Uriah Smith, "The Sanctuary," *Review and Herald* (22 Dec. 1874): 204.

[19]Paul A. Gordon, *The Sanctuary, 1844, and the Pioneers* (Washington DC: Review and Herald, 1983).

[20]Merlin D. Burt, "The Historical Background, Interconnected Development, and Integration of the Doctrines of the Sanctuary, the Sabbath, and Ellen G. White's Role in Sabbatarian Adventism from 1844 to 1849" (Ph.D. diss., Andrews University, 2002); Rolf J. Pöhler, *Continuity and Change in Adventist Teaching: A Case Study in Doctrinal Development* (Frankfurt Am Main: Peter Lang, 2000); George R. Knight, *A Search for Identity: The Development of Seventh-day Adventist Beliefs* (Hagerstown MD: Review and Herald, 2000).

[21]For Bates's development of "great controversy theology," see George R. Knight, *Joseph Bates: The Real Founder of Seventh-day Adventism* (Hagerstown MD: Review and Herald, 2004) 107-51.

[22]See, e.g., James White, "Time to Commence the Sabbath," 168; Knight, *Joseph Bates*, 102-103, 116, 153.

"Book." They seem to have been consistent in theory and practice in their view of the Bible as the only source of doctrinal authority and their acceptance of a modern prophet. But that would change.

The 1888 Era and Authority

The transformation in Adventism's usage of Ellen White's writings in relation to the Bible cannot be pinpointed with complete accuracy. It may have begun in the late 1870s but it is openly evident in the 1880s. That was particularly true as the denomination approached its 1888 General Conference session. That session would be one of the most significant in Adventist history. At stake was the understanding of gospel and law and how they should be related. Side topics were the definition of the law in Galatians and the ten horns of Daniel 7.[23]

In the struggle over the various topics the question of religious authority came to the forefront. Swerving from the earlier Adventist position on the absolute primacy of Scripture, the denomination's second generation leadership sought to solve their theological and biblical issues through the use of human authority related to expert opinion, authoritative position, Adventist tradition, and majority votes.[24] The reforming element that was pushing for a more Christ-centered theology rejected all appeals to human authority in solving theological and biblical issues. Ellen White, the only remaining founder of the denomination, stood firmly with the reformers in their primacy of Scripture position.

But the official leadership of the denomination not only sought to use human authority to shore up what they saw as threats to traditional Adventist theology, but also the authority of Ellen White. In the eyes of General Conference president George I. Butler an authoritative word from the pen of Ellen White would solve both the biblical and the theological issues facing the church.

Butler and his colleagues took two approaches to having Ellen White

---

[23]For discussion of the events surrounding the 1888 General Conference session, see A. V. Olson *Thirteen Crisis Years: 1888–1901* (Washington DC: Review and Herald, 1981); George R. Knight *A User-Friendly Guide to the 1888 Message* (Hagerstown MD: Review and Herald, 1998).

[24]George R. Knight, *Angry Saints: Tensions and Possibilities in the Adventist Struggle over Righteousness by Faith* (Washington DC: Review and Herald, 1989) 100-104.

solve the theological/biblical issues. The first was to have her provide a written statement on the controverted topics related to the interpretation of Galatians and Daniel. Between June 1886 and October 1888 the embattled president wrote Ellen White a series of more than a dozen letters requesting, and at times demanding, that she use her authority to settle the controversial issues.[25]

Significantly, Ellen White refused to let Butler and his colleagues use her writings to settle the theological/biblical issues dividing the denomination. She even went so far as to tell the delegates to the 1888 General Conference session on October 24 that it was providential that she had lost the one writing in which she had purportedly identified the law in Galatians. "God," she asserted, "has a purpose in this. He wants us to go to the Bible and get the Scripture evidence."[26] In other words, she rejected the position of Butler and others that sought to use her writings as an inspired commentary on the Bible.

The second strategy of the Butler coalition in the 1888 era was to use Ellen White's published writings to establish the "correct" interpretation of the controverted issues. In regard to the interpretation of the law in Galatians, for example, they quoted from her *Sketches from the Life of Paul* (1883) to arrive at the correct understanding. Once again, she rejected their maneuver, asserting: "I cannot take my position on either side until I have studied the question."[27] She was not willing to let her writings be used to settle the interpretive issue. For her, Scripture was supreme. While her writings might be used to apply scriptural principles to her context, they were not to be used authoritatively to give the final word on the meaning of Scripture. And to make sure that they would not be used improperly to solve that particular issue she had the quotations on the law in Galatians removed when she revised the book some years later.[28]

No one pounded home the primacy of scripture principle more vigorously and more often during the 1888 era of Adventist history than Ellen White. "We want Bible evidence for every point we advance," she

---

[25]Knight, *Angry Saints*, 104-107.

[26]Ellen G. White, "Morning Talk by Ellen G. White," unpub. MS 9, 24 Oct. 1888.

[27]Ellen White, "Morning Talk"; Knight, *Angry Saints*, 107-108.

[28]D. A. Parsons, in "Inspiration of the Spirit of Prophecy as Related to the Inspiration of the Bible," 1919 Bible Conference Minutes, 1 Aug. 1919, 20.

wrote to Butler in April 1887. In July 1888 she published in the leading Adventist periodical that "the Bible is the only rule of faith and doctrine." And in August she wrote to all the delegates of the forthcoming General Conference session that

> the Word of God is the great detecter of error; to it we believe everything must be brought. The Bible must be our standard for every doctrine and practice.... We are to receive no one's opinion without comparing it with the Scriptures. Here is divine authority which is supreme in matters of faith. It is the word of the living God that is to decide all controversies.[29]

The struggle over authority at the 1888 meetings apparently made an impression on the denomination's ministry. W. C. White, Ellen's son, wrote at the end of the General Conference session that "many go forth from this meeting determined to study the Bible as never before."[30]

The lessons on religious authority related to the 1888 General Conference session are crucial for evaluating the authority of the Bible in relation to prophetic authority in Seventh-day Adventism. Ellen White herself had held to the position of early Adventism. But many of the second generation leaders and ministers had moved from that well defined position and had sought to use Ellen White's prophetic authority to settle theological and exegetical issues.

A. T. Jones Sets the Stage for Problems with Authority in the Twentieth Century

One of the unfortunate developments in Adventism related to authority is that all too many Adventists in the twentieth century would take the position rejected by the founders of the denomination and by Ellen White. The leader in the move, strangely enough, was Alonzo T. Jones, one of Ellen White's reforming associates during the 1888 era. In his widely read week of prayer reading for 1894, titled "The Gifts: Their Presence and Object," Jones pointed out that the Holy Spirit is the only interpreter of the Bible and that the Spirit's "interpretation is infallible." From that proposition he moved to the role of Ellen White's testimonies, correctly using her

[29]E. G. White to G. I. Butler and U. Smith, 5 Apr. 1887; Ellen G. White, "The Value of Bible Study," *Review and Herald* (17 July 1888): 449; E. G. White to Brethren who shall assemble in General Conference, 5 Aug. 1888.
[30]W. C. White to Smith Sharp, 2 Nov. 1888.

statements that the purpose of her writings was not to provide new information, but to lead her readers to the Bible itself.[31]

Up to that point his argument seemed to be solid enough, but then he veered off into a line of thought that contradicted both biblical principles and Adventism's historic position on the relation between Ellen White's gift and the Bible. Jones wrote:

> The right use of the Testimonies, therefore, is not to use them *as they are in themselves*, as though they were apart from the word of God in the Bible; but to study the Bible *through them*, so that the things brought forth in them we shall see and know for ourselves *are in the Bible*; and then present those things to others *not from the Testimonies* themselves, but *from the Bible itself*. . . . This and this alone is the right use of the Testimonies, whether used privately or publicly. . . . This of itself will make us all "mighty in the Scriptures."[32]

Jones's argument, while intended to maintain the primacy of the Bible, actually subordinated it to Ellen White's writings. Thus, for Jones and those sharing his logic, her writings came to be viewed as a divine, infallible commentary on the Bible. That, of course, was the very position that Ellen White had rejected in the theological struggles surrounding the 1888 meetings.

The divine, infallible-commentary use of Ellen White's writings, an approach that gave Ellen White the final word on the meaning of Scripture, was one of several problems related to authority that the influential Jones bequeathed to twentieth-century Adventism.[33] In fifty years the position of many Adventists on the authority of Ellen White in relation to that of the Bible had been totally transformed from the position of the denomination's founders.

Adventists and Religious Authority in the Twentieth Century

The A. T. Jones approach to the authority of Ellen White in relation to the

---

[31]Alonzo T. Jones, "The Gifts: Their Presence and Object," *Home Missionary* extra (Dec. 1894): 12.

[32]Jones, "The Gifts," 12.

[33]On Jones's problematic contributions, see George R. Knight, *From 1888 to Apostasy: The Case of A. T. Jones* (Washington DC: Review and Herald, 1987) 230-39.

authority of the Bible took firm hold of large sectors of Adventism early in the twentieth century, even though there were influential voices arguing against it. The first major struggle in the new century on the authority issue was stimulated by a controversy over the identity of the "daily" (KJV) of Daniel 8:11, 12, 13. In that struggle, those who advocated the older interpretation held that the new one would subvert the denomination's theology because a statement in Ellen White's *Early Writings* supported the traditional Adventist interpretation. The leader of those advocating the older interpretation argued that to make any change in the established position would undermine Mrs. White's authority. He was quite explicit on his view of the relation of her writings to the Bible. "We ought to understand such expressions by the aid of the Spirit of Prophecy [that is, Ellen White's writings]. . . . For this purpose the Spirit of Prophecy comes to us. . . . All points are to be solved" in that manner.[34]

Ellen White disagreed with the argument. She requested that her writings "not be used" to settle the issue:

I entreat of Elders Haskell, Loughborough, Smith, and others of our leading brethren, that they make no reference to my writings to sustain their views of "the daily." . . . I cannot consent that any of my writings shall be taken as settling this matter.[35]

Thus in both the struggles over "the daily" and the law in Galatians, Ellen White took the position that her comments were not to be used as if she were an infallible commentator to settle the meaning of the Bible.

W. C. White also provides us with an interesting insight into the issue of his mother's relationship to the Bible. He wrote that

Some of our brethren are much surprised and disappointed because Mother does not write something decisive that will settle the question as to what is "the daily" and thus bring an end to the present disagreement. At times I have hoped for this, but as I have seen that God has not seen fit to settle the matter by a revelation thru His messenger, I have come more and more to believe that it was the will of God that a thorough study should be made of the Bible and history, till a clear understanding of the truth was gained.[36]

[34]S. N. Haskell to W. W. Prescott, 15 Nov. 1907.
[35]E. G. White, "Our Attitude toward Doctrinal Controversy," unpub. MS 11, 31 July 1910.
[36]W. C. White to P. T. Magan, 31 July 1910.

Ellen White's refusal to function as an infallible Bible commentator should not have surprised anyone. She had not assumed that role in the past, but had always pointed people to their need to study the Bible for themselves. Never did she take the position that "you must let *me* tell you what the Bible really means."

In spite of Ellen White's clarity on the topic, the battle over the identity of "the daily" rumbled along for more than two decades. The topic of "the daily" itself wasn't all that crucial. The real issue was Ellen White's authority as a divine commentator on Scripture. Such titles as *Have We an Infallible "Spirit of Prophecy"?* reflect the sentiments of those who were so concerned with the topic that in 1922 they utilized the issue of Ellen White's authority to overthrow Arthur G. Daniells, who had been president of the General Conference of Seventh-day Adventists since 1901.[37]

The authoritative role of Ellen White was not just a preoccupation with denominational dissidents. Leaders at the center of the church also espoused it. Thus F. M. Wilcox, influential editor of the denomination's *Review and Herald*, could claim in 1921 that her writings "constitute a spiritual commentary on the Scriptures." And in 1946 Wilcox asserted before the General Conference session that Ellen White's writings were

> far above all other commentaries [because they were] inspired commentaries, motivated by the promptings of the Holy Spirit. . . . The one who fails to make this distinction reveals that he has little if any faith in the doctrine of spiritual gifts in their application to the church today.[38]

By mid-century the Wilcox position had become by far the dominant one in the church. So much so that the extensive *Seventh-day Adventist Bible Commentary* (1953–1957) had a section for unpublished and out of print Ellen White remarks at the end of each volume and a list of references to her published usages of various texts after the discussion of each biblical

[37]Claude E. Holmes, *Have We an Infallible "Spirit of Prophecy"?* (N.p.: by the author, 1920); Knight, *A Search for Identity*, 139. For a helpful treatment of issues surrounding the battle over the daily, see Gilbert Murray Valentine, "William Warren Prescott: Seventh-day Adventist Educator" (Ph.D. diss., Andrews University, 1982) 389-426.

[38]F. M. Wilcox, "The Study of the Bible, Aided by the Writings of the Spirit of Prophecy," *Review and Herald* (3 Feb. 1921): 2; F. M. Wilcox, "The Testimony of Jesus," *Review and Herald* (9 June 1946): 75.

chapter. That very arrangement led people to see her writings more than ever as an inspired commentary on the Bible.

The denomination by and large hadn't learned much from its history. Nor had it learned the lessons of Ellen White's refusal to let her writings be used in commentary fashion in such struggles as those over the law in Galatians and the identity of the daily.

Up to her death in 1915 she sounded the same message on the relation of her writings to the Bible that she and her husband had at the beginning of the Adventist movement. In 1903, for example, she wrote that "little heed is given to the Bible, and the Lord has given a lesser light to lead men and women to the greater light."[39] All through her ministry she held that a major function of her writings was to lead people to the Bible.

As to the authority of the Bible, she continued to hold the position that the Adventist pioneers had inherited from the William Kinkade tradition. "In His word," she noted in 1911,

> God has committed to men the knowledge necessary for salvation. The Holy Scriptures are to be accepted as an authoritative, infallible revelation of His will. They are the standard of character, the revealer of doctrines, and the test of experience. . . . The Spirit was not given—nor can it ever be bestowed—to supersede the Bible; for the Scriptures explicitly state that the word of God is the standard by which all teaching and experience must be tested.

She went on, as had Kinkade and the early Adventist leaders, to indicate that "after the close of the canon of the Scripture" the Holy Spirit still continued his rightful work, including the gift of prophecy, and would do so until the Second Advent.[40]

Others may have drifted from the position of early Adventism on the authority of Ellen White in relation to the Bible, but she appears to have kept on course. And she was not the only one. The denomination's 1919 Bible conference of church administrators and religion teachers is remarkable for its openness on the topic. C. L. Benson, for example, pointed out disapprovingly that many Adventists put more emphasis on Ellen White's writings than the Bible.[41] And A. G. Daniells, the denomination's president,

---

[39]Ellen G. White, "An Open Letter," *Review and Herald* (20 Jan. 1903): 15.

[40]Ellen Gould Harmon White, *The Great Controversy between Christ and Satan: The Conflict of the Ages in the Christian Dispensation* (1911; repr.: Mountain View CA: Pacific Press, 1950) vii-ix.

[41]"The Use of the Spirit of Prophecy in Our Teaching of Bible and History,"

was much closer to James and Ellen White and the other pioneers of Seventh-day Adventism than he was to some of his contemporaries when he remarked that "we are to get our interpretation from this Book [the Bible], primarily. I think that the Book explains itself, and I think we can understand the Book, fundamentally, through the Book, without resorting to the Testimonies to prove up on it." W. E. Howell, education director of the General Conference, noted that "the spirit of prophecy says the Bible is its own expositor." To that comment Daniells responded:

> Yes, but I have heard ministers say that the spirit of prophecy is the interpreter of the Bible. I heard it preached at the General Conference some years ago [by A. T. Jones], when it was said that the only way we could understand the Bible was through the writings of the spirit of prophecy.

J. M. Anderson added that "he also said 'infallible interpreter.' " Daniells responded by observing that that "is not our position, and it is not right that the spirit of prophecy is the only safe interpreter of the Bible. That is a false doctrine, a false view. It will not stand."

Daniells went on to note correctly that the Adventist pioneers

> got their knowledge of the Scriptures as they went along through the Scriptures themselves. It pains me to hear the way some people talk, that the spirit of prophecy led out and gave all the instruction, all the doctrines, to the pioneers. . . . That is not according to the writings themselves. . . . We are told how . . . they searched these scriptures together and studied and prayed over them until they got together on them.

He then expressed his dismay at those Adventists "who will hunt around to find a statement in the Testimonies and spend no time in deep study of the Book."[42]

Daniells and his colleagues in 1919 may have had a correct position on the relation of Ellen White's writings to the Bible, but their timing couldn't have been more disastrous. The 1920s would see the fundamentalist crisis over biblical authority reach an explosive climax and Adventism would be drawn into the vortex of a struggle that for them entailed not only biblical issues but also issues related to Ellen White's authority. Those who spoke openly at the 1919 Bible conference, including the denomination's leader,

1919 Bible Conference Minutes, 30 July 1919, 39.

[42]"The Use of the Spirit of Prophecy in Our Teaching of Bible and History," 9-11.

would lose their jobs. Meanwhile, the minutes of this very open meeting were purposefully locked up "in a vault" where they were lost for six decades. The conference was forgotten along with the position on authority held by Ellen White and the founders of Seventh-day Adventism.[43]

The middle decades of the twentieth century found Adventists more and more using Ellen White's writings to both settle biblical issues and to do theology. Few would have openly admitted that they were putting Ellen White's authority above that of the Bible, but their writings and discussions indicated that all too many Adventists (if not most) were spending more time with Ellen White than with the Bible. She had for most of them become the final word on any biblical passage that she had utilized and a doctrinal authority. A word from Ellen White tended to end discussion. The official position of the denomination may not have changed but practice certainly had. By the 1960s the new practices had become firmly entrenched and it appeared to most Adventists that that is how their church had always utilized Ellen White's authority.

Toward a Healthier Perspective

Those days of historical innocence began to crumble in 1970 when *Spectrum* (an Adventist publication independent of the church) and a new generation of academically trained historical and biblical scholars began publishing articles on Ellen White calling for a critical reexamination of her writings. In the next decade and a half nearly every aspect of her work was rigorously examined, including her role in doctrinal formation in early Adventism and the relationship of the authority of her writings to the Bible.[44] Between the early 1980s and the late 1990s the historic pattern of that relationship as outlined earlier in this paper was becoming more well known among significant sectors of the leadership, clergy, and reading laity of the denomination.

Significantly, in 1981 Robert Olson, director of the Ellen G. White

---

[43]Donald E. Mansell, "How the 1919 Bible Conference Transcript Was Found," unpub. MS, 6 July 1975; [Donald E. Mansell], "Sequence of Materials in the 1919 Bible Conference Transcript and Papers," unpub. MS, ca. 1975, xiii; Molleurus Couperus, "The Bible Conference of 1919," *Spectrum* (May 1979): 23-26.

[44]For a brief summary of the debates over Ellen White in the late twentieth century, see Knight, *A Search for Identity*, 184-88.

Estate,[45] faced the problems inherent in the infallible commentary approach when he wrote that

> to give an individual complete interpretive control over the Bible would, in effect, elevate that person above the Bible. It would be a mistake to allow even the apostle Paul to exercise interpretive control over all other Bible writers. In such a case, Paul, and not the whole Bible, would be one's final authority.[46]

Olson went on to note that "Ellen White's writings are generally homiletical or evangelistic in nature and not strictly exegetical." In fact, she often accommodated the words of a text to her own homiletical needs. Thus she could derive quite different meanings from the same passage, depending on her purpose. Olson does note correctly that she sometimes interprets texts exegetically, even though she "generally" spoke homiletically.[47] But that fact does not imply that she ever claimed to be a divine commentary on Scripture.

In the early twenty-first century mainline Adventism has a healthier understanding of the relationship between Ellen White's authority and that of the Bible. Its theologians and biblical interpreters have a better grasp of the biblical position and that of the founders of the church, including Ellen White herself. In practice that means that she is neither a determiner of doctrine nor the final word on the meaning of Scripture. But old habits and ways of thinking die hard for some, even when they know the facts. And there are many mainline Adventists who haven't even caught up with the facts yet. But when all is said and done mainline Adventism is light years ahead of where it was in 1980 in its understanding of Ellen White's authority.

The same cannot be said for sectarian Adventism. The perfectionistic, fundamentalistic subdenominations within the denomination still largely rely on Ellen White for their theology and have no problem viewing her as

---

[45]In her will Ellen White established the Ellen G. White Estate, Inc., to be in charge of her literary estate. Its offices are located in the General Conference of Seventh-day Adventists world headquarters building in Silver Spring MD.

[46]Robert W. Olson, *One Hundred and One Questions on the Sanctuary and on Ellen White* (Washington DC: Ellen G. White Estate, 1981) 41.

[47]Olson, *One Hundred and One Questions*, 41-42; George R. Knight, *Reading Ellen White: How to Understand and Apply Her Writings* (Hagerstown MD: Review and Herald, 1997).

an infallible commentary on the Bible. This sector of Adventism has even developed an Ellen White study Bible that has Ellen White notes and marginal references.[48] Such a Bible would have been totally rejected in early Adventism. Even though the study Bible is published by an independent group it is unfortunately marketed by the main denominational publisher. Some years ago I persuaded the publishing house administration to drop its marketing of the Ellen White study Bible on the grounds that Ellen White would vigorously object to it from what we know of her principles historically. But after some months the publishing house president phoned me, notifying me that they were reversing their decision because there was a demand for the study Bible and it sells well. So much for higher principles!

Sectarian Adventist groups are critical of mainline Adventism for its "betrayal" of the prophet and often consider themselves in one form or another to be the true historic Adventists. Unfortunately, their understanding of history focuses on the period from the 1920s through the 1950s and the approach to Ellen White's writings set forth by A. T. Jones in the 1890s. They have failed to capture the biblical understanding of the founders of the denomination, including that of Ellen White herself.

I mentioned at the beginning of this chapter that the question of religious authority was doubly interesting in a Christian movement that believes in the authority of Scripture but also claims to have had an inspired prophet as one of its founders. It certainly has been so in Adventism in the past and it looks like it will continue to be so in the future. Overall, Adventism since the 1880s has done better in relating the two in theory than in practice. But the founders, including Ellen White, managed to be consistent in both theory and practice. Those Adventists who understand their history on the topic are in an advantaged position to harmonize the two today. But those who remain innocent of that history will most likely continue the problematic approach of the mid-twentieth century, all the while proclaiming that they have it right.

---

[48]*KJV Study Bible with Ellen White Comments* (Hagerstown MD: Review and Herald Publishing Association, 2007) and *Holy Bible: Color Study Bible, Authorized King James Version* (Harrah OK: Mission Publishing, 2009) "E. G. White comments" and "Scripture index to the writings of Ellen G. White."

LIVING GOD'S MISSION IN A CREATED WORLD

David Neff

In an October 2005 e-mail message to the conference presenters, Professor Millet observed that a number of us had made transitions from one tradition to another. And he thought that would bring an interesting flavor to the discussion. So, I beg your leave to begin this reflection on a personal note.

Most of us don't have to ponder questions of religious authority most of the time. In his *Westminster Handbook to Evangelical Theology*, Roger Olson says that "some critics might say evangelical theologians are obsessed with issues of authority for belief."[1] And given the way some evangelical theologians have written in the past, *obsession* is not an entirely inapt word.

But as an evangelical Protestant believer, I don't sit about wondering whether the Bible is really authoritative for faith and practice. Nor do I worry that maybe my forebears got it wrong and that really I should be guiding my life by papal pronouncements. It is in the nature of our lives as religious persons that when we are convinced members of a believing community we turn our attention to other questions—usually to the presenting issues that require us to *apply* our received source of authority.

As an evangelical in the Episcopal Church USA, I have in recent years had to ask how to *apply* what the Bible says about same-sex eroticism to the contemporary scene. The Episcopal Church's general laxity on this issue was transformed into a crisis of identity by the 2003 election, consent, and consecration of V. Gene Robinson as bishop of New Hampshire. A openly gay man, divorced from his wife and now living with a male partner, his elevation to the office of bishop posed a series of questions that pitted the "authority" of the church's governing body against the "authority" of Scripture, the "authority" of prior church teaching, and the "authority" of the worldwide Anglican communion to which the Episcopal Church belongs (at least for the time being). The past few years have been devoted to the sorting out of the way these competing authorities relate to each other. The process is not over, and I ask myself whether my patience will last as long as the process takes. One thing I do know: my sense of the authority of Scripture is stronger than my sense of these other authorities, and the form of my future commitments will definitely be shaped by that fact.

With consideration of these competing authorities, comes a crisis in

---

[1]Roger E. Olson, *The Westminster Handbook to Evangelical Theology* (Louisville: Westminster/John Knox Press, 2004) 151.

identity, for it is now difficult to believe that one is governed by the authority of Scripture and that one is fully Episcopalian at the same time; it is difficult to believe that one is fully Episcopalian and fully Anglican at the same time; it is difficult to think of oneself as belonging to a church that values its catholicity and to a church that vaunts itself as progressive at the same time.

In October 2003, just several months after the consecration of Gene Robinson, my own bishop held a public forum in which he tried to address the concerns of lay Episcopalians about his support for Robinson's consecration. In that forum, I had the opportunity to pose two questions, and my bishop's answers were very revealing.

The first question was relatively open-ended and allowed him simply to explain himself. I asked: "What theology or theological principle guided your decision to support Bishop Robinson's election?"

His answer was that it was no theology that guided him, but his own years of pastoral experience with gays and lesbians when he had been a parish priest in Los Angeles.

My second question was more specific: "Given our confession that the church is *catholic*, and given the time-honored rule of catholicity—St. Vincent's famous dictum that "that which has been believed everywhere, always, and by all. That is truly and properly 'Catholic'—and given the radical break that this action made with two millennia of belief and practice, how can you still affirm the church's catholicity?"

The bishop dismissed the received notion of catholicity and suggested that for some people, catholicity is to be found in the ever-increasing diversity of the church.

In these exchanges, it became clear to me that my own bishop did not think theologically, did not employ any principle of authority in considering such a volatile and potentially destructive problem, and certainly did not pay attention to what G. K. Chesterton dubbed "the democracy of the dead."

I was stymied. I had no idea how I could in the future have any fruitful dialog with this church leader. By his empty answers he effectively destroyed his own authority for believers like me. My ability to continue to function within the Episcopal Church was now tied to the organic vitality of my local congregation, the continuing fidelity of my own pastor to the Scriptures, and my sense of participation in the worldwide Anglican Communion—something that was seriously enhanced by means of internet communication with likeminded believers across the continent and the globe. That I placed congregational identity above identification with my bishop and diocese was a very un-Episcopal thing to do. Perhaps it was a very Baptist thing to do. But during a difficult time of transition, it has served to help keep me sane.

This is not the first time my belief in scriptural authority put me in tension with the religious community that was my spiritual family. I was born into a Seventh-day Adventist home, raised in a Seventh-day Adventist church, educated in Seventh-day Adventist schools, ordained into Christian ministry by Seventh-day Adventist hands, and employed as pastor and teacher by the Seventh-day Adventist Church. In the 1970s, I found myself torn between the teachings of the Seventh-day Adventist Church and what I believed to be the best scholarly reading of Scripture—and torn between what appeared to be the exercise of brute "authority" by church leadership and loyalty to an honorable and careful scriptural scholar whose teaching was at odds with that denomination's traditions. In this earlier chapter in my life, the renegade figure was not someone (as in the case of Bishop Robinson) whose life and ministry were at odds with fidelity to Scripture. Instead, the renegade— Australian Desmond Ford—was a careful scholar, trained under F. F. Bruce, devoted to Scripture and the integrity of the faith. Ford's reading of Scripture was not my only point of contention with received Seventh-day Adventist tradition, but it was the catalyst that brought to a head the assorted tensions that already existed.

At that time in my life (the late 1970s), I made a conscious decision to relocate into another religious community. And I identified with the broad stream of Evangelical Protestantism as I had come to understand it, largely through contact with the campus ministry InterVarsity Christian Fellowship. In the event, I relocated from Walla Walla, Washington, to Downers Grove, Illinois; I left the employ of the Seventh-day Adventist Church and went to work for InterVarsity Press; and I left membership in the Adventist Church and followed the train of other evangelicals on the so-called "Canterbury Trail."[2]

---

[2]Robert Webber et al., *Evangelicals on the Canterbury Trail: Why Evangelicals Are Attracted to the Liturgical Church* (Waco TX: Word Books, 1985).

Transition and Eschatology

As I said above, times of crisis do not usually force us to reevaluate our sources of authority, but simply to think afresh about how those sources of authority are applied. In both the Adventist debates of the 1970s and Anglican debates at the beginning of the twenty-first century, I have simply thought afresh about the meaning and import of scriptural authority for the presenting issues of the day.

But times of crisis may also throw us into periods of transition, and in this liminal experience of transition, we reflect more deeply not merely on how to apply our sources of authority, but on the very nature of those authorities. Such was my experience as I moved away from the church of my childhood into I knew not what, and such is my experience now, as I continue to function in my Episcopal congregation, but with my sense of religious identity teetering on a threshold.

There is something of the eschatological in every time of transition: some old context is unraveling, coming apart, and coming to an end, even as something new (though unknown) is beginning. The writers of the New Testament clearly had that liminal sense—but unlike my own personal transitions, they claimed that their time of transition was cosmic in scope—and a critical hinge in history. Paul believed that "the end of the ages had come upon" him and other first-generation followers of Jesus. The old revelation that came through Moses had been fulfilled; the seed that was there had sprouted, put forth its leaves, and borne its fruit. The firstfruits of the harvest had come in the life, death, and resurrection of Jesus the Messiah. And indeed, "if anyone is in Messiah, creation is new" (εἴ τις ἐν Χριστῷ, καινὴ κτίσις·, 2 Cor. 5:17). The sweep of God's story has come full circle: Creation. Fall. Promise. Covenant. Torah. Apostasy. Prophecy. Restoration. Incarnation, death, and resurrection. Creation renewed. And the creation renewed in Jesus will be completely renewed for all.

The apostle Paul relates this sense of eschatological transition to scriptural authority in 1 Corinthians 10. There he expounded the meaning of the received Scriptures for his time, and he did so by means of a midrash on Psalm 78. The point of that Psalm is the necessity of passing on to the next generation knowledge of God's torah.

> He decreed statutes for Jacob
> and established the law in Israel,
> which he commanded our forefathers

> to teach their children,
>   so the next generation would know them,
>   even the children yet to be born,
>   and they in turn would tell their children.   (Ps. 78:5-6 NIV)

That is the positive purpose: to ensure the inclusion of the future generations in the torah-guided covenant people. Negatively, this is done so that
future generations will not repeat the idolatrous apostasy of their forebears.

> Then they would put their trust in God
>   and would not forget his deeds
>   but would keep his commands.
> They would not be like their forefathers—
>   a stubborn and rebellious generation,
> whose hearts were not loyal to God,
>   whose spirits were not faithful to him.   (Ps. 78:7-8 NIV)

Then follows a recital of God's saving miracles, his mighty acts in
providing escape through the Red Sea, of guiding his people with a cloud
by day and fire by night, of providing water from the rock, of giving manna
in the wilderness, and so forth.

Then the Psalmist writes:

> But they continued to sin against him,
>   rebelling in the desert against the Most High.
> They willfully put God to the test
>   by demanding the food they craved.   (Ps. 78:17-18 NIV)

Now we turn to 1 Corinthians 10. Paul recalls the same elements of the
Exodus story: the passage through the sea, the cloud, the food in the
wilderness, the water from the rock. And he interprets these in sacramental
terms: baptism, Eucharist, and beneath it all, the Rock, who is Christ. Then
he follows with a series of warnings against the infidelities God's people
committed in the desert: idolatry, sexual immorality, putting God to the test,
and grumbling. And he adds:

> These things happened to them as examples and were written down as
> warnings for us, on whom the fulfillment of the ages has come. So, if you think
> you are standing firm, be careful that you don't fall!   (1 Cor. 10:11-12 NIV)

Whereas Psalm 78 is focused on the well-being of future generations,
Paul is focused on the wholeness and holiness of a transitional generation,
a generation standing at a threshold—the generation "upon whom the ful-

fillment of the ages has come." And his wisdom for the transitional generation is twofold. Negatively it is to avoid idolatry, sexual immorality, grumbling, and putting God to the test. Positively, it is to perceive and receive Christ.

This perceiving and receiving is *sacramental* (that is, it happens in the one-time baptismal washing and in the regular, repeated anamnesis meal of the believing community).

This perceiving and receiving of Christ is also *scriptural*: these narratives of Israel's experience with God were written not only so that we can avoid incurring God's wrath, but also so that we can see Christ embedded in the stories of water gushing from a rock and the manna.

And beyond this, the perceiving and receiving of Christ is also *creational*, that is, it is in finding the proper Jesus-like relation to the created world of which Jesus is Lord. In the verses that follow, Paul discusses Christian freedom and the dangers of living in a pagan culture by reminding his readers that "the earth is the Lord's and everything in it" (1 Cor. 10:26; cf. Ps. 24:1) and by pointing them to their appointed purpose: "Whether you eat or drink, or whatever you do, do all to the glory of God" (1 Cor. 10:31).

Creation, Holiness, Narrative

I would like to use Paul's figural reading of Psalm 78 and indeed of Israel's history to highlight three impulses or urges regarding scriptural authority that I see in myself and in my particular corner of the evangelical movement. I will summarize the recent contributions of several evangelical theologians: two New Testament scholars, one systematic and one historical theologian, and one prominent spiritual writer. I will introduce them one at a time, but first, let me list those three impulses. Those impulses/urges are first, the creational, second, the impulse toward holiness, and third, the revisioning of authority in narrative terms.

These three are intertwined. The creational dimension is related to the sacramental and the scriptural. In the sacramental dimension we come to see God's ways of being present to us through created things. And in the scriptural dimension, we learn God's story in order to learn his ways, and to learn what chapter in that story we are living out, and finally, because we know his ways, and we know what part of the story we are living, we live both our quotidian routines and our challenges to heroic sacrifice in the concrete context of a creation that is both passing away and being renewed.

Second, our concept of biblical authority is shaped by this creational context in order that we might use the Bible for its right purpose or purposes. (I taught my children when they were young how important it is to use a toy or a tool for the purpose it is made for. Misuse makes for broken toys and dull tools. How much more important with Scripture.)

To be creational means, among other things, to be concerned with our embodied state, and therefore with our behavior and the way that behavior shows love for God and love for neighbor—how it contributes to or detracts from God's mission to renew his creation and how it builds up others who share our creatureliness.

Some older Protestant treatments of biblical authority have had a tendency to treat the Bible as a repository of truths. This is an essentially epistemological notion of Scripture, which, if it fails to take into account everything else Scripture is, fails us. Listen to the emphasis on reformation of life and active goodness in 2 Timothy 3:16-17, the locus classicus for Protestant thinking about Scripture:

> All Scripture is God-breathed and is useful for teaching, rebuking, correcting, and training in righteousness, so that the man of God may be thoroughly equipped for every good work.   (2 Timothy 3:16-17 NIV)

The word *teaching* here should be understood to reflect the notion of *torah*, which is divine wisdom for living. Think of the Psalms that celebrate the benefits of personally appropriating God's teaching. For example, these verses from Psalm 119:

> Teach me, O LORD, to follow your decrees;
>   then I will keep them to the end.
> Give me understanding, and I will keep your law
>   and obey it with all my heart.   (Ps. 119:33-34 NIV)

And note the rest of the 2 Timothy passage is clearly ethical: "rebuking, correcting, and training in righteousness, so that the man of God [that is, messenger of God] may be thoroughly equipped for every good work."

James Edwards, who teaches New Testament at Whitworth College, recently devoted his *Edwards Epistle* newsletter to the authority of Scripture. He also sees practical wisdom as the point of Paul's teaching about Scripture. Here is an extended extract from Edwards.

> The value and power of Scripture, we could say, are "practical" as opposed to "theoretical." Scripture exists to do something, not merely to be regarded as something. . . .

Curiously, theory is what Paul avoids in his definition of "God-breathed." We receive and honor Scripture in its God-intended way when we allow it to have its God-intended effect in our lives, both individual and communal. It is *ophelimos,* says Paul, "useful" or "beneficial" for the ordering and common good of the Christian community, for teaching, reproof, training in righteousness, and so forth. These practicalities have a sanctifying effect in the lives of believers: they make us *artios,* "complete," "capable," or "proficient" as God-persons, who are likewise equipped for doing good in the world. Paul seems to be saying that the authority of Scripture is not something we profess, but something we *live.* We may claim to have a high view of Scripture and not live it. It is in *living* that we show whether or not we have a high view of Scripture. . . . [G]ood works presuppose right belief, but right belief itself does not necessarily lead to good works. . . .

Jesus, the living Word of God, did not first call people to form an opinion of him and then follow him. He called them to follow him and learn in so doing who he was. Something similar happens with Scripture. Scripture does not first ask for a proper theory, but rather whether we are willing to allow it to set the saving course of our lives. When it does so, then we experience its God-breathed authority.[3]

Privileging the Script

The metaphor in 2 Timothy is one of being equipped for action. But the drama metaphor employed by Kevin Vanhoozer in *The Drama of Doctrine* also points us in this direction of lived-out wisdom. Vanhoozer, who is research professor of systematic theology at Trinity Evangelical Divinity School, does not want to deny that Scripture is a source of doctrine. After all, he is in the doctrine business. After referring to some of the challenges to the use of Scripture alone as a criterion for doctrine (such as a focus on "traditions of use" or on Scripture's sacramental and poetic uses), he states, "An even happier scenario would be one in which we did not have to choose between the Bible's truth and its affective power!"[4]

But even as Vanhoozer is working to keep space open for doctrine, he is pushing our understanding of doctrine in the direction of *wisdom.* In his introduction to *The Drama of Doctrine,* he writes, "The present work seeks to move theology away from theoretical knowledge in order to reorient it

---

[3]James Edwards, *The Edwards Epistle* 14/3 (Fall 2005).
[4]Kevin Vanhoozer, *The Drama of Doctrine: A Canonical Linguistic Approach to Christian Theology* (Louisville: Westminster/John Knox Press, 2005) 12.

toward wisdom."[5] And in the next paragraph, "Theological knowledge is neither merely theoretical nor instrumental; it has less to do with *scientia* than with *sapientia*."[6] He then unpacks the distinction by quoting Ellen Charry, "Sapience includes correct information about God but emphasizes attachment to that knowledge. Sapience is engaged knowledge that emotionally connects the knower to the known."[7]

Now we turn to Vanhoozer's dramatic metaphor, which is worked out in detail and in dialogue with many critical and postmodern voices. If we think of the narrative of Scripture, with all its moments of tragedy and triumph, and we think of doctrine as a kind of script that tells us the various acts and scenes and roles—and that also tells us where we as players are in that story—then we can see that doctrine essentially calls us to act out our part as the time has come for our turn in the drama. "According to our revitalized Scripture principle," Vanhoozer writes, "the divine author is not merely a teacher, who passes on propositional truths or a narrator who conveys the discourse of others but a dramatist who does things in and through the dialogical action of others."[8]

In dealing with the *performance* of doctrine, Vanhoozer urges on us a particular kind of performance, which he calls Performance I. Performance always requires interpretation. (Think of all the different actors you've seen play Hamlet and how widely their interpretations differ.) The kind of performance we are called to is not to act as a second author (as some stage actors might do). We are instead called to "answerability"—"*acknowledging* what the playwright is doing in the many voices in Scripture and *responding* to it in an appropriate manner." This approach to performance, he says, "privileges the script, . . . yet it does so without neglecting the significance of the reader's response or the context of the interpreting community."[9]

We are not called just to speak our lines, Vanhoozer says, but to improvise. But when he speaks of improvisation, he does not mean some kind of "out of the blue" spontaneity. Rather, he says, the church improvises "not out of a desire to be original, but out of a desire to minister the gospel

---

[5]Vanhoozer, *The Drama of Doctrine*, 13.
[6]Vanhoozer, *The Drama of Doctrine*, 13.
[7]Vanhoozer, *The Drama of Doctrine*, 13.
[8]Vanhoozer, *The Drama of Doctrine*, 179.
[9]Vanhoozer, *The Drama of Doctrine*, 180.

in new contexts."

His historical example? "Rote memorization of one's lines falls short of understanding," he writes. "The Arians could affirm Jesus' statement 'The Father and I are one' (John 10:30), but it fell to Athanasius to explain what the words meant. *Homoousios* was Athanasius's 'improvised' response to the new question concerning the nature of the Son of God. The answer was improvised, not out of the blue but out of the canonical script, out of passages that spoke of [the] Son's being 'only begotten' and the like."[10]

Vanhoozer's dramatic notion of doctrine and scriptural authority thus push us in the direction of acting faithfully in response to the divine playwright's authorial intent, having to improvise new lines to act out the gospel in new contexts.

A Five-Act Hermeneutic

Other thinkers are not far behind Vanhoozer in employing similar narrative approaches. In his 2005 book *The Last Word: Beyond the Bible Wars to a New Understanding of the Authority of Scripture*, N. T. Wright, builds on the work of Vanhoozer as well as on his previous New Testament scholarship. Wright, who is the Anglican Bishop of Durham, wants to rescue the notion of biblical authority from various challenges. But he also thinks we cannot simply turn the clock back to the Reformation. "What we miss today, as we read the Reformers," he says,

> is something which is vital within scripture itself but which, in their attention to the details, they were not concerned to stress: [and that is] the great *narrative* of God, Israel, Jesus, and the world coming forward into our own day and looking ahead to the eventual renewal of all things.[11]

In *The New Testament and the People of God*, Wright outlined a "five-act hermeneutic" in which the five acts are creation, fall, Israel, Jesus, and the church. These "constitute the differentiated stages in the divine drama which scripture itself offers."[12]

Here is how scriptural authority works, Wright says:

---

[10]Vanhoozer, *The Drama of Doctrine*, 128.

[11]N. T. Wright, *The Last Word: Beyond the Bible Wars to a New Understanding of the Authority of Scripture* (San Francisco: HarperSanFrancisco, 2005) 76.

[12]Wright, *The Last Word*, 121.

Those who live in this fifth act [the church] have an ambiguous relationship with the four previous acts, not because they are being disloyal to them but precisely because they are being loyal to them as part of the story. . . . We must act in the appropriate manner for *this* moment in the story; this will be in direct continuity with the previous acts (we are not free to jump suddenly to another narrative, a different play altogether), but such continuity also implies discontinuity, a moment where genuinely new things can and do happen. We must be ferociously loyal to what has gone before and cheerfully open about what must come next.[13]

Notice again that the emphasis here is on how Scripture informs our action. At another point in *The Last Word*, Wright draws on Telford Work's book *Living and Active*[14] to affirm that

It is enormously important that we see the role of scripture not simply as being to provide *true information about*, or even accurate running commentary upon, the work of God in salvation and new creation, but as taking an active part *within* that ongoing purpose. . . . Scripture is there to be a means of God's action in and through us—which will include, but go far beyond, the mere conveying of information.[15]

Ancient-Future Authority

Another evangelical voice who understands authority in terms of God's story is Robert Webber, who holds the Myers Chair of Ministry at Northern Seminary. Webber has been a theological guru to many within the postmodern evangelical conversation called "Emergent." And Webber's books *Ancient-Future Faith* (1999), *Ancient-Future Evangelism* (2003), and *Ancient-Future Time* (2004)[16] have all recalled evangelicals to take on the strategic mode of the ancient church, which itself faced a pagan culture that resembles our dawning postmodern culture. Webber has consulted with about 300 scholars and pastors in drafting a document entitled "A Call to an Ancient Evangelical Future." This document runs only a few pages; it

---

[13]Wright, *The Last Word*, 122-23.
[14]Telford Work, *Living and Active: Scripture in the economy of salvation* (Grand Rapids MI: Eerdmans, 2001).
[15]Wright, *The Last Word*, 30.
[16]All three titles published by Baker Book House, Grand Rapids MI.

was made public in September 2006.[17] Kevin Vanhoozer and others have been very influential in its formulation, and I expect it to get a good hearing. David Neff said that three conferences have been held. Nothing is in published form yet.

In contrast to postmodernism, which attacks all metanarratives and privileges no particular story, Webber's "ancient evangelical future" asks us to rediscover the essentially narrative character of Scripture and of any truly biblical theology, while reappropriating the authority of that story for our lives—privileging it above all other narratives. Let me quote just one paragraph from this document:

> Today, as in the ancient era, the Church is confronted by a host of master narratives that contradict and compete with the gospel. The pressing question is: who gets to narrate the world? The Call to an Ancient Evangelical Future challenges Evangelical Christians to restore the priority of the divinely inspired biblical story of God's acts in history. The narrative of God's Kingdom holds eternal implications for the mission of the Church, its theological reflection, its public ministries of worship and spirituality and its life in the world. By engaging these themes, we believe the Church will be strengthened to address the issues of our day.

Following this brief statement, the document engages various aspects of the church's worship, mission, theological reflection, and spiritual formation. Like the work of Vanhoozer and Wright, the stress is on embodied holiness as part of God's mission in the world.

Webber has also written a book on the history of how Christian spirituality went wrong and the historical resources for repairing faulty spiritualities. While *The Divine Embrace* is not explicitly addressed to the question of religious authority in the way that Wright's *The Last Word* and Vanhoozer's *The Drama of Doctrine* are, it sketches out many of the same themes.

After describing the rational hermeneutic he was taught in the 1950s, Webber recalls its impact on his spirituality:

---

[17]The was in *Christianity Today* 50/9 (September 2006) and is available online at <www.christianitytoday.com/ct>; Robert Webber's own website <www.ancient futureworship.com>; that of the Grow Center at Northern Seminary where Webber taught until his death in 2007 <www.growcenter.org>; and a site dedicated to the Call for an Ancient-Evangelical Future <www.aefcall.org>.

This method of reading Scripture . . . resulted in a dry and intellectual view of the faith. The more I employed *only* the biblical, historical, and theological method, the more remote God became for me. Falling into what has been traditionally known as the "God in the box" syndrome, I became increasingly dead to Scriptures and found my study led to lifeless propositions that I could easily defend. Something was missing.

What was missing was the very heart of the Bible—the embrace of God expressed in the images that connected the two Testaments and envisioned God restoring the world. I had exchanged the divine embrace for a list of propositions. The story had become lost to me. The faith became merely an intellectual construct.[18]

Webber's remedy for this spiritual dryness is to read the Bible as the narrative of God's embrace—and to read it in a particular way, the figural and typological reading of the church fathers.

So, I invite you to read the Bible, not for bits and pieces of dry information, but as the story of God's embrace of the world told in poetic images and types. This visionary way of reading the Bible whole was the way the Bible was approached by the New Testament writers and by the early church fathers, and it was highly valued until the advent of modern biblical criticism. Today the visionary way of reading the Bible is being recovered because we live in a culture of images and types. . . . The typological reading of the Bible discloses the story of God's embrace in a pictorial way and invites us to see God not as an object of study but as the subject who acts in the world and in us to redeem and restore both.[19]

Webber's *The Divine Embrace* also echoes Wright and Vanhoozer in their emphasis on the *performance* of God's story found in Scripture: "The second part of the spiritual life is to *participate* in the purposes of God in history. We live in a theological consciousness of life shaped by the mystery of the Triune God reconciling all of life to himself."[20]

Webber argues that this theological consciousness "arises from a cluster of biblical teachings that form the Christian vision of reality." This is, he says, "a *revelational spirituality* because God has made all this known to us

---

[18]Robert E. Webber, *The Divine Embrace: Recovering the Passionate Spiritual Life* (Grand Rapids MI: Baker, 2006) 128. *The Divine Embrace* is the fourth volume in Webber's Ancient-Future series published by Baker.

[19]Webber, *The Divine Embrace*, chap. 6.

[20]Webber, *The Divine Embrace*, chap. 2.

in his mighty deeds, culminating in his Son, who is the Alpha and Omega of the universe, the one who reconciles all things to himself—authoritatively recorded for us in the inspired texts of Scripture."[21] Thus Webber affirms the essential core of the traditional evangelical approach to scriptural authority, but transforms it by insisting on its narrative character, its necessarily figural reading, and its participatory purpose.

The Truly Sovereign Self

Vanhoozer, Wright, and Webber bring different disciplines to bear on the role of the Bible and its authority. Vanhoozer specializes in hermeneutics. Wright is a New Testament scholar and a Church of England bishop. Webber is a theologian who has focused on patristics and liturgics. Yet they all sound the same themes: the authority of Scripture must be understood in terms of its narrative character and in terms of its purpose, which is to help the people of God to play their role in his mission. Eugene Peterson, a popular (but never lightweight) spiritual writer, travels in their company. A Presbyterian pastor, who was well trained in Hebrew, he came to his fame by translating *The Message*. He is currently emeritus professor of Spiritual Theology at Regent College.

Peterson begins his recent volume, *Eat This Book*, by asserting, "What is neglected is reading the Scriptures formatively, reading in order to live."[22]

Like Vanhoozer, Wright, and Webber, Peterson wants to outline an understanding of authority that is different from the factual, cognitive emphasis of neoevangelicals like Carl F. H. Henry, Harold Lindsell, and others who were reacting to the threat posed by neoorthodoxy. The "encounter" theology of the continental neoorthodox theologians was perceived as undermining confidence in the historicity of the scriptural witness. And so Henry et al. focused almost exclusively on the "propositional" nature of scriptural revelation.

Peterson, like Webber, wants to recall evangelicals from the spiritual aridity that often resulted from such propositionalism, and calls attention to the intensely personal nature of revelation. Ironically, he cites Karl Barth to underscore the inherently personal nature of revelation. "He showed, clearly and persuasively, that this 'different' kind of writing (revelatory and

---

[21]Webber, *The Divine Embrace*, 45.

[22]Eugene Peterson, *Eat This Book: A Conversation in the Art of Spiritual Reading* (Grand Rapids MI: Eerdmans, 2006) xi.

intimate instead of informational and impersonal) must be met by a different kind of reading (receptive and leisurely instead of standoffish and efficient)."[23]

> The authority of the Bible is immediately derived from the authorial presence of God. In other words, this is not an impersonal authority, an assemblage of facts or truths. This is not the bookish authority that we associate with legislation codified in a law library, or the factual authority of a textbook on mathematics. This is revelation, personally revealed—letting us in on something, telling us person to person what it means to live our lives as men and women created in the image of God.[24]

Peterson's emphasis on the personal, however, is not meant to suggest the slightest support for the autonomous self that rules over the realm of so much modern religion (whether the religion of consumerism or that of self-serving spiritualities). He contrasts the Holy Trinity that authored Scripture with the modern liberal counterfeit. In this counterfeit, "[t]he sovereign self expresses itself in Holy Needs, Holy Wants, and Holy Feelings."[25] And this substitute trinity is subtle, like the serpent. "The new Trinity doesn't get rid of God or the Bible, it merely puts them to the service of needs, wants, and feelings."[26]

For Peterson, the follower of the true Trinity does not use the Scriptures, but listens in obedience and serves: "When we privatize Scripture we embezzle the common currency of God's revelation. But Scripture is never that—the revelation draws us out of ourselves, out of our fiercely guarded individualities, into the world of responsibility and community and salvation—God's sovereignty. "Kingdom" is the primary biblical metaphor for it."[27]

Scripture is, for Peterson as for the others, essentially narrative in character, and, like the others, he understands it as not just any story, but *the* story.

> The Christian community has always read this story as not just one story among others but as the metanarrative that embraces, or can embrace, all

---

[23]Peterson, *Eat This Book*, 6.
[24]Peterson, *Eat This Book*, 24.
[25]Peterson, *Eat This Book*, 32.
[26]Peterson, *Eat This Book*, 33.
[27]Peterson, *Eat This Book*, 46.

stories. If we fail to recognize the capaciousness of this form, we will almost certainly end up treating our biblical text anecdotally as "inspiration" or argumentatively as polemic.[28]

But Peterson does not develop the dramatic metaphor to the degree that Vanhoozer and Wright do. They write of *performance*, but Peterson, standing in the tradition of ascetic theologians, focuses on *formation*. Nevertheless, the notion of dramatic performance is not entirely missing from Peterson. One chapter is titled, "Scripture as Script: Playing Our Part in the Spirit,"[29] In that context, he alludes to the dramatic metaphor: "We have our part to play in this text, a part that is given to us by the Holy Spirit. As we play our part we become *part*-icipants."[30]

It is important to realize that we have a script, writes Peterson, because

if we are "unscripted," . . . we spend our lives as anxious stutterers in both our words and actions. But when we do this rightly—performing the score, eating the book, embracing the holy community that internalizes the text—we are released into freedom: "I will run in the way of thy commandments when thou enlargest my understanding" (Ps. 119:32).[31]

Thus is freedom realized from living under the authority of the Word.

The Mission of God

Let us call to mind once again the passage from 1 Corinthians 10. Understanding that the scriptural narratives are for our instruction "upon whom the fulfillment of the ages has come," helps us keep our focus on God's intention, on the mission of God. And that mission is the restoration of wholeness to his people and to his creation through the grace and truth that have come in Messiah Jesus.

We were made to live as God's representatives in the context of creation. He is the ultimate authority; we exercise his delegated authority

---

[28]Peterson, *Eat This Book*, 46.

[29]Peterson, *Eat This Book*, 59.

[30]Peterson, *Eat This Book*, 69.

[31]Peterson, *Eat This Book*, 77. Peterson derives the notion of "performing the score" from Frances Young's *Virtuoso Theology* (Cleveland: Pilgrim, 1993). Also on p. 77, he cites Young's assertion that "music has to be 'realized' through performance and interpretation" (Young, 22) as an analogy to "the interrelated complexities of reading and living the Holy Scriptures" (Peterson, 76).

in our respective spheres of influence, whether work, home, family, church, school, etc. We were not meant to be extracted from human society, as some pictures of heaven seem to have it. While surfing the web the other day, I ran across this statement: "The Bible speaks the Creator's directions to us, like a detailed road map that clearly shows the exit ramp directly into heaven."[32]

I'm sorry, but I don't think the Bible tells me of an "exit ramp . . . to heaven." I think it tells me that the kingdom of heaven—that is, the rule of God—has broken into our world in the person of Jesus. My task is not to escape this world, but to help the world welcome the rule of God, and ultimately the renewal of creation.

In summary, I am an evangelical Protestant with a chastened belief in Scripture as the "norming norm" for Christian faith and practice. That chastened view owes a lot to John Calvin, who seemed to understand the pneumatological dimension of Scripture's inspiration and our interpretive task better than many later evangelicals. It also owes a lot to the English Puritans, who were the ultimate practitioners of a creational approach to biblical authority. It also owes a lot to the emphasis on narrative which began in the 1970s, but which is now ripening and maturing in the work of people like Vanhoozer and Wright. A lot of nonsense has been written in the name of narrative theology, but whereas appeal to narrative was once an escape from a reality-based understanding of truth, today it can be a useful tool in combating postmodern relativism.

Seattle pastor Mark Driscoll addressed this in a recent issue of the *Criswell Theological Review*. There he vented his dissatisfaction with the Emergent conversation, a small but influential current of young evangelical pastors and thinkers who play the amateur with postmodern ideas. The article is significant, because Driscoll has been one of the key voices in the so-called "Emergent conversation."

Driscoll caps his list of eight areas of concern with Emergent by addressing the issue of authority:

> This issue is perhaps the most difficult of all. Much of this conversation is happening online with blogs and chat rooms. However, as the conversation becomes a conflict, the inherent flaw of postmodernism is becoming a practical obstacle to unity because there is no source of authority to determine what

---

[32]"What Adventists Believe" <http://www.adventist.org/beliefs/>.

constitutes orthodox or heretical doctrine

With the authority of Scripture open for debate and even long-established Church councils open for discussion . . . , the conversation continues while the original purpose of getting on mission may be overlooked because there is little agreement on the message or the mission of the Church.[33]

Driscoll's lament joins with the concerns of Vanhoozer, Wright, Webber, and Peterson in focusing us on the link between scriptural authority and God's mission. Without a clear sense of scriptural authority, we may all be stuck in a mere conversation (postmodern or otherwise) and forget to act our part in the drama of creation redeemed and restored.

---

[33]Mark Driscoll, "A Pastoral Perspective on the Emergent Church," *Criswell Theological Review* 3/2 (Spring 2006): 91-92.

ON LOVING TRUTH MORE THAN RELIGION: CONFESSIONS OF A REBELLIOUS CHRISTIAN MIND

Roger E. Olson

One can hardly do justice to the subject of religious authority in a brief reflection essay. I'll have to jump in the middle and ask my audience to be generous as I make some philosophical and theological assumptions. What I intend to present here is my own interpretation and perhaps permutation of a Free Church Protestant vision of religious authority. It is influenced by baptist (with a small "b") theologian James William McClendon, Jr. who argues in his *Systematic Theology* 2, *Doctrine*, that ultimate authority is another name for the Godhood of God; all other authorities are proximate or even false authorities.[1] McClendon places Jesus Christ at the center of Christian authority and views the Bible as inspired narrative of Jesus Christ; it shares in subsidiary fashion his authority.[2] He argues that all traditions at best point toward the greater authority of Scripture and Jesus Christ and should not be allowed to "monopolize the voice of God in Scripture."[3]

McClendon's conclusion about authority resonates with the spirit of Free Church theology in general:

> In summary, when full authority is assigned to God alone, the result is the subordination of every human locus of authority. The *disciple* whose soul is competent, the *book* whose word is divine, the *church* whose fellowship is spiritual can make their claims only as *proximate* authorities, each beneath the sovereign authority of God."[4]

What I want to say here is an "Amen" to McClendon and yet point further along the trajectory he has laid out toward an identity between real religious authority and truth itself. This is not so different from what McClendon intends because we cannot separate God from truth; the two are inextricably linked. However, I want to say that even God is authoritative *because* he is the locus of truth in order to make clear that his authority is not located in his power.

With regard to liberal and conservative theologies, my impression (and that of most Free Church Protestants, I hope) is that their extremes can be

---

[1] James Wm. McClendon, Jr., *Doctrine*, vol. 2 of *Systematic Theology* (Nashville: Abingdon, 1994) 458.

[2] McClendon, *Doctrine*, 463.

[3] McClendon, *Doctrine*, 468.

[4] McClendon, *Doctrine*, 481.

and often are pernicious. The individualistic, relativistic approach taken by many liberal theologians and ministers reduces religious belief to a matter of personal taste. If Gumby can replace Jesus in the manger (as one liberal minister in my community reportedly did at a Christmas pageant) and all paths lead to God, what about Satanism? What do you say, then, to the person who wants to put Satan in the manger or, perhaps more realistically, who wants to say that Christian identity is white to the exclusion of people of color? I asked a religious liberal about that and he simply said such people would be "moral imbeciles." Oh, really? Who says? With what warrant is that the case? But the rigid, authoritarian approach of many conservatives is little better. It reduces religious belief to a matter of mindless obedience to hierarchical power. Truth can be and often is the victim of both approaches. One tosses truth aside in an orgy of relativism; the other crushes truth under a boot of ecclesiastical power.

I would like to back up from the usual starting point in this discussion of religious authority and raise a metaquestion about authority along the lines suggested by McClendon. What is authority? Or, to be more specific and therefore clearer, how do I know when to accept my own or someone else's claim to my mental agreement with an assertion or proposition? I put "my own" in that question because nobody starts out with a tabula rasa. Everyone always already has beliefs. A mature, reflective person questions his or her beliefs from time to time. But by what standard? Against what norm? And when I encounter assertions that ask for or insist on my agreement or disagreement (which often happens in religious forms of life) what should I do? I grew up under the motto "Doubt your doubts and believe your beliefs." But from a very early age I wondered if that should apply just to me and people in my church or to others as well? Would the evangelist who preached that to my congregation say it to Latter-day Saints, Roman Catholics, Muslims, Buddhists, and others not of his faith tradition? I developed a rebellious mind very early on. The very first time I heard of Descartes's principle of methodological doubt it appealed to me: Doubt everything. Of course, I hid my preference for doubt over blind belief for years because even hinting at it brought my spiritual life if not my salvation under suspicion. And now, years later, I recognize the philosophical and theological problems with giving doubt pride of place in epistemology. I prefer the motto "faith seeking understanding" and yet, I believe, honest questioning of authority is a healthy policy and practice.

But then, in my immaturity, I couldn't help but question and doubt the religious authorities of my environment. I noticed almost against my will that many of my own spiritual mentors were contradicting themselves and each other. And I noticed that some of the beliefs of churches and denominations and even religions and philosophies other than my own made sense. In spite of my nagging doubts I attended a Bible college and engaged in a four-year-long study of pastoral ministry and theology. I often tried gently to raise obvious questions about some of what was being taught and preached and the response was almost always the same. I was shut down very harshly and told not to question things but just to accept them. I was told to pray for a submissive mind and spirit. Even when I saw blatantly abusive, irresponsible, and even immoral behavior on the parts of some leaders of our denomination and college I was supposed to lay it before God and never question the leaders—even to other leaders. The atmosphere at that college was one of pervasive spiritual abuse; shame was used to manipulate and control active, inquiring minds. I was labeled "rebellious" for no other reason than that I asked difficult questions to which my teachers had no answers. I kept all the rules and was never accused of pushing the envelope in any other way; my only crime was questioning authority.

I don't remember the first time I saw the bumper sticker that says "Question Authority," but it immediately resonated with my spirit. I regarded it as self-evidently a good policy insofar as "authority" means human power to enforce conformity or submission. Authority can be merely a form of power and power corrupts, so questioning authority in the right spirit and in the right way is not only good but imperative. But I learned early on that it is also dangerous. One day I laid myself down on my bunk bed in my dormitory room and thought long and hard about all this. The provoking event was the appearance of an evangelist at our college for a "spiritual emphasis week." He was saying and doing things in chapel that seemed obviously wrong to me. His antics and teachings went against the grain of everything I had read in scripture and been taught by my best mentors and teachers and yet they were submissively sitting there allowing him to carry on. In the middle of the week I tried to approach the evangelist to ask a question but was blocked by the college president who ordered me away. Up until that point I had not said a word but had only sat at the back of the chapel observing and mentally checking everything. The president had noticed my reticence. I was branded rebellious for not going with the holy flow but doubting and questioning.

As I looked around the chapel I saw the fruit of a favorite hymn by nineteenth-century evangelist Gypsy Smith: "If I Am Dreaming, Let Me Dream On." Some of what was going on was so blatantly unreal, so manifestly contrary to common sense and even our own spiritual beliefs and practices, that I felt like I was in a dream. And the attitude of my mentors and teachers and many fellow students was "If this is a dream let us dream on because it feels so good." The truth issue was not even in question; everything was spiritual authority and spiritual submission and emotionalism. It didn't even matter that some of it just flat out contradicted plain teachings of Scripture and our own denomination's policies.

As I lay there on my back on my dorm room bed a thought occurred to me; it seemed to come out of nowhere. I was far too wet behind the ears to have heard and absorbed it or been taught it or come up with it on my own. I was just a callow and sheltered Pentecostal boy of nineteen. But the thought was this: Authority and truth are the same thing; nobody has a right to exercise authority over truth. No matter how young or inexperienced you may be if you have truth on your side even the person holding the highest office of human authority has no right to demand your mental submission. You must follow truth no matter where it leads you. Of course, I'm putting the thought into my own fifty-something-year-old words. But I believe they are faithful to the idea that fell like a bombshell on the playground of my adolescent mind in that winter of 1971. It was the most rebellious idea anyone could ever have and I immediately knew that. What suddenly became clear to me was that I was responsible for my own beliefs and had no right to give someone else the right to dictate them. But that I was responsible to truth and therefore could not just believe whatever I wanted to believe or was told to believe.

Later I encountered two sayings that became confirmations of that impression and remain mottos for my own intellectual life. First generation Anabaptist leader Balthasar Hubmaier ended each of his rebellious essays with "Truth is deathless." His appeal was always to truth even against the highest religious and political authorities and even against the greatest magisterial traditions of both Catholics and Protestants. In contrast the pusillanimous Zwingli gave the city council the right to determine the course of the Swiss Reformation along pragmatic and utilitarian lines. He reversed himself on baptism and even condoned the torture of Hubmaier when he—Zwingli—knew Hubmaier was right. (At least that is what seems to be the case; Zwingli had not long earlier agreed with the Anabaptists but turned against them when the city council threatened to stop supporting the Protestant Reformation if Zwingli continued on that course.)

Nineteenth-century English poet, critic, and philosopher Samuel Taylor Coleridge said "He who begins by loving Christianity better than Truth, will proceed by loving his own sect or church better than Christianity and end in loving himself better than all."[5] That was the second saying that captured my mind and heart; together with Hubmaier's "Truth is deathless" it serves as a compass for my own attitude and approach to religious authority. My quarrel is with folks who love Christianity or their particular sect better than truth itself. And their name is Legion. If what we are after in religion (including Christianity) is not truth we are sunk in a swamp of notions. The problem is that too many religious folks care too little about truth itself and too much about order and submission or about unfettered spiritual excitement; for them religious devotion is subservience to tradition and authority or a spiritual journey without a goal and not a search for truth.

I have come to believe firmly what occurred to me in a somewhat nebulous manner while lying on my dormitory room bed that winter day in 1971: *A person is only authoritative insofar as his or her pronouncements conform to reality or faithfully point toward it, which is just another way of saying insofar as they are true.* Put negatively, my philosophy is that *insofar as an authority's affirmations and directions fall short of being true they lack authority regardless of how high the person's throne may be.* That means that, as a teacher, I must be open to all sincere questioning of what I teach. I must be prepared to deal with honest challenges and not sweep them aside by appeal to what has always been believed or what our tradition has always said or what some authority says. "Just because I say so" not only doesn't sit well with inquiring minds, it also falls short of intellectual integrity and intellectual integrity and spiritual authority cannot be divided.

I will never forget a Baptist minister under whose pastoral leadership I sat while studying theology in Munich, Germany. He was a missionary of the Southern Baptist Convention. His closing line of a sermon on the Christian and secular culture was "The Christian's attitude toward secular culture should be 'Don't confuse me with the facts, my mind is already made up.'" With that declaration he gave up intellectual and spiritual integrity. While knowing what the "facts" are is always problematic, once one believes something to be indeed a fact, closing the mind to it is wrong.

---

[5]Samuel Taylor Coleridge, *Aids to Reflection*, aphorism xxv.

So, what is true authority in religion and in Christianity? All kinds of people, books and institutions claim authority. Some people believe that holding a certain office in the church automatically gives a person authority. I say he may have power to enforce edicts, but whether he has true authority is another matter. Some people believe ultimate authority rests in the philosophical, spiritual, and moral preferences of the transcendental self. I say truth and therefore authority transcends the self. Others believe the Bible possesses absolute authority for all matters of faith and practice. I tend to agree with them. But if it is so, it isn't because the Bible possesses authority in and of itself but because it has been found to be true. What about God? "Let God be true and every man a liar," says scripture. Indeed, God is the ultimate authority, as McClendon reminds us, but not because he has absolute power to enforce his will; even in God's case might does not make right. Rather, God's authority is linked inextricably with his being the ground and source of all truth as creator and redeemer of the universe. A God who is not true would not be God but a demiurge at best.

True religious authority, then, lies in truth itself which is ultimately in God. But under God it is correspondence with reality. Truth is the real—what really is (or was or will be) and not illusion or mere appearance or wishful thinking or what excites or comforts me. In practical terms (we Americans are always interested in cash value) this means that if the emperor has no clothes even the smallest child of no account who says so is right and ought not to be punished or silenced. In that moment the child holds the scepter of authority on that particular issue. Of course, there are better and worse settings for speaking the truth and some ways of speaking truth are better than others, but who is doing the speaking ought not to matter at all. "Let no one despise your youth," so said Paul the Apostle to Timothy (1 Tim. 4:12). And yet ever since Christians have been despising youth and poverty and low income and lack of credentials by shaming and silencing people who are simply speaking the truth. A case in point is Galileo who was only finally exonerated of all charges against him by his church in 1992. According to most historians, the church of his day knew he was right about the solar system, but he was imprisoned and persecuted for speaking the truth against the church's authority. (Please don't think I'm singling out the Catholic church here; Protestants have their share of history with suppressing and punishing dissenters!) My philosophy says Galileos must never be shut up; whenever someone discovers truth and we are convinced it is indeed the truth we must grant the authority of what he or she says regardless of how uncomfortable or inconvenient it may be.

Among evangelical Christians one of my heroes is theologian Bernard Ramm who railed against Christian obscurantism in *A Christian View of Science and Scripture.*[6] There he argued that Christians do God no service by shutting out the brute facts of science or any other discipline. Once something is a brute fact that cannot seriously be refuted without intellectual suicide, adjustments to doctrine or traditional interpretation must be made because what is at stake is truth and nothing matters more than truth. But many evangelical Christians have not heeded Ramm's advice and some have even vilified Ramm for allegedly pitting truth against the Bible. Of course, he did no such thing. He was simply insisting on a distinction between the Bible itself and anyone's interpretation of the Bible. Like Ramm, I give no human being the right to dictate how the Bible must be interpreted. To me, this is what the Baptist doctrine of soul competency means. But it isn't an expression of Enlightenment individualism or autonomy of the self; it is an expression of Hubmaier's "Truth is deathless." It is also an expression of Scripture's "The truth shall make you free" (John 8:32).

Authoritarianism that insists on mental agreement with human pronouncements regardless of truth is dangerous even, and perhaps especially in religious life. But that is not to denigrate all human authority. So what makes a person or group or written statement authoritative? That is the case when he, she, or it conforms to truth. Or, better stated, a person, group or written statement is authoritative insofar as he, she or it conforms to reality in his, her or its affirmations. Holding an office is no guarantee of that. Nor is being an ancient or widely accepted standard. Luther discovered this and insisted on it even if later he waffled. Luther was of a rebellious Christian mind. He dared to question authority and appealed to truth against it. Unfortunately, later, like Zwingli, he bowed to the authority of princes and nobility to keep them supporting the Protestant Reformation. Then Hubmaier and others had to pick up the fallen torch of "deathless truth" and many of them like Hubmaier died for questioning authority.

Nevertheless, in spite of Luther's occasional lapses, I consider him a Christian authority. I appeal to him all the time—"Luther said. . . ." I disagree with him only with fear and trembling. But he was a mere mortal and a child of his times. Even he could be and was occasionally wrong and

---

[6]Bernard L. Ramm, *The Christian View of Science and Scripture* (Grand Rapids MI: Eerdmans, 1954; repr. 1976).

insofar as he was wrong he is not an authority. He is an authority where he was right. All this, of course, raises the question of knowing when a person, group, or written affirmation is true. If he, she, or it is not authoritative and *therefore* true but only authoritative *insofar* as true, how can a person know truth in order to grant authority to another? This is where postmodernism sweeps in. Are all truth claims but masks for will to power? Think of the implications. Ultimately, avowal of that policy would lead to a war of all against all or totalitarianism. Might then makes right. Surely common sense if nothing else tells us truth is. Even most postmoderns admit it in spite of themselves. But they rightly raise the question "Whose truth?" How do we recognize truth in order to grant authority in religious life?

There cannot really be any other reliable, viable path to truth than *reason* insofar as we are talking about intersubjective truth and reason in its broadest sense. (I should make clear that in this entire essay I am bracketing out and setting aside the issue of the truth-status of rules in games and the authority of umpires; that's a different subject for a different day. Throughout this essay I am talking about "objective truth" or "True Truth," as Francis Schaeffer liked to refer to it. That is, correspondence with reality "out there" beyond social construction, subjective preference and merely analytical statements.) If I have inner conviction that God told me something I need no reason insofar as I keep it to myself and my belief in it doesn't impact others. But the moment I expect others to believe it and especially insofar as I attempt to impose it on others through any means I *must* offer reasons beyond my own inner conviction. I can ask others to be open to the same inner conviction and if they are and receive it from God, fine. Now our common reason is inner conviction. But if someone says "I don't have that inner conviction" and I expect him or her to conform to what I believe solely by inner conviction I do that person and the entire human community a disservice and injustice by attempting to make him or her accept my belief and live by it. Unless I can give reasons that persuade. One such reason is the community's common inner conviction and its transforming fruits. But hopefully I can offer other warrants such as coherence with other beliefs, "metaphysical fit" with reality, historical explanatory power, etc., etc. But merely to say "Because I say so" or "Because we say so" is not enough. It opens the door to totalitarianism and abuse. Even Scripture says "Always be prepared to offer a reason for the hope that you have in Christ Jesus" (1 Peter 3:15). Even Luther said "unless I am convinced by scripture *and reason*. . . ."

So is this just a recommendation for rational apologetics in religion? Well, if it were that would be better than a recommendation for mindless submission to authority. If the gospel and theology do not have the power to persuade reasonable and open minds they are not worth believing. Socrates said the unexamined life is not worth living; a modern philosopher of religion said that the unexamined faith is not worth believing. I agree. But that does not enshrine "autonomous, individualistic reason" as the ultimate authority. I am no fan of what theologian Helmut Thielicke called "Cartesianism" that enthrones the subjective self or the transcendental self as the source and norm of truth.[7] Truth is elusive to the individual. We are blinded by our vested interests, our limited contexts and our sinfulness. Finitude and fallenness infect all our reasoning toward truth. The solution is not abject submission to unquestionable authority but participation in a large and diverse community of seekers after truth. That is why I don't just go and sit on a mountain top and use my reason to discover truth. Because there is no such thing as a "view from nowhere." As philosopher Alisdair MacIntyre reminds us, every search for truth follows a path laid out by tradition and takes place within a community shaped by a tradition. But truth itself is higher than any person within that community or even than the community itself. Whenever a person on the path with the community discovers an unnoticed landmark that should alter the course he or she has the right and duty to say "Hey! Wait a minute! Look at this!" and hold up the whole parade until proper examination has dealt with the issue.

On a very practical note I argue that every religious community (and probably every human community) needs to nurture faithful questioners within the community. Their role would be something like the role of the jester in medieval royal courts, only instead of making jokes about the court and the crown the questioner would have the job of raising valid questions about beliefs and practices of the community. He or she would be a kind of devil's advocate. Are there beliefs that just seem not to be true because they have no basis in fact or are inconsistent with other beliefs and practices? What do outsiders think of the community's beliefs and practices and how might they need to be adjusted to appear more reasonable and attractive to sincere seekers? Are some beliefs or practices in need of reconsideration? Making this role official would declare a community's commitment to truth

---

[7]Helmut Thielicke, *The Evangelical Faith*, vol. 1, *Prolegomena* (Grand Rapids MI: Eerdmans, 1974) 30-37.

and lower the level of authoritarianism that tends to arise within especially religious traditions. Furthermore, I argue that faithful but questioning inquiring minds ought never to fear religious officials when raising questions and concerns about the truth status of their community's beliefs and practices. If the officials cannot do better than say as one Pentecostal leader said to me when I challenged the doctrine of speaking in tongues as the only initial physical evidence of Spirit-baptism "If we didn't believe it we wouldn't be Pentecostals, would we?" then they expose themselves as simply silly and irrelevant; they prove the emperor has no clothes.

In my case I left my particular Pentecostal community because authority and truth were there torn apart; religious obscurantism was the order of the day. That doesn't mean everything I believed as a Pentecostal I now believe to be false. It only means that I no longer believe in the authority of the men and women who claimed to have religious authority over me because they could not persuade me of the truth of their assertions. I thank God for the freedom so hard-won by Hubmaier and Roger Williams and others in the Free Church tradition to follow the truth elsewhere than in the place one grew up or first found religious faith. Now I live and work and worship within a different religious tradition-community. Because I don't trust my own individual judgment about truth I consult my fellow strugglers toward truth whenever I have a doubt or a question about our common beliefs. Occasionally I keep something to myself. But if the day ever comes when I am convinced we are wrong about something important I will not hesitate to question it. And one reason I'm where I am is because I've been assured that is okay; it's what I'm expected to do and even paid to do. Am I naive enough to think there won't be consequences? No. I expect them. But in principle I am committed to truth itself more than to any human authority. That even applies to the Bible (to jump right over a whole lot of other, lesser authorities in my tradition-community). I believe in the Bible's authority and submit to it insofar as I believe it to be true. Truth stands even above (or beneath—whichever metaphor works best) Scripture. Scripture is but an instrument of truth; it is only a pointer to the truth which is for me embodied in God as God is revealed in Jesus Christ. Why do I believe in Jesus Christ as God? Because of his resurrection. Why do I believe in his resurrection? Because it is the best explanation of the historical events ("it is true beyond a reasonable doubt") *and* because "he lives within my heart."

In the final analysis, then, reason *broadly conceived* guides me toward truth. If any of my beliefs can be shown to be flat-out irrational or unreason-able, which would not be as easy as many think, I would have to abandon them. For me, however, reasonableness transcends the threadbare and thin existence of logical or evidential "proof." Most important matters in life are immune to proof and disproof. Does my wife love me? I believe so. Can I prove it? Hardly. Do I have good evidence? Yes, but perhaps not the kind that would persuade someone determined to doubt her love for me. But if she hired an assassin to "do me in," I would have to question her love for me. Some things are simply incompatible with other things. Something that is compatible with anything and everything is strictly meaningless. Even in my religious faith, reason, evidence, logic play a role. But so do tradition and community as well as inner conviction. But these latter cannot serve as substitutes for intellectual persuasion. No authority of office or tradition or even community consensus can convince me to believe what my intellect cannot accept. Nor should it.

All of this inevitably raises the question of the authority of a religious community to hold and enforce beliefs and practices. Doesn't every religious community have the right to set up a *magisterium*, whether formal or informal, to sustain its distinctives and hold doctrinal drift and relativism at bay? Of course it does. But my argument is that such authority ought to be secondary to the authority of truth itself, so that should the case ever arise where a person within the community presents a convincing argument against the truth-status of one of the community's beliefs the community should bow to that greater authority and change its beliefs. However, if the dissenter cannot persuade, the community has a right to expel him or her. Then the dissenter has the right to set up his or her own new community. My question is which one—the original community and its leadership or the dissenter—has real authority in the particular situation of the issue under debate? If the dissenter was right, real authority was on his or her side whether anyone recognizes that or not. I am making a distinction here between metaphysical authority—"rightness," if you will—and legal or judicial authority which is mere power to enforce consent and conformity. But I hope we agree that might does not make right.

What I am saying is that true authority, authority of this highest and most important kind, lies on the side of right and not might. In deciding what is "right" a person ought to take into account many factors, including tradition and community consensus, but in the final analysis the person seeking truth must go with true authority against tradition and community consensus if reason in the broadest and best sense demands it. It is never right to go against reason. When rational proof is unavailable, as is often the case, a person may legitimately go with "reasons of the heart" or simply submit to tradition and community. But when these contradict themselves or prove baseless except on whims and fancies of religious leaders, the person has every right and even should break away from traditional belief and community consensus or hold belief in suspension until greater light dawns. Religious communities should respect this necessity and responsibility more than they tend to.

So, have I simply come around full circle to Kant's (after Horace) *Sapere aude!*—"Dare to know," that is, "Think for yourself"—and modernity's solipsistic emphasis on the authority of the individual, reasoning and thinking subject? First of all, if I had to choose between that and religious totalitarianism I would choose the way of the Enlightenment.

Second, however, I don't think the motto "Think for yourself" is necessarily solipsistic so long as truth is elevated above the individual's personal preferences and insofar as the individual's reasoning toward truth respects the paths forged by tradition and community. "Think *for* yourself" does not have to mean "Think *by* yourself."

Third, in the final analysis the individual really is the only one who can and must decide what he or she believes to be true—especially in matters of ultimate concern. The individual should follow reason in its broadest sense, consulting tradition and community but also interrogating them using evidence and logic in deciding what is right and true. And when the individual is *sure* he or she has discovered truth there lies his or her authority. So authority is higher than the self even if the self must ultimately recognize and acknowledge it.

CONTRIBUTORS

STEVEN C. HARPER is associate professor of Church History and Doctrine at Brigham Young University in Provo, Utah.

PETER A. HUFF is T. L. James Associate Professor of Religious Studies at Centenary College in Shreveport, Louisiana.

GEORGE R. KNIGHT is professor emeritus of Church History at Andrews University in Berrien Springs, Michigan.

GERALD R. MCDERMOTT is Jordan-Trexler Professor of Religion at Roanoke College in Salem, Virginia.

ROBERT L. MILLET is Abraham O. Smoot University Professor and professor of Religious Education at Brigham Young University in Provo, Utah.

BRADLEY NASSIF is professor of Biblical and Theological Studies at North Park University in Chicago, Illinois.

DAVID NEFF is editor-in-chief of *Christianity Today* in Carol Stream, Illinois.

RICHARD JOHN NEUHAUS, before his death in 2009, was president of the Institute on Religion and Public Life and editor-in-chief of *First Things*.

ROGER E. OLSON is professor of Theology at George W. Truett Theological Seminary of Baylor University in Waco, Texas.

ROBERT M. RANDOLPH is institute chaplain at Massachusetts Institute of Technology in Cambridge, Massachusetts.

STEPHEN D. RICKS is professor of Asian and Near Eastern Languages at Brigham Young University in Provo, Utah.

INDEX